Oracle Press™

Oracle NoSQL
Database

D1736478

Oracle Press™

Oracle NoSQL Database: Real-Time Big Data Management for the Enterprise

Maqsood Alam

Aalok Muley

Ashok Joshi

Chaitanya Kadaru

New York   Chicago   San Francisco
Athens   London   Madrid   Mexico City
Milan   New Delhi   Singapore   Sydney   Toronto

Cataloging-in-Publication Data is on file with the Library of Congress

McGraw-Hill Education books are available at special quantity discounts to use as premiums and sales promotions, or for use in corporate training programs. To contact a representative, please visit the Contact Us pages at www.mhprofessional.com.

Oracle NoSQL Database: Real-Time Big Data Management for the Enterprise

1234567890 DOC DOC 109876543

ISBN 978-0-07-181653-3
MHID   0-07-181653-4

Sponsoring Editor	**Developmental Editor**	**Production Supervisor**
Paul Carlstroem	Dave Rubin	George Anderson
Editorial Supervisor	**Copy Editor**	**Composition**
Patty Mon	Nancy Rapoport	Cenveo Publisher Services
Project Manager	**Proofreader**	**Illustration**
Hardik Popli,	Paul Tyler	Cenveo Publisher Services
Cenveo® Publisher Services	**Indexer**	**Art Director, Cover**
Acquisitions Coordinator	Ted Laux	Jeff Weeks
Amanda Russell		

*To my wife, Suraiya; my marvelous angels,
Zuha and Firas; and my parents; for their unconditional,
extraordinary, and incredible love and support, as always!*
—Maqsood Alam

*To my parents; my wife, Sheela; and my amazing kids,
Dhruv and Anusha. Without their love and
support, this project would not have been possible.*
—Aalok Muley

*To my wife, Anita, and my children, Avina and
Nishant, whose love, support, and encouragement
made this possible, and to the amazing NoSQL Database
development team for creating this wonderful product!*
—Ashok Joshi

*This book is dedicated to my family, especially my mom;
my beautiful wife, Deepthi; and my little angel, Tanya.*
—Chaitanya Kadaru

About the Authors

Maqsood Alam is a Director of Product Management at Oracle and has over 17 years of experience in architecting, building, and evangelizing enterprise and system software. Maqsood is a pure technologist at heart and has a wide range of expertise, ranging from parallel and distributed systems to high performance database applications and big data. His current initiatives at Oracle are focused on Oracle NoSQL Database, Oracle Exadata, Oracle Database 12*c*, and the Oracle Big Data Appliance. He is a coauthor of the book *Achieving Extreme Performance with Oracle Exadata* published by McGraw-Hill Education, and also the author of several whitepapers and best practices dealing with various Oracle technologies. He is an Oracle Certified Professional and holds both bachelor's and master's degrees in computer science.

Aalok Muley is a Senior Director of Product Management at Oracle. He is responsible for driving adoption of Oracle's family of database products: Oracle NoSQL Database, Oracle Big Data Connectors, Oracle Database 12*c*, and engineered systems such as Oracle Big Data Appliance and Oracle Exadata. Aalok has over 19 years of experience; he has led teams working on database industry standard benchmarks, database product development, and Fusion Middleware technologies. He has been part of the technology integration of many Oracle acquisitions. As part of the product development organization, Aalok is currently focused on working closely with partners and customers to design high-throughput, highly available enterprise-grade solutions. He holds a master's degree in computer engineering from Worcester Polytechnical Institute in Massachusetts.

Ashok Joshi is the Senior Director of Development for Oracle NoSQL Database, Berkeley DB, and Database Mobile Server. Ashok has been involved in database systems technology for over two decades as an individual contributor, as well as in a management role. Ashok has made extensive contributions to indexing, concurrency control, buffer management, logging and recovery, and performance optimizations in a variety of products, including Oracle Rdb, Oracle Database, and Sybase SQL Server. He is the author or coauthor of several papers as well as 12 patents on database technology. Ashok graduated from the Indian Institutes of Technology, Bombay with a bachelor's degree in electrical engineering and received a master's degree in computer science from the University of Wisconsin, Madison.

Chaitanya Kadaru is an accomplished software professional with over 12 years of industry experience. He has spent the majority of his time with Oracle, working in databases, middleware, and Oracle applications in various roles, including developer, evangelist, pre-sales, consulting, and training. He recently co-founded Extuit, a premier Oracle consulting company, and has architected solutions involving engineered systems, such as Oracle Exadata, Oracle Exalogic, and Oracle Big Data Appliance, for a wide range of customers. He is currently responsible for a large-scale Oracle

Database consolidation to Oracle Exadata for a large financial services company. Chaitanya holds a bachelor's degree in engineering from BITS, Pilani, and a master's degree in information systems from Carnegie Mellon University.

About the Developmental Editor

Dave Rubin is the Director of Oracle NoSQL Database Product Development at Oracle, and has an extensive background in big data systems. Prior to Oracle, Dave was with Cox Enterprises, where he ran the infrastructure engineering organization responsible for developing big data systems for online advertising. Previously, he ran the engineering teams at Rapt, Inc., delivering price optimization and inventory forecasting solutions to online media companies. Dave started his career at Sybase and holds four U.S. patents in the areas of query optimization and advanced transaction models.

Contents at a Glance

Contents

Foreword

Long before the term "NoSQL databases" entered our lexicon, Berkeley DB was built with many of the goals that have recently propelled the NoSQL databases movement. Its main guiding principle was that through a simple key-value model, the system could achieve the best performance and most flexibility.

Developed in the late 1980s at the University of California, Berkeley, and acquired by Oracle in 2006, Oracle Berkeley DB is an open-source software library that is deployed as an embedded database. By supporting a simple key-value model, Oracle Berkeley DB eliminates much of the complexity of relational databases and can thus support very high transaction rates. Oracle Berkeley DB supports thousands of concurrent ACID transactions, recovery from system failures, and self-managed replication for high availability. Oracle Berkeley DB is one of the most widely used databases because of its high performance, robustness, and flexibility.

Oracle Berkeley DB achieves many of the goals of NoSQL databases, namely: very high transaction rates, support for unstructured data, and high availability. However, Oracle Berkeley DB does not have scalability as a core feature. To achieve scalability, an application would have to build it explicitly on top of Oracle Berkeley DB.

Oracle NoSQL Database was developed to augment Oracle Berkeley DB with elastic horizontal scalability, a feature much needed by Big Data applications, and to complement Oracle's Big Data offering. With Oracle NoSQL Database, data is distributed automatically over a number of servers and is replicated over a configurable number of these servers. Servers can be added and removed dynamically to adapt to an application's data management requirements. As the number of servers varies, Oracle NoSQL Database redistributes data automatically to achieve load balancing. Data is redistributed concurrently with other application operations, thus guaranteeing continuous and uninterrupted service. The transaction throughput and the data capacity of Oracle NoSQL Database scale linearly with the number of servers.

Oracle NoSQL Database uses Berkeley DB as its underlying storage manager and augments it with a data distribution layer for scalability. It thus leverages the robust ACID properties and high availability of Berkeley DB. Oracle NoSQL Database offers a simple programming model and JSON support. It is integrated with Oracle Database and Hadoop, and is a base component of Oracle's Big Data Appliance.

The authors are members of the Oracle NoSQL Database development and product management team. They have deep expertise in data management technology and Big Data requirements. They have a thorough understanding of the product and the motivation for its design. They have a close relationship with customers, understand their use cases, and have driven the product to support their requirements.

Oracle NoSQL Database: Real-Time Big Data Management for the Enterprise provides a comprehensive description of Oracle NoSQL Database, its architecture, design guidelines, installation, and use. It also includes a description of how Oracle NoSQL Database is integrated into Oracle's Big Data platform, and a description of a number of use cases.

Marie-Anne Neimat

Marie-Anne Neimat was the former Vice President of Development for Oracle's embedded databases, which includes Oracle NoSQL Database, Oracle Berkeley Database, and Oracle TimesTen In-Memory Database. Prior to Oracle, she was a co-founder, Vice President of Engineering, and a board member of TimesTen, Inc., which was acquired by Oracle in 2005. Before TimesTen, she worked at HP Labs and managed several research projects, including an object-oriented database (IRIS, which later became the OpenODB product), an extensible database, and an in-memory database.

Marie-Anne was awarded her PhD in computer science from the University of California, Berkeley, and has a bachelor's degree in mathematics from Stanford University. She holds several patents, is a popular technical conference presenter, and is the author of many publications in refereed conferences and journals.

Acknowledgments

My sincere thanks to the McGraw-Hill Education editorial team, Paul and Amanda, for giving me the opportunity to write (once again), and for providing outstanding support during the authoring process. Many thanks to Dave Rubin for his exceptional work in reviewing the content; we all acknowledge it was not easy. And of course I should thank everyone in my family who cooperated and at times wondered why I would willingly put myself through this ordeal.

Special thanks also to Oracle Corp. for giving me the opportunity to work on wonderful products throughout my career. Also, thanks to my fellow coauthors for finally getting the chapters done.

—Maqsood Alam

First and foremost, we must acknowledge the contributions of the Oracle NoSQL Database development team. This book would not be possible if they had not done such a stellar job of creating Oracle NoSQL Database! We are grateful to the team at McGraw-Hill Education who encouraged us, cajoled us, and at times, pushed us to meet deadlines. Special thanks to Paul and Amanda. Dave Rubin spent a huge amount of time reviewing and editing various chapters—this book has benefited tremendously from his tireless diligence and efforts.

—Ashok Joshi

I would like to thank McGraw-Hill Education and Maqsood Alam for believing in me and giving me a chance to contribute to this book. I would also want to thank Maqsood for guiding me throughout the process and for reviewing the content. I would like to thank Paul and Amanda for working tirelessly with us and helping us bring out a great book on Oracle NoSQL Database. Most importantly, I would like to thank the reviewer, Dave Rubin, for doing a wonderful job reviewing my work.

—Chaitanya Kadaru

Introduction

The roots of NoSQL databases can be traced back to the mid-60s when databases such as MUMPS (aka M Database) and PICK (aka MultiValue) came into existence. The main purpose at that time was to build a schema-less implementation of the relational database management system (RDBMS) that would be lightweight and optimized, highly scalable, provide high-transaction throughput, and most importantly, provide an alternative method for data access than the traditional SQL interface.

The term "NoSQL" was initially coined by Carlo Strozzi in 1998 when he named his lightweight, open source relational database management system as NoSQL. Although his database still used the relational database paradigm, his main intention was to provide an alternative interface for data access besides SQL. The term "NoSQL" later resurfaced in 2009 as an attempt to categorize the large number of emerging databases that defied the attributes of traditional RDBMS systems. The key attributes of NoSQL databases are mainly to support non-relational structures; provide a distributed implementation that is highly scalable; and at most times, to not support the key transaction guarantee features inherent to RDBMS systems, such as ACID properties (atomicity, consistency, isolation, and durability).

Berkeley DB (BDB) originated at University of California, Berkeley (1986–1994) as a byproduct of the effort to convert BSD 4.3 (aka Berkeley Unix) to BSD 4.4. In 1996, Netscape requested a few additional enhancements to BDB in order to make it usable in the browser, which led to the formation of Sleepycat Software. The purpose of Sleepycat was to provide enterprise-level support to BDB and to make further enhancements to the product. Sleepycat Software was later acquired by Oracle in February 2006.

Oracle NoSQL Database is a distributed key-value database that uses the BDB engine underneath the covers, and provides a variety of additional features such as dynamic partitioning, load balancing, predictable latency, monitoring, and other features that enable Oracle NoSQL Database to be used in enterprise-level deployments. This book introduces the basics of NoSQL databases, followed by the architecture of Oracle NoSQL Database. Topics related to installation and configuration of the software, application development using APIs and Avro, and sizing and integration of Oracle NoSQL Database with external systems are also covered. Here is a brief overview of each chapter.

Chapter 1: Overview of Oracle NoSQL Database and Big Data

We start off by introducing big data and the role that NoSQL databases play in solving real-time big data problems in enterprises. Multiple flavors of the NoSQL databases are discussed, along with Oracle's approach to NoSQL and big data with optimized software and preconfigured engineered systems.

Chapter 2: Introducing Oracle NoSQL Database

This chapter introduces the foundational concepts of NoSQL systems, along with a description of Oracle Berkeley DB, which is the foundation for Oracle NoSQL Database.

Chapter 3: Oracle NoSQL Database Architecture

In this chapter, we discuss the detailed architecture of Oracle NoSQL Database.

Chapter 4: Oracle NoSQL Database Installation and Configuration

This chapter covers the installation and configuration steps of Oracle NoSQL Database. You start with downloading the software, proceed through the software installation process, and finally wrap up by configuring a distributed cluster of Oracle NoSQL Database.

Chapter 5: Getting Started with Oracle NoSQL Database Development

In this chapter, you are introduced to the basics of NoSQL development. You start with a basic Hello World program and learn about modeling the key space. The basics of reading and writing data are also covered in this chapter.

Chapter 6: Reading and Writing Data

In this chapter, you learn about the options available for reading and writing data into the Oracle NoSQL key-value store. Consistency and durability policies are explained with real-world examples.

Chapter 7: Advanced Programming Concepts: Avro Schemas and Bindings

In this chapter, you learn about the Avro schemas and how they are used, manipulated, and maintained. You also learn about different kinds of Avro bindings available, and we provide sample code to explain the use of bindings.

Chapter 8: Capacity Planning and Sizing

The performance and availability of any enterprise software is dependent on the choice and capacity of the underlying hardware. In this chapter, you are presented with the best practices of sizing an enterprise-grade deployment of Oracle NoSQL Database.

Chapter 9: Advanced Topics

In this chapter, we cover topics related to integration of Oracle NoSQL Database with other products commonly found in enterprise datacenters, such as the Oracle Relational Database Management System, Oracle Event Processing, and Hadoop.

Intended Audience

This book is suitable for the following readers:

- Developers who need to write NoSQL applications using Oracle NoSQL Database

- Big data architects looking for different methods of storing unstructured data for real-time analysis

- Database administrators who like to get into installation, administration, and maintenance of NoSQL databases

- Technical managers or consultants who need an introduction to Oracle NoSQL Database and to see how it compares to other NoSQL databases

No prior knowledge of Oracle NoSQL Database, big data, or any NoSQL database technology is assumed.

CHAPTER
1

Overview of Oracle NoSQL Database and Big Data

S ince the invention of the transistor, the proliferation and application of computer technologies has been shaped by Moore's Law. The growth in CPU compute capacity, high-density memory, and low-cost data storage has resulted in the invention and mass adoption of a variety of computing devices over time. These devices have become ubiquitous in our life and provide various modes of communication, computation, and intelligent sensing. As more and more of these devices are connected to the cloud, the amount of online data generated by these devices is growing tremendously. Until recently, there did not exist a very cost-effective means for businesses to store, analyze, and utilize this data to improve competitiveness and efficiency. In fact, the sheer volume and sparse nature of this data has necessitated the development of new technologies to store and analyze the data. This book covers those technologies, and focuses specifically on the role that Oracle NoSQL Database plays in that space.

Introduction to NoSQL Systems

In recent years, there has been a huge surge in the use of big data technologies to gain additional insights and benefits for business. *Big data* is an informal term that encompasses the analysis of a variety of data from sources such as sensors, audio and video, location information, weather data, web logs, tweets, blogs, user reviews, and SMS messages among others. This large, interactive, and rapidly growing data presents its own data management challenges. *NoSQL data management* refers to the broad class of data management solutions that are designed to address this space.

The idea of leveraging non-intuitive insights from big data is not new, but the work of producing these insights requires understanding and correlating interesting patterns in human behavior and aggregating the findings. Historically, such insights were largely based on the use of secret, custom-built, in-house algorithms, and systems. Only a handful of enterprises were able to do this successfully, because it was very difficult to analyze the large volume of data and the various types of data sources involved.

During the first decade of the twenty-first century, techniques and algorithms for processing large amounts of data were popularized by web enterprises such as Google and Yahoo!. Because of the sheer volume of data and the need for cost-effective solutions, such systems incorporated design choices that made them diverge significantly from traditional relational databases, leading to their characterization as *NoSQL* systems. Though the term suggests that these systems are the antithesis of traditional row and column relational systems, NoSQL solutions borrow many concepts from contemporary relational systems as well as earlier systems such as hierarchical and CODASYL systems. Therefore, NoSQL systems are probably better characterized as *Not only SQL* rather than *Not SQL*.

Brief Historical Perspective

It is useful to review a brief history of data management systems to understand how they have influenced modern NoSQL systems. Database systems of the early 1960s were invented to address data processing for scenarios where the amount of data was larger than the available memory on the computer. The obvious solution to this problem was to use secondary storage such as magnetic disks and tapes in order to store the additional data. Because access to secondary storage is typically a few hundred (or more) times slower than access to memory, early research in data processing was focused on addressing this performance disparity. Techniques such as efficient in-memory data structures, buffer management, sequential scanning, and batch processing and access methods (indices) for disk resident data were created in order to improve the performance of such systems.

The issue of data modeling also posed significant challenges because each application had its own view of data. The manner in which information was organized in memory as well as on disk had a huge influence on application design and processing. In the early days, data organization and modeling was largely the responsibility of the application. As a result, any changes to the methods in which data was stored or organized forced drastic changes to applications. This was hugely inefficient, and gave the impetus to decouple data storage from applications.

Early database management systems were based on the *hierarchical data model*. Each entity in this model has a parent record and several sub-records that are associated with the parent record organized in a hierarchy. For example, an employee entity might have a sub-record for payroll information, another sub-record for human resource (HR) information, and so on. Modeling the data in this manner improves performance because an application needs to access only the sub-records that are required, resulting in fewer disk accesses and better memory utilization. For example, a payroll application needs to reference only the payroll sub-record (and the parent record that is the "root" of the hierarchy). Application development is also simplified because applications that manage separate sub-records can be modularized and developed independently. Figure 1-1 illustrates how an employee entity might be organized in the hierarchical model.

The CODASYL model improved upon the hierarchical data model by providing indexing and links between related sub-records, resulting in further improvements in performance and simplified application development. If we use the earlier example of modeling Employee records, the CODASYL data model allows the designer to link the records of all the dependents of an employee, as shown in Figure 1-2.

Despite these improvements, the issue of record structure and schema design continued to be the dominant factor in application design. To add to the complexity, the data model was relatively inflexible; making a significant change to the organization of data often necessitated significant changes to the applications that used the data. In spite of these limitations, it is important to remember that these early systems provided excellent performance for data management problems of

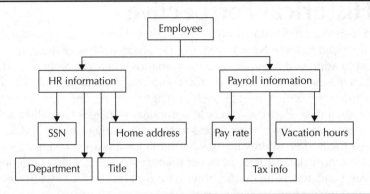

FIGURE 1-1. *Employee entity represented in the Network model of data*

the day. The overall simplicity of the system also contributed to better stability and reliability of the software. To this day, several common database applications such as airline reservation systems and banking applications are based on these architectures, a testament to their simplicity, performance, and reliability.

Ted Codd's seminal research on relational database theory in the early 1970s, the introduction of Structured Query Language (SQL) for data manipulation, and the subsequent work on relational database management systems revolutionized the data management industry. Relational database systems support logical relationships between data items and provide a clean separation between the data model and the

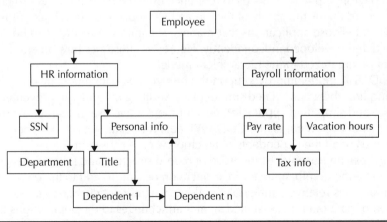

FIGURE 1-2. *Employee entity and child records in the CODASYL model*

application. The database system assumes the responsibility of mapping logical relationships to physical data organization. This data model independence has several important benefits, including significant acceleration of application development and maintenance, ease of physical data reorganization, and evolution and use of the relational data repository in multiple ways for managing a variety of data for multiple applications. Relational data is also referred to as *structured data* to highlight the "row and column" organization of the data. Since the mid-1980s, the use of relational database systems has been growing exponentially; it is fair to say that present-day enterprise data management is dominated by SQL-based systems.

In addition to the advances in data modeling and application design, the last 40 years have also seen major architectural and technological innovations such as the concept of transactions, indexing, concurrency control, and high availability. Transactions embody the intuitive notion of the all-or-nothing unit of work, typically involving multiple operations on different data entities. Various indexing techniques provide fast access to specific data quickly and efficiently; concurrency control ensures proper operation when multiple operations simultaneously manipulate shared resources. Recovery and high availability ensure that the system is resilient to a variety of failures. These technologies have been adapted and used in a variety of ways in modern NoSQL solutions.

Modern NoSQL systems were developed in the early 2000s in response to demands for processing the vast amounts of data produced by increasing Internet usage and mobile and geo-location technologies. Traditional solutions were either too expensive, not scalable, or required too much time to process data. Out of necessity, companies such as Google, Yahoo!, and others were forced to invent solutions that could address big data processing challenges. These modern NoSQL systems borrowed from earlier solutions but made significant advances in horizontal scalability and the efficient processing of diverse types of data such as text, audio, video, image, and geo-location.

Big Data and NoSQL: Characteristics and Architectural Trade-Offs

Big data is often characterized by the three Vs—*volume, variety,* and *velocity.* Volume obviously refers to the terabytes and petabytes of data that need to be processed, often in unstructured or semi-structured form. In a relational database system, each row in a table has the same structure (same number of columns, with a well-defined data type for each column and so on). By contrast, each individual entity (row) in an *unstructured* or *semi-structured* system can be structurally very different and therefore, contains more, less, or different information from another entity in the same repository. This variety is a fundamental aspect of big data and can pose interesting management and processing challenges, which NoSQL systems can address. Yet another aspect of big data is the velocity at which the data is generated. For data capture scenarios, NoSQL systems need to be able to ingest data at very high throughput rates (for example, hundreds of thousands to millions of entities per second). Similarly, results often need to be delivered at very high throughput as well as very low latency (milliseconds to a few seconds per recipient).

Unlike data in relational database systems, the intrinsic value of an individual entity in a big dataset may vary widely, depending on the intended use. Take the common case of capturing web log data in files for later analysis. A sentiment analysis application aggregates information from millions or billions of individual data items in order to make conclusions about trends and patterns in the data. An individual data item in the dataset provides very little insight, but contributes to the aggregate results. Conversely, in the case of an application that manages user profile data for ecommerce, each individual data item has a much higher value because it represents a customer (or potential customer). Traditionally, every row in a relational database repository is typically a "high *value*" row. We will refer to this *variability* in value as the fourth V of big data.

In addition to this "four Vs" characterization of big data, there are a few implicit characteristics as well. Often, the volume of data is variable and changes in unpredictable or unexpected ways. For example, it may arrive at rates of terabytes per day during some periods and gigabytes per day during others. In order to handle this variability in volume, most NoSQL solutions provide dynamic horizontal scalability, making it possible to add more hardware to the online system to gracefully adapt to the increased demand. Traditional solutions also provide some level of scalability in response to growing demand; however, NoSQL systems can scale to significantly higher levels (10 times or more) compared to these systems.

Another characteristic of most NoSQL systems is high availability. In the vast majority of usage scenarios, big data applications must remain available and process information in spite of hardware failures, software bugs, bad data, power and/or network outages, routine maintenance, and other disruptions. Again, traditional systems provide high availability; however, the massive scalability of NoSQL systems poses unique and interesting availability challenges. Unlike traditional relational database solutions, NoSQL systems permit data loss, relaxed transaction guarantees, and data inconsistency in order to provide availability and scalability over hundreds or thousands of nodes.

Types of Big Data Processing

Big data processing falls into two broad categories—*batch* (or analytical) processing and *interactive* (or "real-time") processing. Batch processing of big data is targeted to derive aggregate value (data analytics) from data by combining terabytes or petabytes of data in interesting ways. MapReduce and Hadoop are the most well-known big data batch processing technologies available today. As a crude approximation, this is similar to data warehousing applications in the sense that data warehousing also involves aggregating vast quantities of data in order to identify trends and patterns in the data.

As the term suggests, interactive big data processing is designed to serve data very quickly with minimal overhead. The most common example of interactive big data processing is managing web user profiles. Whenever an ecommerce user connects to the web application, the user profile needs to be accessed with very low latency (in a few milliseconds); otherwise the user is likely to visit a different site. A 2010 study by Amazon.com found that every 100 millisecond increase in latency results in a 1 percent reduction in sales. Oracle NoSQL Database is a great example of a database that can handle the stringent throughput and response-time requirements of an interactive big data processing solution.

NoSQL Database vs. Relational Database

Relational database management systems (RDBMS) have been very effective in managing transactional data. The Atomicity, Consistency, Isolation, and Durability (ACID) properties of relational databases have made them a staple for enterprises looking to manage data that spans various critical business functions. Examples include Enterprise Resource Planning (ERP), Customer Relationship Management (CRM), data warehouse, and a multitude of similar applications.

The Oracle Database has a 30-year legacy of high performance, scalability, and fault tolerance. Enterprise customers demand a high level of security, disaster recovery capabilities, and rich application development functionality. Relational databases, like the Oracle Database, provide a very comprehensive functionality to manage a multitude of data types and deployment options. These capabilities result in a rich and complex database engine.

NoSQL databases were created at the other end of this spectrum; their primary goal was to provide a very quick and dirty mechanism to retrieve information without all the varied capabilities of the RDMBS that we have highlighted in the preceding paragraph. NoSQL databases are highly distributed, run on commodity hardware, and provide minimal or no transactional support; they also have a very flexible or nonexistent schema definition requirement, and this makes them very suitable for fast storage, retrieval, and update of unstructured data. NoSQL databases have developed into a very lightweight, agile, developer-centric, API-driven database engine. NoSQL database developers are comfortable using low-level APIs to interact with the database, and don't rely on higher-level languages such as SQL (Structured Query Language), which is a standard for an RDBMS.

It is recommended that NoSQL databases be used for high volume, rapidly evolving datasets, with low latency requirements, and where you need the complete flexibility of its APIs to develop a very specialized data store. An RDBMS has enterprise-grade features for high availability and disaster recovery, which are essential for transactional systems. When availability requirements are more flexible and the possibility of data loss or consistency can be tolerated, NoSQL databases prove to be a cost-effective solution. Also, applications that require a very efficient mechanism to retrieve individual records without the need for operations such as complex joins will also benefit from the use of the Oracle NoSQL Database. NoSQL databases make efficient use of commodity servers and storage; they do not rely on specialized hardware and can scale to thousands of servers and hence can manage petabytes of data with very good scalability characteristics.

Both RDBMS and NoSQL databases provide significant benefits in their individual use case scenarios. It is therefore very important to choose the appropriate technology based on the need, and it is also critical to realize that the two can complement each other, to provide a very comprehensive solution for big data.

While it is critical to choose a NoSQL technology that meets your specific use case scenario, may it be key-value pair, graph, or document store (terms explained in the next section), it is also important to realize that like any other data management technology, NoSQL databases do not operate in a vacuum. Choose a NoSQL database implementation that integrates very well with data ingestion tools, RDBMS, Business Intelligence tools, and enterprise management utilities. Such an integrated NoSQL database will allow you to combine information across different database types, and data types (structured and unstructured), resulting in a big data deployment that brings tremendous value to your enterprise.

Types of NoSQL Databases

In a highly distributed database management system, it is important to realize that Consistency, Availability, and Partition Tolerance come at a price. The *CAP Theorem* states that it is impossible to provide all three capabilities simultaneously. Different NoSQL systems provide varying degrees of Consistency, Availability, and Partition Tolerance, and it is important to choose the right implementation based on your application needs.

In addition to the distributed system properties that are mentioned in the preceding paragraph, you can also classify NoSQL database implementations based on the mechanisms they use to store and retrieve data. These are important for the application developer to consider before choosing the appropriate implementation. There are four broad implementation types: key-value store, document store, columnar, and graph.

Key-Value Stores

The key-value implementation stores data with unique keys, and the system is opaque to the contents of the data. It is the responsibility of the client to introspect the contents. This architecture allows for a highly optimized key-based lookup.

Scalability is achieved through the *sharding* (a.k.a. partitioning) of data across nodes. To protect against data loss, key-value store implementations replicate data over nodes, and this can potentially lead to consistency issues when you have network failures and inaccessible nodes. Many systems therefore leave it up to the client to handle and resolve any consistency issues.

Key-value stores are very useful for applications such as user profile lookup, storing and retrieving online shopping carts, and catalog lookups. These applications have a unique user ID or an item ID associated with the data, and the key-value store provides a clean and efficient API to retrieve this information.

Document Stores

The document stores at their foundation are very similar to key-value implementation. An important distinction, however, is their capability to introspect the data that is associated with the key. This is possible because the document store understands the format of the data stored. This opens up the possibility to carry out aggregates and searches across elements of the document itself. Also, bulk update of the data is possible. Document stores work with multiple formats including XML and JSON. This allows for storage and retrieval of data without an impedance match.

The scalability, replication, and consistency characteristics of document stores are very similar to those of KV stores. Typical use cases for document stores include the storage and retrieval of catalogs, blog posts, news articles, and data analysis.

Graph Stores

Graph stores are different from the other methods in that they have the capability not only to capture information about objects, but can also record the relationships between these objects. Within each graph store, there are objects and relationships, which have specific *properties* attached to them. At the application level, these properties can be used to create specific subsets of relationships or objects best suited to a specific enterprise purpose. For example, the developer of a social network gaming application may wish to target a promotion of free in-game currency to those users who are friends of a gamer who ranks amongst the top 10 percentile of the highest scorers. Such data would be difficult to retrieve in other NoSQL database implementations, but the capability to traverse relationships in graph databases makes such queries very intuitive. For social networks, this analytical capability of graph stores allows for quick analysis and monetization of relationships that have been captured in their application. Graph databases can be used to analyze customer interactions, social media, and scientific application where it is crucial to traverse long relationship graphs to better understand data.

Column Stores

Column stores are the final type of NoSQL database that we will review. These store data in a columnar fashion; the result is a table where each row can have one or more columns, and the number of columns in each row can vary from row to row. This provides a very flexible data model to store your data, and a clear demarcation of similar attributes, which also acts as an index to quickly retrieve data. To further demarcate by columns, you can combine similar columns to build column families. This concept of grouping helps with more complex queries as well. At the core, each column and its associated data is essentially a key-value pair. As data is organized into columns, you have better indexing (and therefore visibility) compared to other key-value stores. Also, when it comes to updates, multiple column block updates can be aggregated. Column store databases were born when Google open sourced its implementation of a Column store NoSQL database called Big Table. Apparently, the data for the well-known Google e-mail service, Gmail, is stored in the Google Big Table NoSQL Database.

Based on the discussion of the four different types of NoSQL databases, it is evident that this family of products provides a rich set of functionality for storing and retrieving data in a very cost-effective, fault-tolerant, and scalable manner.

Big Data Use Cases

The initial use of NoSQL technology began with the social media sites as they were looking at ways to deal with large sets of data generated by their user communities. For example, in 2010 Twitter saw data arriving at the rates of 12TB/day, and that resulted in a 4PB dataset in a year. These numbers have grown significantly as Twitter usage has expanded globally.

While the social media sites such as Twitter gave users an option to share their thoughts, ideas, and pictures, there was no easy way to make sense of such a large tsunami of information as it arrived from millions of users. HDFS is used to store such data in a distributed and fault-tolerant manner, and MapReduce technology, with its batch processing capability, is used to analyze the data. However, this wasn't the right technology for answering real-time analytics on the data. Each tweet is stored with a unique identifier, and Twitter also saves the user ID. This key-value store could potentially take advantage of the capability of NoSQL databases. NoSQL database technologies could be used to run queries such as user searches, tweets from a specific user, and graph database capabilities could be used to find friends and followers.

Present-day enterprises have come to value the insight that social media provides into customer behavior, opinions, and market trends. Combining social media data with CRM data can provide a holistic view about the customer, something that was not possible just a few years ago. Customer data is no longer just limited to the past interactions; it can now include images, recordings, Likes (as in Facebook likes), web pages visited, preferences, loyalty programs, and an evolving set of artifacts. This requires a system that can handle both structured and unstructured data. As more channels of communication and collaboration come and go, the data format keeps constantly changing, requiring that developers and data management systems know how to operate in a schema-less fashion. While each record in a transactional system is very critical for the operation of the business, the new customer data is high volume and sparse. This requires a distributed storage and computing environment.

Customer profile data is predominantly a read-only lookup and requires a simple key-based access. NoSQL databases, with their support of unstructured and semi-structured data, key-value store, and distributed deployments, are ideal candidates. When it comes to operational analysis, you might want to combine the customer profile data with that in your OLTP or DW systems. The tight integration between Oracle NoSQL Database and the Oracle Database makes it possible for you to join data across both of these systems. Therefore, enterprises now deploy NoSQL databases alongside RDBMS, and MapReduce technologies.

Another use case that will illustrate how the different data management and analysis technologies work together is that of online advertisers. Advertisers are always in search of a new set of eyes, and the fast growth of mobile devices has made that a key focus.

Usage patterns on mobile devices are characterized by short intermittent access, as compared to that of a desktop interface, and this puts stringent constraints on the time publishers have to make the decision about which ad to display. Typically, this is of the order of 75 milliseconds, and a medium-sized publisher might have more than 500 million ad impressions in a day. The short time intervals, the large number of events, and the huge amount of associated data that gets generated require a multifaceted data management system. This system needs to be highly responsive, be able to support high throughput, and be able to respond to varying loads and system fault conditions. There is no single technology that can fulfill these requirements.

To be effective, the publisher needs to be able to quickly analyze the user so as to decide which ad to display. A user lookup is carried out on a NoSQL database and the profile is loaded. The profile might include details on demographics, behavioral segments, recency, location, and a user rating, which might have been arrived at behind the scenes through a scoring engine.

In addition to displaying the ad, there are campaign budgets to manage, client financial transactions to track, and campaign effectiveness to analyze. NoSQL database technologies, in conjunction with MapReduce and relational databases, are used in such a deployment, as shown in Figure 1-3.

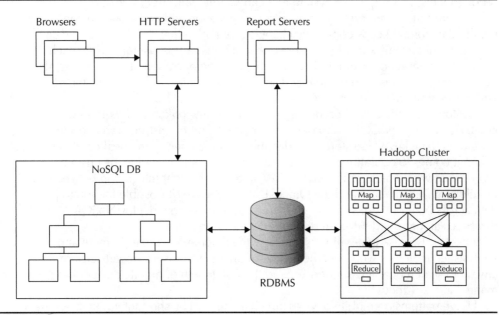

FIGURE 1-3. *Typical big data application architecture for an advertising use case*

Oracle's Approach to Big Data

The amount of data being generated is on the verge of an explosion, and according to an International Data Corporation (IDC) 2012 report, the total amount of data stored by corporations globally would surpass a zettabyte (1 zettabyte = 1 billion terabytes) by the end of 2012. Therefore, it is critical for the data companies to be prepared with an infrastructure that can store and analyze extremely large datasets, and be able to generate actionable intelligence that in turn can drive business decisions. Oracle offers a broad portfolio of products to help enterprises acquire, manage, and integrate big data with existing corporate data, and perform rich and intelligent analytics.

Implementing big data solutions with tools and techniques that are not tested or integrated is too risky and problematic. The approach to solve big data problems should follow best practice methodologies and toolsets that are proven in real-world deployments. The typical best practices for processing big data can be categorized by the flow of data in the processing stream, mainly the data acquisition, data organization, and data analysis. Oracle's big data technology stack includes hardware and software components that can process big data during all the critical phases of its lifecycle, from acquisition to storage to organization to analysis.

Oracle engineered systems such as Oracle Big Data Appliance, Oracle Exadata, and Oracle Exalytics, along with the Oracle's proprietary and open source software, are able to acquire, organize, and analyze all enterprise data, including structured and unstructured data, to help make informed business decisions.

Acquire

The *acquire* phase refers to the acquisition of incoming big data streams from a variety of sources such as social media, mobile devices, machine data, and sensor data. The data often has flexible structures, and comes in with high velocity and in large volumes. The infrastructure needed to ingest and persist these big datasets needs to provide low and predictable latencies when writing data, high throughput on scans, and very fast and quick lookups, and it needs to support dynamic schemas. Some of the popular technologies that support the requirements of storing big data are NoSQL databases, Hadoop Distributed File System (HDFS), and Hive.

NoSQL databases are designed to support high performance and dynamic schema requirements; in fact, they are considered the real-time databases of big data. They are able to provide fast throughput on writes because they use a simple data model in which the data is stored as-is with its original structure, along with a single identifying key, rather than interpreting and converting the data into a well-defined schema. The reads also become very simple: You supply a key and the database quickly returns the value by performing a key-based index lookup. The NoSQL databases are also distributed and replicated to provide high availability and reliability, and can linearly scale in performance and capacity just by adding more Storage Nodes to the cluster. With this lightweight and distributed architecture, NoSQL databases can rapidly store a large number of transactions and provide extremely fast lookups.

NoSQL databases are well suited for storing data with dynamic structures. NoSQL databases simply capture the incoming data without parsing or making sense of its structure. This provides low latencies at write time, which is a great benefit, but the complexity is shifted to the application at read time because it needs to interpret the structure of stored data, which is often a great trade-off because when the underlying data structures change, the effect is only noticed by the application querying the data. Modifying application logic to support schema evolution is considered more cost-effective than reorganizing the data, which is resource-intensive and time-consuming, especially when multi-terabytes of data are involved. Project planners already assume that change is part of an application lifecycle, but not so much for reorganization of data.

Hadoop Distributed File System (HDFS) is another option to store big data. HDFS is the storage engine behind the Apache Hadoop project, which is the software framework built to handle storage and processing of big data. Typical use of HDFS is for storing data warehouse–oriented datasets whose needs are store-once and scan-many-times, with the scans being directed at most of the stored data.

HDFS works by splitting the file into small chunks called *blocks*, and then storing the blocks across a cluster of HDFS servers. As with NoSQL, HDFS also provides high scalability, availability, and reliability by replicating the blocks multiple times, and providing the capability to grow the cluster by simply adding more nodes.

Apache Hive is another option for storing data warehouse–like big data. It is a SQL-based infrastructure originally built at Facebook for storing and processing data residing in HDFS. Hive simply imposes a structure on HDFS files by defining a table with columns and rows—which means it is ideal for supporting structured big datasets. HiveQL is the SQL interface into Hive in which users query data using the popular SQL language.

HDFS and Hive are both not designed for OLTP workloads and do not offer update or real-time query capabilities, for which NoSQL databases are best suited. On the flip side, HDFS and Hive are best suited for batch jobs over big datasets that need to scan large amounts of data, a capability that NoSQL databases currently lack.

Organize

Once the data is acquired and stored in a persistent store such as a NoSQL database or HDFS, it needs to be *organized* further in order to extract any meaningful information on which further analysis could be performed. You could think of data organization as a combination of knowledge discovery and data integration, in which large volumes of big data undergo multiple phases of data crunching, at the end of which the data takes a form suitable to perform meaningful business analysis. It is only after the organization phase that you begin to see a business value from the otherwise yet-to-be-valued big data.

Multiple technologies exist for organizing big data, the popular ones being Apache Hadoop MapReduce Framework, Oracle Database In-Database Analytics, R Analytics, Oracle R Enterprise, and Oracle Big Data Connectors.

The MapReduce framework is a programming model, originally developed at Google, to assist in building distributed applications that work with big data. MapReduce allows the programmer to focus on writing the business logic, rather than focusing on the management and control of the distributed tasks, such as task parallelization, inter-task communication, and data transfers, and handling restarts upon failures.

As you can imagine, MapReduce can be used to code any business logic to analyze large datasets residing in HDFS. MapReduce is a programmer's paradise for analyzing big data, along with the help of several other Apache projects such as Mahout, an open source machine learning framework. However, MapReduce requires the end user to know programming language such as Java, which needs quite a few lines of code even for programming a simple scenario. Hive, on the other hand, translates the SQL-like statements (HiveQL) into MapReduce programs behind the scenes, a nice alternative to coding in Java since SQL is a language that most data analysts are already familiar with.

Open source R along with its add-on packages can also be used to perform MapReduce-like statistical functions on the HDFS cluster without using Java. R is a statistical programming language and an integrated graphical environment for performing statistical analysis. R language is a product of a community of statisticians, analysts, and programmers who are not only working on improvising and extending R, but also are able to strategically steer its development, by providing open source packages that extend the capability of R.

The results of R scripts and MapReduce programs can be loaded into the Oracle Database where further analytics can be performed (see the next section on the *analyze* phase). This leads to an interesting topic—integration of big data with transactional data resident in a relational database management system such as the Oracle Database. Transactional data of an enterprise has extreme value in itself, whether it is the data about enterprise sales, or customers, or even business performance. The big data residing in HDFS or NoSQL databases can be combined with the transactional data in order to achieve a complete and integrated view of business performance.

Oracle Big Data Connectors is a suite of optimized software packages to help enterprises integrate data stored in Hadoop or Oracle NoSQL Database with Oracle Database. It enables very fast data movements between these two environments using Oracle Loader for Hadoop and Oracle Direct Connector for Hadoop Distributed File System (HDFS), while Oracle Data Integrator Application Adapter for Hadoop and Oracle R Connector for Hadoop provide non-Hadoop experts with easier access to HDFS data and MapReduce functionality.

Oracle NoSQL Database also has the capability to expose the key-value store data to the Oracle Database by combining the powerful integration capabilities of the Oracle NoSQL Database with the Oracle Database external table feature. The external table feature allows users to access data (read-only) from sources that are external to the database such as flat files, HDFS, and Oracle NoSQL Database. External tables act like regular database tables for the application developer. The database creates a link that just points to the source of the data, and the data continues to reside in its original location. This feature is quite useful for data analysts who are accustomed to using SQL for analysis. Chapter 9 has further details on this feature.

Analyze

The infrastructure required for analyzing big data must be able to support deeper analytics such as data mining, predictive analytics, and statistical analysis. It should support a variety of data types and scale to extreme data volumes, while at the same time deliver fast response times. Also, supporting the ability to combine big data with traditional enterprise data is important because new insight comes not just from analyzing new data or existing data, but by combining and analyzing together to provide new perspectives on old problems.

Oracle Database supports the *organize* and *analyze* phases of big data through the in-database analytics functionality that is embedded within the database. Some of the useful in-database analytics features of the Oracle Database are Oracle R Enterprise, Data Mining and Predictive Analytics, and in-database MapReduce. The point here is that further organization and analysis on big data can still be performed even after the data lands in Oracle Database. If you do not need further analysis, you can still leverage SQL or business intelligence tools to expose the results of these analytics to end users.

Oracle R Enterprise (ORE) allows the execution of R scripts on datasets residing inside the Oracle Database. The ORE engine interacts with datasets residing inside the database in a transparent fashion using standard R constructs, thus providing a rich end-user experience. ORE also enables embedded execution of R scripts, and utilizes the underlying Oracle Database parallelism to run R on a cluster of nodes.

In-Database Data Mining offers the capability to create complex data mining models for performing predictive analytics. Data mining models can be built by data scientists, and business analysts can leverage the results of these predictive models using standard BI tools. In this way the knowledge of building the models is abstracted from the analysis process. *In-Database MapReduce* provides the capability to write procedural logic conforming to the popular MapReduce model, and seamlessly leverage Oracle Database parallel execution. In-database MapReduce allows data scientists to create high-performance routines with complex logic, using PL/SQL, C, or Java.

Each one of the analytical components in Oracle Database is quite powerful by itself, and combining them creates even more value to the business. Once the data is fully analyzed, tools such as Oracle Business Intelligence Enterprise Edition and Oracle Endeca Information Discovery help assist the business analyst in the final decision-making process.

Oracle Business Intelligence Enterprise Edition (OBI EE) is a comprehensive platform that delivers full business intelligence capabilities, including BI dashboards, ad-hoc queries, notifications and alerts, enterprise and financial reporting, scorecard and strategy management, business process invocation, search and collaboration, mobile, integrated systems management, and more.

OBI EE includes the BI Server that integrates a variety of data sources into a Common Enterprise Information Model and provides a centralized view of the business model. The BI Server also comprises an advanced calculation and integration engine, and provides native database support for a variety of databases, including Oracle. Front-end components in OBI EE provide ad-hoc query and analysis, high precision reporting (BI Publisher), strategy and balanced scorecards, dashboards, and linkage to an action framework for automated detection and business processes. Additional integration is also provided to Microsoft Office, mobile devices, and other Oracle middleware products such as WebCenter.

Oracle Endeca Information Discovery is a platform designed to provide rapid and intuitive exploration and analysis of both structured and unstructured data sources. Oracle Endeca enables enterprises to extend the analytical capabilities to unstructured data, such as social media, websites, e-mail, and other big data. Endeca indexes all types of incoming data so the search and the discovery process can be fast, thereby saving time and cost, and leading to better business decisions. The information can also be enriched further by integrating with other analytical capabilities such as sentiment and lexical analysis, and presented in a single user interface that can be utilized to discover new insights.

Oracle Engineered Systems for Big Data

Over the last few years, Oracle has been focused on purpose-built systems that are engineered to have hardware and software work together, and are designed to deliver extreme performance and high availability, while at the same time making them easy to install, configure, and maintain. The Oracle engineered systems that assist with big data processing through its various phases are the Oracle Big Data Appliance, Oracle Exadata Database Machine, and Oracle Exalytics In-Memory Machine. Figure 1-4 shows the best practice architecture of processing big data using Oracle engineered systems. As the figure depicts, each appliance plays a special role in the overall processing of big data by participating in the acquisition, organization, and analysis phases.

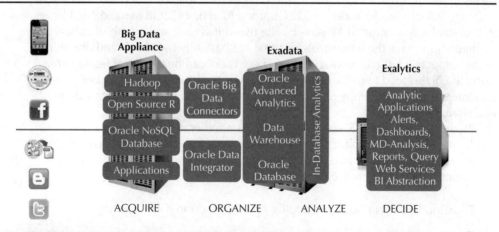

FIGURE 1-4. *Oracle engineered systems supporting acquire, organize, analyze, and decide phases of big data*

Oracle Big Data Appliance

The Oracle Big Data Appliance is an engineered system built with optimized hardware and a comprehensive set of software designed to provide big data solutions in a complete, easy-to-deploy offering for acquiring, organizing, and analyzing big data. Oracle Big Data Appliance delivers an affordable, scalable, and fully optimized big data infrastructure in-a-box, as compared to building a custom system from scratch, which could be time-consuming, inefficient, and prone to failures. Oracle Big Data Appliance, along with Oracle Exadata Database Machine and Oracle Exalytics In-Memory Machine, creates a complete set of technologies for leveraging and integrating big data, and helps enterprises quickly and efficiently turn information into insight.

The Oracle Big Data Appliance provides the following benefits:

- Rapid provisioning of large and highly available big data clusters that can linearly scale and process massive amounts of data

- Cost control benefits of deploying a pre-integrated, engineered system that can be installed and managed easily

- High performance by engineering state-of-the-art hardware and pre-optimized software to assist with acquiring, organizing, and analyzing big data

The Oracle Big Data Appliance comes in multiple configurations of different-sized racks: the full rack, two-thirds rack, and one-third rack. The full-rack configuration comprises 18 Sun servers and provides a total raw storage capacity of 648TB. Every server in the rack has 2 CPUs, each with 8 cores for a total of 288 cores, and 64GB memory that can be expanded to 512GB, for a total of 1152GB expandable to over 9TB of total memory for all 18 servers. The two-thirds rack and one-third rack configurations have the hardware specs that are basically two-thirds and one-third of the respective full-rack configuration. These racks can be easily cabled together using the high-speed InfiniBand network in order to provide rapid scalability and incremental growth, thereby enabling the cluster to handle extreme data volumes and storage capacity.

As shown in Figure 1-5, the software preinstalled on the Oracle Big Data Appliance includes a combination of open source software and specialized software developed by Oracle to address enterprise big data needs. The Oracle Big Data Appliance integrated software includes:

- Cloudera's distribution including Apache Hadoop (CDH)

- Cloudera Manager

- Oracle NoSQL Database Community Edition (CE)

- Oracle Big Data Connectors

- Oracle R Distribution (Oracle's redistribution of Open Source R)

Oracle NoSQL Database Community Edition (CE) comes preinstalled on the Oracle Big Data Appliance by default, and configured upon the customer's request at install time. You have the capability to run Oracle NoSQL Database on all the 18 nodes in the cluster, with each node having a dedicated space of 3TB or 6TB (one disk or two disks, other custom configurations are also possible). Oracle NoSQL Database is rack aware and its block placement algorithms minimize data loss when multiple racks are interconnected by placing mirrored blocks on different racks to enhance availability. The customer can purchase the Enterprise Edition (EE) license of Oracle NoSQL Database and get enterprise-level features (see Chapter 2 for more details).

Cloudera's Distribution including Apache Hadoop (CDH) consists of open source Apache Hadoop and a comprehensive set of open source software components needed to use Hadoop, with Cloudera's branding and support. Cloudera Manager is a proprietary product from Cloudera that provides an end-to-end management application that provides monitoring and administration capabilities of CDH clusters. It also incorporates a full range of reporting and diagnostic tools to help optimize cluster performance and utilization.

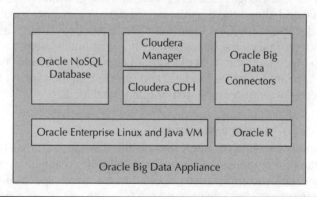

FIGURE 1-5. *Oracle Big Data Appliance software overview*

Oracle Exadata Database Machine

The Oracle Exadata Database Machine is an engineered system built to support all types of database workloads, ranging from data warehouse applications that scan large amounts of data, to OLTP applications supporting highly concurrent and real-time transactions. It has an award-winning combination of smart software that runs in the storage layers called Exadata Storage Server Software, the intelligent Oracle Database 11g software, and the latest industry hardware components from Oracle, all combined to deliver extreme performance in a highly available, reliable, and highly secure environment out-of-the-box.

The Database Machine has large amounts of memory and PCIe-based Flash storage, which allows caching and storage of frequently accessed data into entities that are hundreds of times faster than the hard disks, which helps boost OLTP-like workload performance. The smart features of the Exadata Storage Server Software offloads processing to run near the disks where the data resides, thereby eliminating a lot of unnecessary data movement between the database CPUs and disks, a feature that can provide ten- or twenty-fold speed-up for data warehousing workloads.

The Database Machine is also well-suited for consolidating multiple databases onto a single grid by utilizing the resource management, clustering, workload management, and the pluggable database features of the Oracle Database. Also, the award-winning Exadata Hybrid Columnar Compression feature allows you to achieve 10- to 50-times compression of data on disk, thereby offering cost savings and performance improvements because you store and scan less data.

The Oracle Exadata Database Machine has the capability to perform the *organize* and *analyze* stages of big data processing. The In-Database Analytics offers powerful features for knowledge discovery and data mining, which helps extract hidden intelligence and allows the organization of data in a manner suitable for making business decisions. The Oracle business intelligence tools, such as Oracle BI EE and Oracle Endeca, rely on the data residing in a relational system, for which the Exadata Database Machine is the ideal platform of choice. Connections between Oracle Big Data Appliance, Oracle Exadata, and Oracle Exalytics are via InfiniBand, enabling high-speed data transfer for batch or query workloads.

Oracle Exalytics In-Memory Machine

In the world of rapidly evolving economy and business dynamics, it has become even more important for organizations to perform real-time, visual analysis, and enable new types of analytic applications in order to assist with speed-of-thought decision process, in order to help them stand out from the rest. Static reports and dashboards have become passé; enterprises are now utilizing tools and techniques such as business modeling, planning, forecasting, and predictive analytics, and using rich and interactive visualizations to assist with actionable intelligence and real-time decisions.

Oracle Exalytics In-Memory Machine is an engineered system built to deliver high-performance business intelligence (BI) and enterprise planning applications. The hardware consists of a single server that is optimally configured for business intelligence workloads and includes powerful compute capacity and abundant memory to assist with in-memory analytics. The InfiniBand network connectivity provides an extremely fast option to connect Exalytics to other Exalytics or Oracle engineered systems such as Exadata. For example, this option can augment the business intelligence capabilities of Exalytics with powerful embedded in-database analytics capabilities of Exadata.

The software included in the Oracle Exalytics In-Memory Machine is the optimized Oracle BI Foundation Suite (Oracle BI Foundation) and Oracle TimesTen In-Memory Database. Business Intelligence Foundation takes advantage of the Exalytics hardware and system configuration to deliver rich and actionable intelligence. Exalytics also provides better query responsiveness and higher user scalability compared to standalone installation of Oracle BI Foundation. The TimesTen In-Memory Database for Exalytics is an optimized in-memory database that offers some exclusive features especially enabled for Exalytics, such as columnar compression to reduce the footprint for in-memory data.

Summary

NoSQL databases provide a simple and lightweight mechanism for storing new and diverse sets of digital data streams, which oftentimes would not be appropriate to store in a traditional RDBMS. NoSQL databases are optimized to handle quick reads and writes of large datasets by allowing the application to define loose durability and consistency models in order to favor read and write performance, which is a key factor for a big data application with real-time needs.

Oracle NoSQL Database is a distributed key-value database designed to provide highly reliable, scalable, and available data storage across a configurable set of systems. Oracle NoSQL Database plays a key role in the overall portfolio of Oracle's big data offerings, to assist in analyzing enterprise big data. The rest of the chapters cover Oracle NoSQL Database in much greater depth.

CHAPTER
2

Introducing Oracle
NoSQL Database

O racle NoSQL Database is a scalable, highly available, key-value store that can be used to acquire and manage vast amounts of interactive information. It is intended to address the "last mile" requirements of interactive big data applications. We begin this chapter with an introduction to Oracle Berkeley DB (or Berkeley DB for short), which is the foundation for Oracle NoSQL Database as well as several other NoSQL systems.

Oracle NoSQL Database uses Oracle Berkeley DB Java Edition as the underlying data storage engine. Berkeley DB Java Edition is a mature product that also provides many, but not all, of the features and characteristics that are necessary for building a distributed key-value store such as Oracle NoSQL Database.

Oracle Berkeley DB

The Berkeley DB family of embeddable database products was developed by *Sleepycat Software, Inc.,* beginning in the early 1990s. Sleepycat Software, Inc. was later acquired by Oracle in 2006. Since the acquisition, Oracle has continued to invest in the Berkeley DB family of products by adding features and enhancements to meet the needs of a large and growing base of users. In addition to a SQL interface (the SQL API is available for Berkeley DB, but not for Berkeley DB Java Edition) for supporting ad hoc queries, there have been major performance and reliability enhancements as well as support for enterprise mobility. Enterprise mobility support is available through the SQL API for Berkeley DB.

Berkeley DB is a highly flexible, embeddable database engine that provides the application designer with a wide variety of choices for configuring and using the data management library. For example, you can run Berkeley DB as a pure in-memory database, change transactional constraints, run it on a wide variety of servers as well as embedded operating systems, and choose the appropriate API from a variety of

Products in the Berkeley DB Family

The Berkeley DB family of products encompasses three products: Berkeley DB, Berkeley DB Java Edition, and Berkeley DB XML. Berkeley DB is implemented in C and provides transactional key-value access to data. Berkeley DB supports a variety of programmatic and scripting APIs, including a SQL interface. Berkeley DB Java Edition is a pure Java implementation that provides similar functionality and features (except the SQL API) as Berkeley DB. Berkeley DB XML is designed to manage XML documents; it provides transactional XQuery access to XML documents. Berkeley DB XML uses Berkeley DB as the storage engine.

available APIs. Further, Berkeley DB supports advanced data management features such as B-tree indexing and hash indexing (only available in Berkeley DB, but not Berkeley DB Java Edition) as well as replication and high availability. Figure 2-1 illustrates the architecture of the Berkeley DB family of products.

Though Berkeley DB (we use the terms "Oracle Berkeley DB," "Berkeley DB," and "Berkeley DB family of products" interchangeably in this discussion) was originally focused on providing simple, fast key-value access to large amounts of disk-resident data in a small, embeddable library, several enhancements and modes of operation (for example, pure in-memory support) have been added to the products over the years. The Berkeley DB founders recognized the widespread need of applications to efficiently manage large quantities of disk-resident data; after all, programs are a combination of data, data structures to represent information, and algorithms to manipulate that data. Very often, the application also needs capabilities such as concurrency, fast indexed access, transactions, and recovery. These key observations led to the genesis of Berkeley DB. Berkeley DB provides all the data management capabilities that we have come to expect from traditional database systems packaged into an embeddable database library. Because Berkeley DB is an embeddable database library, database capabilities are built into the application, as opposed to

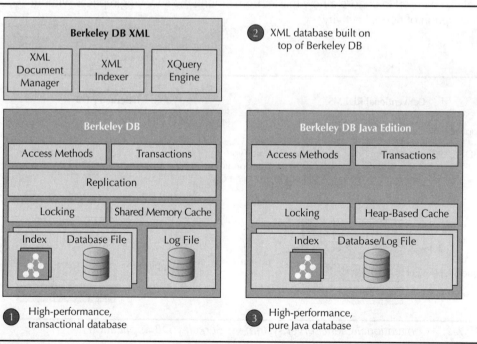

FIGURE 2-1. *Berkeley DB product family*

the application accessing data managed by a separate server. Berkeley DB APIs are intentionally designed from an application programmer's point of view, rather than a database application developer's point of view. Rather than specifying a data request declaratively in SQL, the Berkeley DB application developer accesses data using intuitive get() and put() API calls. This simple and intuitive interface eliminates the overhead of query parsing and optimization associated with SQL. In that sense, Berkeley DB applications are similar to the proprietary hierarchical database systems of the 1960s, where the data management engine was tightly coupled with the application. This tight coupling and simplicity of access enable the Berkeley DB application to get dramatic performance improvements for accessing vast quantities of data. Figure 2-2 illustrates the differences between an application using a SQL client-server system and an embeddable database such as Berkeley DB.

Berkeley DB's high availability and replication feature allows an application to survive machine failures as well as improve read scalability. A highly available Berkeley DB application runs on multiple computers configured as a high availability *cluster*; updates to the database are allowed only on one machine, designated as a *master*. The application running on the other nodes (called *replicas*) can read the data. Berkeley DB propagates changes to the data on the master node to all the replicas on the other machines in the cluster to keep the replicas updated and current. If the machine running the master should fail, Berkeley DB provides an *election* mechanism that can be used to choose a new master from among the surviving replicas without interruption of normal activity.

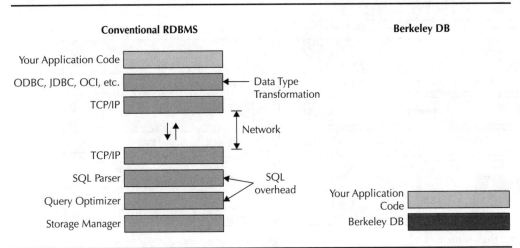

FIGURE 2-2. *Conventional client-server system vs. Berkeley DB application*

Due to the ease of use and robust database features, Berkeley DB products are extremely popular; there are over 200 million deployments of Berkeley DB worldwide. A wide variety of production applications, ranging from mobile phone applications to special-purpose appliances such as LDAP and e-mail servers to ecommerce websites, are based on Berkeley DB. It is fair to say that Berkeley DB is one of the most mature, high-performance, and high-function embeddable databases available today.

In recent years, several customers have built their own distributed key-value stores using Berkeley DB as a foundation. For example, Voldemort, the database engine for LinkedIn, one of the most popular social websites, uses Berkeley DB Java Edition for managing information for millions of subscribers. It is no surprise, then, that the developers of Oracle NoSQL Database also chose Berkeley DB Java Edition as the foundation for building a distributed key-value store. Besides the high-performance transactional indexed access capabilities, the high availability and replication features of Berkeley DB Java Edition are crucial architectural components of Oracle NoSQL Database.

Oracle NoSQL Database

Oracle NoSQL Database leverages the features and functionality of Oracle Berkeley DB Java Edition. We begin with a high-level description of the features and characteristics of the system and then explore some of the topics in more detail in the following sections.

Oracle NoSQL Database is a shared-nothing system designed to run and scale on commodity hardware. Key-value pairs are hash partitioned across server groups known as *shards*. At any point in time, a single key-value pair is always associated with a unique shard in the system. The major key (described shortly) of the key-value pair is hashed in order to determine which shard the record will belong to. Most Oracle NoSQL Database deployments use multiple machines (also referred to as *nodes*) per shard; each shard is configured as a highly available system using Berkeley DB Java Edition's high availability feature. The recommended configuration requires a minimum of three machines per shard; this is called the *replication factor* for the configuration. Depending on application requirements, a replication factor greater or less than 3 might be more appropriate. For example, a highly available 10-shard system with a replication factor of 3 would be deployed on 30 nodes. Of course, other configurations are possible in practice.

At the API level, Oracle NoSQL Database provides a key-value paradigm that is similar to Berkeley DB's key-value API. Oracle NoSQL Database supports the notion of a primary key (called *major key*) of a key-value pair, which is used to determine which shard the key-value pair should belong to. Because Oracle NoSQL Database is a shared-nothing, sharded, key-value client-server system, there are some key differences between the features offered in Berkeley DB Java Edition and Oracle NoSQL Database.

Oracle NoSQL Database supports the notion of minor keys. The combination of major and minor keys can be used to identify and address specific portions of the information in a key-value pair record. Minor keys are optional, but provide a significant convenience to the application developer. The combination of major and minor keys serves as the fully qualified unique primary key. Oracle NoSQL Database provides APIs for accessing all the contents of a specific key-value pair record as well as APIs for accessing parts of the record identified by a major and minor key combination. For example, a record in Oracle NoSQL Database might contain textual information about a user as well as the user's photo (image). The textual information and the image would each have a minor key; of course, the major key would be the person's identifier key. The value associated with a minor key can be retrieved and updated without having to access or modify other content in a key-value pair. Thus, the notion of minor keys not only provides a significant convenience to the application developer, but also results in performance improvements.

Oracle NoSQL Database leverages Berkeley DB Java Edition's ACID transaction capabilities in order to provide transactional semantics for data access. The notion of Berkeley DB Java Edition transactions is more general and can support multiple operations on multiple records within a single transaction. Unlike Berkeley DB, an operation in Oracle NoSQL Database can only affect the contents of a single major key. Further, Oracle NoSQL Database operations are *single-API call* transactions (except for scanning the contents of the entire database) where each API request from the client to the server is an atomic unit of work. Within the context of a single major key, a client request might modify the contents of some minor keys, delete others, and add some new minor keys (and values); all these activities are executed as a single transaction. Robust ACID transaction support is one of the key distinguishing features of Oracle NoSQL Database.

Oracle NoSQL Database leverages the high availability features in Berkeley DB in order to provide resiliency, fault tolerance, and read scalability. In the event of a node failure, Oracle NoSQL Database manages elections automatically and transparently to the application. Other than a momentary delay while the election is in progress, the application is not affected by node failures. Further, Oracle NoSQL Database automatically optimizes the placement of masters and replicas on the hardware servers in order to ensure the best performance of the system.

Berkeley DB provides APIs for administering and monitoring the database. Maintenance activities such as backups and log archiving can be initiated by the application by invoking the appropriate APIs. The application can also monitor resource usage, performance, and other metrics of the system using the provided APIs. Administering and monitoring a distributed system such as Oracle NoSQL Database is significantly more complex than managing a Berkeley DB application. Oracle NoSQL Database provides an administration console, a command-line interface and APIs for managing and monitoring all components of the system. This provides a tremendous convenience to the system administrator running a production Oracle NoSQL Database application. Besides support for activities such as backups and troubleshooting, it is possible to configure and alter the topology of the system, add more shards to the cluster in response to increased demand and data volumes, identify hotspot nodes, and redistribute the data as needed in order to maintain optimal performance. These simple-to-use but powerful administration capabilities are critical for smooth operation of a large production Oracle NoSQL Database deployment.

Let us now look at some of the features of Oracle NoSQL Database in more detail.

Database System Architectures

Database systems are generally categorized as shared memory (database system runs in a single, shared address space), shared-disk (the database system runs in multiple processes and multiple address spaces on different computers with access to shared storage—Oracle pioneered the concept of shared-disk database systems in the 1980s), or shared-nothing systems (the database system runs in multiple processes and multiple address spaces on multiple machines *without any shared storage*; database system processes communicate with each other using network messages). Tandem Non-Stop SQL pioneered the concept of scalable shared-nothing database systems in the mid-1980s. A shared-nothing system partitions the data into disjoint subsets (called *shards*), each shard managed by a node (along with replicas for providing high availability).

Berkeley DB is a shared memory database system; this means that a Berkeley DB application is generally constrained to run on a single computer. Though the high availability and replication features do support running Berkeley DB on multiple computers, this is still considered to be a shared memory architecture since

Shared Memory, Shared-Disk, and Shared-Nothing Systems

A shared memory system's performance is limited by the hardware (memory, processor, disk). To get additional performance, you need to get a bigger system. A shared-disk system needs to synchronize and coordinate access to shared data. The performance of such a system is limited by the performance of low-level synchronization primitives. A shared-nothing system's performance is constrained by the limits of the messaging infrastructure. One of the keys to getting scalable performance from shared-nothing systems is to reduce the messaging overhead to the minimum possible. Besides the obvious solution of using a faster network, NoSQL systems optimize messaging requirements by limiting the kinds of operations that can be performed by the application. As we shall see, this is a key aspect of all big data systems.

the total amount of data managed by Berkeley DB is constrained by the capacity of one computer. On the other hand, Oracle NoSQL Database is a shared-nothing system. Oracle Real Application Clusters is an example of a shared-disk architecture. Figure 2-3 illustrates the differences between the three types of database system architectures.

Unlike Berkeley DB Java Edition, which is an embeddable database library, Oracle NoSQL Database is a client-server system. Figure 2-4 illustrates the architecture of the system in a typical deployment; in this example, there are two client nodes and six server nodes, configured as two shards, for managing the data. Each shard is a highly available cluster of three nodes and manages a subset of the data. The system is designed to be dynamically scalable in the number of clients as well as the number of shards. In short, a highly available shard is the building block for implementing a highly scalable, shared-nothing system. Similarly, a node is the building block for implementing a highly available shard.

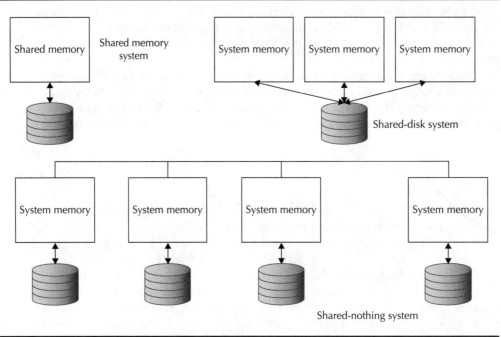

FIGURE 2-3. *Shared memory, shared-disk, and shared-nothing database architectures*

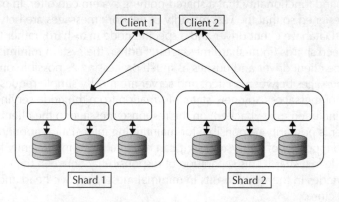

FIGURE 2-4. *Typical Oracle NoSQL Database deployment architecture*

Partitioning and Sharding

The primary goal of shared-nothing systems is to achieve horizontal scalability by using additional compute and storage hardware in order to keep pace with growing demands for data capacity and data retrieval. This "army of ants" approach requires that the storage and processing be partitioned across the individual nodes. In contrast, data and processing are managed by a single compute and storage resource in a shared memory system; similarly, in a shared-disk system, the data are shared, but processing is partitioned across multiple compute nodes.

A shared-nothing system is composed of *shards*; each shard in the cluster manages a distinct and disjoint dataset. Each shard is termed the *owner* of the subset of data that it manages. There are various alternatives to partitioning the data across shards. The partitioning algorithm uses a key (specified by the user) in order to partition the data. The most popular technique is to hash-partition the data, with the intent of distributing data evenly across shards. Hash partitioning works well when user requests are limited to accessing a single entity in the system and there is no relationship between consecutive data requests. Another technique is to range partition the record key. Range partitioning is advantageous when multiple related records (records with adjacent keys) are accessed by the application. Range partitioning is vulnerable to skewed distribution of data and "hotspots" in data access if a disproportionate number of requests have to be satisfied by the same shard. Thus, range partitioning is not widely used in practice.

A request for a specific record is routed to the owning shard. The owner processes the request and returns the answers to the client. The key to achieving scalability is to eliminate any single point of control and minimize the network messages that are required to satisfy a request. This architectural requirement has a significant impact on the features and functionality that a shared-nothing system can offer. In particular, the system is designed so that the vast majority of network messages are between the Oracle NoSQL Database client driver and a specific node in a shard, rather than messages between shards (intra-shard messages). Further, the system minimizes data processing in the client driver and pushes as much processing as possible onto the shard so that messages between a client and server are mostly simple request-response kinds of messages. Any new state information from the node serving the request is also included (piggybacked) on the response message to the client driver. The client driver is primarily responsible for maintaining information about data distribution and topology of the system so it can route requests intelligently to the appropriate node in a shard. This separation of responsibility between the client driver and the nodes in the shard results in minimal messaging overhead and a highly scalable architecture.

Most often, the amount of data managed by a system keeps growing over time. Oracle NoSQL Database supports the ability to add new hardware resources as data and processing demands grow. When one or more new shards are added, data on existing shards must be repartitioned across all the shards in the cluster. The simplest approach is to disable user requests temporarily, redistribute the data, and resume normal operation. However, this is unacceptable in practice, because the temporary outage for adding new capacity can last for a significant period of time (several hours or days), depending on the volume of data to be repartitioned. Most systems, including Oracle NoSQL Database, redistribute data online and dynamically, without compromising availability of the system. This is not a trivial exercise; the data movement needs to be correct and atomic (all or nothing), the client drivers need to be updated to reflect the new distribution, and the repartitioning needs to be done in a way that takes maximum advantage of the newly added resources. Careful implementation of data migration within a highly available system is a key metric of a product's maturity. Maximizing throughput, minimizing the impact on user queries, allowing for operation failure and restart, and updating the system with the new topology are all key functions and design considerations in Oracle NoSQL Database.

If the data and/or processing requirements decrease, then it is possible to free up some of the resources, thus reducing the amount of hardware needed by the system. When the usage of the system is cyclical over time, or follows a predictable pattern (for example, dramatic spike in processing demand for ecommerce systems during the holiday season), there is a temporary need to grow the number of shards. At the end of the peak demand period, the number of shards can be reduced to handle "steady-state" requirements. Data redistribution required to shrink the cluster is also an online activity.

We will use the term *dynamic elasticity* to refer to the ability of the system to add and remove resources dynamically in response to changes in data and processing requirements. Dynamic elasticity is a key characteristic of shared-nothing systems that makes them very attractive for big data applications. Oracle NoSQL Database provides administrative tools to support dynamic elasticity.

Availability

High availability is another key characteristic of Oracle NoSQL Database. Processors, memory, storage, software, and networks can fail in unpredictable ways. As the number of such components in a system increases, the probability of failure of *some* components increases dramatically. For example, the failure rate of an individual disk may be one failure during a period of two years. Statistically, a shared-nothing system with 1,000 disks will experience at least one disk failure every day! If you also take processors, memory, software, and network components into account, the frequency of a failure is even higher! A distributed system needs to be designed to handle these failures without impact to the application.

Availability is achieved by adding redundancy to the system. In NoSQL systems, redundancy is commonly achieved by maintaining multiple copies of the data on multiple nodes. Each shard comprises two or more nodes (called *replicas*) that have identical copies of the data. As changes are made to the data on one node, they are propagated to the other replicas to keep them current. Monitoring tools are used to detect and repair failures. Should one of the nodes fail, the system automatically detects and handles the change in the membership of a shard without any noticeable impact to the application. It is not trivial to determine whether a particular node is currently a member of a shard since a node might fail or there may be a temporary network outage that makes the node temporarily unreachable.

There are two alternative approaches to handling data updates in a highly available shard. One approach is to designate one of the replicas as the *master* node; a master can serve update requests as well as read requests, while all other nodes can only serve read requests. This architecture is called *single-master*. Note that it is possible to have passive, standby replicas, but this is not common in practice. Another approach is to allow updates at any node of the shard and then propagate those changes to the other replicas. This architecture is called *multi-master*.

The advantage of a single-master architecture is that there cannot be concurrent changes to the same record on multiple replicas; the master always has the most current value of any record in the shard. This property of single-master architectures simplifies the job of the application developer because there is no possibility of lost updates, or conflicting, concurrent changes to the same record. A single-master system needs to have a mechanism to elect a new master from one of the surviving replicas in the shard, should the current master fail. Master re-election uses a distributed quorum-based algorithm to unambiguously choose a new master. This is why most highly available systems have three (or an odd number of) replicas; this ensures that it is possible to gather a majority of votes to correctly determine the outcome of a master election. Electing a new master is typically a very quick process, lasting no more than a second or two; during this period, update activity to the shard is temporarily suspended. Figure 2-5 illustrates the process of master re-election in a shard with a master and two replicas.

The advantage of a multi-master system is that any node can handle application requests to change a record. In fact, it is possible that the same record is changed concurrently on two different replicas. If a node fails, a request can simply be routed to another surviving node without any pause in update activity (there is no need for master election). As in the single-master case, changes to records are constantly propagated to the other replicas in the shard. Resolving conflicting changes to the same record provides interesting challenges in a multi-master system. Because the changes occur on separate and distinct machines, it is not easy to determine the timing and sequence of the conflicting changes. In some cases, the system can resolve the change on its own. Most often, however, conflicts are detected when a record is retrieved, and conflict resolution is left up to the application (or even the end user, in some cases). Update operations (even concurrent updates to the same record on different replicas) proceed normally. For read requests, the application

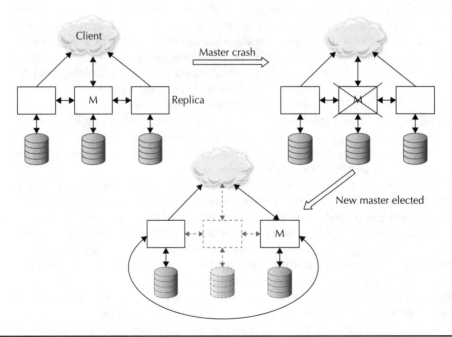

FIGURE 2-5. *Electing a new master*

typically requests the same record from multiple replicas of the shard. If the versions (along with the timestamp of the latest change) returned by different replicas are not identical, then it is necessary to determine which is the most current version using timestamps, application-specific semantics, and knowledge of the data. Oracle NoSQL Database is a single-master per shard system.

Eventual Consistency

A discussion about distributed systems such as Oracle NoSQL Database would not be complete without a mention of *eventual consistency*. A distributed system maintains copies of data on multiple machines in order to provide high availability and scalability. When an application makes a change to a data item on one machine, that change has to be propagated to the other replicas. Because the change propagation is not instantaneous, there's an interval of time during which some of the copies will have the most recent change, but others won't. In other words, the copies will be mutually inconsistent. However, the change will eventually be propagated to all the copies. In a single-master system, if an application makes a change to a record, that request will be handled by the master node. As soon as the update request completes, if the application retrieves the same record (same major key), it is possible that the request will be routed to one of the replicas in the shard. If the master has not yet propagated the changes to that replica, the application will see the older version of the data. However, if the application requests the data after the changes on the master have been propagated to the replica, then the application will see the latest version of the record. Depending on the relative timing of the read request, the application might see different values!

Thus, the notion of *eventual consistency* is simply an acknowledgment that there is an unbounded delay in propagating a change made on one machine to all the other copies. Eventual consistency is not relevant in centralized (single-copy) systems because there is no need for change propagation.

Various distributed systems address consistency in different ways because there is a trade-off between operation latency, availability, and consistency. In some systems, the machine where the change originates will simply send asynchronous (and possibly unreliable) messages to the other machines and declare the operation as successful. This is fast, but at the cost of potential data loss if the originating machine fails before the replica(s) have received the update. Other systems send synchronous (blocking) messages to all other machines, receive acknowledgments, and only then, declare the operation as successful. These systems favor consistency and availability at the cost of performance. Finally, a system might implement some variant of these two extremes (for example, wait for acknowledgments from a majority of the replicas).

Oracle NoSQL Database allows the application designer to choose the consistency level required, on a per-operation basis; of course, there is a default setting of consistency as well. The developer can either choose to use the default semantics of consistency or specify consistency on a per-operation level for critical operations. Per-operation choice of consistency is the most flexible and the most application-friendly option because the application designer has a clear understanding and control on the performance as well as the consistency guarantees without additional complexity in the application program.

Oracle NoSQL Database offers several choices for read consistency. The application can specify absolute consistency if it needs the most recent version; in this case, the client driver will route the request to the master node of the shard. The application developer can also specify time-based or transaction ID–based consistency for read operations. For example, an application might be willing to tolerate reading data that is no more than one second out-of-date with respect to the most recent update. Transaction ID-based consistency is useful in scenarios where the application modifies a record at a certain point in time and wants to ensure that a subsequent read operation will read a version of that same record that is at least as current as the change it made to that record (it is okay to read a more recent version). The client driver keeps track of the change propagation between each master and its replicas, so it is able to route the request to the replica that can satisfy such a request. Finally, the application can also specify that it doesn't care how consistent the data are for a particular read request. The Oracle NoSQL Database client driver is free to route the request to any of the replicas of the shard.

Thus, depending on the kind of read consistency required, the client driver will route the request to the most appropriate replica of the shard. This also serves to distribute the workload across the various nodes of the shard, thus achieving better system utilization and improved performance.

Durability—Making Changes Permanent

Generally, a database system ensures that a change is made permanent (durable) by writing the updated version to stable storage. Making a change durable means that the change survives processor and memory failure. However, I/O is very expensive compared to memory access. As a first approximation, I/O is 1,000 times slower (millisecond latency) than accessing memory (microsecond latency). Over the years, relational database system designers have invented several optimizations such as write-ahead logging in order to alleviate the cost of I/O for providing durability.

Some demanding applications require more performance than what is achievable in a cost-effective manner using the traditional optimizations such as write-ahead logging. Quite often, these applications are willing to relax the durability guarantees in order to achieve better performance. Some database systems (and NoSQL systems, in particular) have implemented a variety of relaxed durability guarantees in order to meet the needs of such applications.

For example, some systems buffer changes in memory and only propagate changes to disk periodically. A system might choose to write the contents of the buffer to disk every 5 seconds. Clearly, this strategy alleviates the I/O overhead significantly, resulting in dramatic performance benefits. However, if there is a failure (memory loss), the most recent set of changes will be lost. Other systems might choose to issue the I/O to operating system buffers and declare the change to be durable before the operating system writes the buffered data to disk. In this case, a process failure (but not operating system failure) will not affect the durability of the changes; however, an operating system failure will result in data loss of the most recent changes. Of course, the most stringent (and most expensive) method to ensure durability is to issue the I/O and then wait for the write operation to complete. It is also possible to write multiple disks (usually, this is done by the operating system or storage subsystem) to ensure that the changes can also survive a disk failure.

A distributed system such as Oracle NoSQL Database can take advantage of the multiple replicas to ensure durability. Because the goal of durability is to protect against processor, memory, and operating system failures, distributed systems leverage the fact that an update can be made durable by propagating the change to one or more replicas concurrently while writing the change to the local disk. The system can declare an operation to be durable after receiving acknowledgments for the update from the replicas, without waiting for the disk I/O to complete because the replicas have received the update (it is durable on another node). Depending on the speed of the network, the message delivery and receipt may be faster than the time it takes to complete a local write (I/O) operation.

Oracle NoSQL Database supports the notion of varying degrees of durability for update operations and exposes these options through the API so that the application designer can make the appropriate trade-offs between performance and durability on a per-operation basis. Three independent dimensions of durability are supported and the application developer can choose the option that best suits the requirements of the application. In the case of the master node, the application designer can choose whether the change should be considered durable when it is written to the log buffer, when it is written to the file system buffers, or when it is written to disk. The application designer can also choose whether the change should be propagated to the replicas asynchronously or synchronously (with acknowledgment). Finally, when the change has been propagated to the replicas, the application can also choose whether the change is considered durable when it is written to the log buffer, when it is written to the file system buffers, or when it is written to disk on the replicas. Thus, the developer has complete control over the degree of durability and required performance for each operation. For example, the choice of "write to local disk, wait for acknowledgments from all replicas, write to replica disk" is the most stringent option an application can choose.

Figure 2-6 illustrates the durability and consistency options that are available in Oracle NoSQL Database. Oracle NoSQL Database allows the user to choose the durability policy on a per-operation basis. Oracle NoSQL Database uses this information during transaction commit processing in order to achieve the best performance while honoring the durability requirements of the operation.

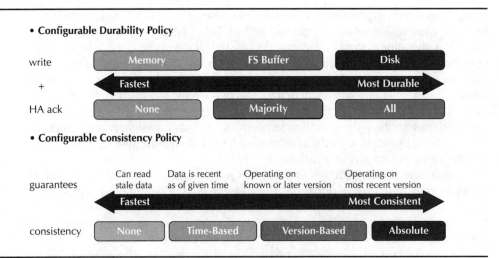

FIGURE 2-6.   *Configurable durability and consistency policies*

Transactions

Atomicity, consistency, isolation, and durability (ACID) are the key characteristics provided by transactions. Oracle NoSQL Database leverages the transaction capabilities of the underlying Berkeley DB storage engine. Berkeley DB supports row-level locking and two-phase locking to ensure that the effects of one transaction are isolated from other, concurrent transactions. We've already discussed the semantics of consistency and durability. In the rest of this section, we discuss the property of atomicity.

Transactional access to data is a critical requirement in many Oracle NoSQL Database applications. Transactions provide atomicity ("all or nothing" semantics) to ensure that either all or none of the changes in a transaction are made durable. Consider an Oracle NoSQL Database application that stores the list of items that the user intends to purchase (popularly referred to as the *shopping cart*) during a particular shopping session. Most often, the shipping costs depend on when the user expects the items to be delivered. For example, overnight delivery is more expensive than delivery within 8 business days. If the user changes the delivery dates for some items during the session, then it is important that the total cost of the transaction be updated to reflect the changes in delivery costs. Thus, the changes to the delivery date for each item and the shipping total cost of the purchase (including shipping costs) need to be updated atomically. Oracle NoSQL Database supports atomicity for all changes performed on various contents of the same major key, as long as all those changes are specified in a single request to the server.

Data Modeling

Data modeling is a critical aspect of proper application design for Oracle NoSQL Database applications. The data model is very flexible and enables the application designer to model a wide variety of data structures, without compromising efficiency of storage or data access. Let us examine these capabilities in more detail below.

Major Keys, Minor Keys, and Values

Oracle NoSQL Database provides a key-value paradigm to the application developer. Every entity (record) is a set of key-value pairs. A key has multiple components, specified as an ordered list. The major key identifies the entity and consists of the leading components of the key. The subsequent components are called minor keys. This organization is similar to a directory path specification in a file system (for example, /Major/minor1/minor2/). The "value" part of the key-value pair is simply an uninterpreted string of bytes of arbitrary length.

This concept is best explained using an example. Consider storing information about a person, John Smith, who works at Oracle Headquarters, start date January 1, 2012, and has a telephone number +1-650-555-9999. The employee ID might be a logical choice for the major key for the person entity (for example, 123456789). In addition, the "person" entity might contain personal information (such as the person's telephone number) and employment information (such as work location and hire date). The application designer can associate a minor key (for example, personal_info) with the personal information (+1-650-555-9999) and another minor key (for example, employment_info) with the employment information (Oracle Headquarters, start date January 1, 2012). Specifying the major key "123456789" would return "John Smith." Specifying "/123456789/personal_info" as the key would access John Smith's personal information; similarly, "/123456789/employment_info" would be the key to access the employment information. Leading components of the key are always required. Oracle NoSQL Database internally stores these as separate key-value pair records; one for the user_id, a second for user_id/personal_info, and the third for user_id/employment_info.

The API for manipulating key-value pairs is simple. The user can insert a single key-value pair into the database using a put() operation. Given a key, the user can retrieve the key-value pair using a get() operation or delete it using a delete() operation. The get(), put(), and delete() operations operate on only a single (multi-component) key. Oracle NoSQL Database provides additional APIs that allow the application to operate on multiple key-value pairs within an entity (same major key) in a single transaction.

The major key determines which shard the record will belong to. All key-value pairs associated with the same entity (same major key) are always stored on the same shard. This implementation enables efficient, single-shard access to logically related subsets of the record. Figure 2-7 illustrates the concept of major and minor keys. Note that minor keys can be nested.

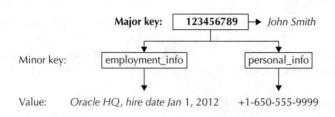

FIGURE 2-7. *Major and minor keys*

Oracle NoSQL Database also provides an unordered scan API that can be used to iterate over all the records in the database; unordered scans do not have transaction semantics, although only committed data will be returned to the application.

Large Object Support

An Oracle NoSQL database is often used to store large objects such as images, audio, videos, and maps. In the vast majority of usage scenarios, once such content is stored in the database, it is either retrieved or deleted, but never updated. For example, an audio or video streaming service might store vast amounts of such media content and then serve it up on demand.

Oracle NoSQL Database provides efficient support for managing large objects in the database and a streaming API for easy access to the information. A large object is stored internally as a sequence of object fragments (or chunks). Because each object fragment is much smaller than the entire object, this design is much more efficient in terms of memory requirements in the user application as well as the server. Further, the streaming API ensures that the fragments can be fetched efficiently from the containing shards.

JSON Schemas

Oracle NoSQL Database manages key-value pair data; the key and value can be arbitrary byte strings that are interpreted only by the application. Minor keys are a great convenience for representing the structure of the record. These capabilities provide a lot of flexibility in terms of evolving and changing the structure of content stored in Oracle NoSQL Database. However, the interpretation of the contents of a record is left entirely up to the application; the contents (value portion of the key-value pair) are represented as byte-arrays, which can make it difficult to share the data between multiple applications.

Oracle NoSQL Database also supports JSON schemas (http:// json-schema.org/) and Apache Avro (http://avro.apache.org/) for specifying the structure of the value in a key-value pair. JSON schemas are self-describing, support schema evolution, and are widely used in big data applications. Apache Avro is an extremely space-efficient serialization format for JSON schemas; thus, the use of JSON schemas and Avro serialization enables ease of application design and data exchange between various applications and systems. For example, JSON schemas enable easy sharing of data between Oracle NoSQL Database applications and MapReduce (Hadoop). Very often, big data applications use a variety of tools and technologies such as key-value stores, map-reduce processing, relational databases, and analytics in order to derive new insights; the easy and efficient exchange of data from one system to another is critical in such scenarios.

Oracle NoSQL Database is often used for managing web and ecommerce data. JSON and Javascript are popularly used in these applications. Hence, support for JSON schemas makes it very convenient for the developer to implement the application without having to interpret and translate data from one format to another each time it is stored or accessed in the database.

Performance

Oracle NoSQL Database has been designed for applications that need fast, predictable, low latency access to vast amounts of data. Let us examine how Oracle NoSQL Database benefits such applications by considering a typical ecommerce environment. Such systems manage vast numbers of user profiles and have stringent response-time requirements. Whenever a user visits the site, the retailer provides a personalized web page based on the user's profile. If no such profile exists, the site must create one. These user profiles will change over time as the retailer learns more about the users. Different user profiles may contain radically different information and the retailer may decide to collect new information at any time. Oracle NoSQL Database addresses this use case by virtue of its flexible key-value paradigm and scales to meet increasing customer demand. Oracle NoSQL Database has been optimized extensively to provide excellent scalable throughput and low latency. As of this writing, Oracle NoSQL Database has been benchmarked at over 1.2 million operations per second with an average latency of 1 millisecond for the 95 percent reads and 5 percent updates workload in the Yahoo! Cloud Serving Benchmark test suite. This test was performed on a 15-machine cluster running 10 shards with over 2 terabytes of data. To put these numbers in perspective, credit card fraud scoring applications typically require a throughput of less than 10,000 operations per second. Thus, Oracle NoSQL Database delivers performance that is more than sufficient to meet the requirements of the most demanding applications.

Administration

A distributed system is composed of large numbers of hardware and software components. This necessitates a comprehensive and easy-to-use monitoring and administration tool to manage the system.

Oracle NoSQL Database includes administration utilities to manage operational tasks such as configuring the system, defining the topology of the system configuration, as well as adding new resources as needed. It also includes monitoring tools to track the health of the overall system as well as individual components, detect performance issues and hotspots, and dynamically redistribute the work as needed. These monitoring capabilities are invaluable for ensuring that the system continues to operate smoothly in spite of component and software failures.

Oracle NoSQL Database also provides JMX (Java Management Extensions) and SNMP (Simple Network Management Protocol) APIs for programmatic monitoring of the system. This makes it easy to integrate Oracle NoSQL Database with other monitoring and administration tools that might already be in use. This is a huge convenience to system administrators because it allows them to minimize the number of separate tools that might be required in order to ensure smooth operation of a production system.

Integration with Other Products

Most big data applications use multiple technologies including Oracle NoSQL Database in order to derive value from big data. For example, an ecommerce site might use Oracle NoSQL Database for the customer-facing application, a relational database repository to store master data, data warehousing and business intelligence tools for tracking key business parameters, and a MapReduce system to process and analyze unstructured information. It is crucial that the components of a big data application be well integrated so as to simplify the task of the application designer as well as the system administrator.

Oracle NoSQL Database integrates well with these related technologies and tools. The *external tables* capability allows the developer to query data stored in Oracle NoSQL Database from Oracle Database using SQL. SQL is arguably the most popular programming language today; being able to query Oracle NoSQL Database data using SQL is a tremendous benefit to many developers. This also provides a huge benefit for applications that need to reference key-value data along with relational data. For example, this is very useful in data warehousing applications that need to have a unified view of all data.

Oracle NoSQL Database also integrates with MapReduce technologies. MapReduce typically reads input data from a file system (most commonly, HDFS). Oracle NoSQL Database provides an interface that allows the *mapper* in a MapReduce job to read data directly from Oracle NoSQL Database. Because MapReduce is designed to process all semi-structured and unstructured data, this capability is very important in big data applications.

Oracle NoSQL Database is integrated with Oracle Event Processing. Data stored in Oracle NoSQL Database can be referenced by the event processing engine in interactive time in order to provide real-time alerts and notifications for meaningful events. For example, the event processing engine might be used for real-time monitoring and trading of stocks. If a user is "watching" a particular stock, then the event processing engine can look up the user's parameters (buy, sell thresholds) and alert the user immediately when the specified conditions are satisfied.

Oracle Coherence is an in-memory data grid solution that enables organizations to predictably scale mission-critical applications by providing fast access to frequently used data. Oracle NoSQL Database is integrated with Oracle Coherence; Coherence is used to cache the most frequently accessed data in memory, while NoSQL Database provides a scalable persistent repository for vast amounts of data stored on disk.

Oracle NoSQL Database is also integrated with Oracle RDF Graph; this makes it easy to discover relationships between key-value pair records stored in the Oracle NoSQL Database. The most obvious example of this capability is social networking to discover new friends and contacts, as popularized by Facebook and LinkedIn. There are many other scenarios such as fraud detection and security where graph traversal capabilities for big data are important as well.

Licensing

Oracle NoSQL Database is distributed as an open source version as well as an enterprise version. The Community Edition is available under the open source AGPLv3 license and is intended for use in open source applications. Oracle NoSQL Database Enterprise Edition is available under a commercial license and is intended for proprietary applications.

Both versions of the product provide the same basic capabilities that are needed to manage large amounts of key-value data. The Enterprise Edition also offers tighter integration between Oracle NoSQL Database and other related Oracle products such as RDF Graph, Oracle Event Processing, Oracle Coherence, and Oracle Database. These additional capabilities make it easy to use Oracle NoSQL Database within a larger data management ecosystem that may include semantic data and streaming event data as well as relational data. Most big data applications use a combination of products and technologies in order to derive new insights and business value from multiple data sources. Oracle NoSQL Database Enterprise Edition is an excellent choice for a scalable key-value store in such deployments.

Summary

In this chapter, we discussed Oracle Berkeley DB, which is the foundational building block for Oracle NoSQL Database. We discussed the three types of database architectures and then examined some of the characteristics of Oracle NoSQL Database like partitioning and sharding, availability, consistency and durability options, support for transactions and data modeling. We discussed the need for integrating Oracle NoSQL Database with related technologies such as MapReduce, Oracle Database, Oracle Event Processing, and Oracle Coherence. All these features and capabilities make Oracle NoSQL Database a compelling solution for today's big data processing needs.

CHAPTER
3

Oracle NoSQL
Database Architecture

The previous chapter discussed some of the underlying concepts and technologies used in Oracle NoSQL Database. Building on this foundation, let us take a closer look at the implementation of Oracle NoSQL Database and how it operates. We will start with the high-level architecture, including clients, servers, and datacenters, followed by a discussion of how records are stored. Next, we will discuss the underlying log-structured storage architecture and how it impacts performance of the system; we will conclude with a discussion of durability and transactions.

High-Level Architecture and Terminology

Oracle NoSQL Database is a client-server system. The server actually comprises one or more shards; each shard manages a distinct subset of all the data managed by the system. Each shard comprises Replication Nodes. Generally (and this is true of other NoSQL systems as well), each shard comprises at least three Replication Nodes. Together, the Replication Nodes in a shard serve requests for the subset of the data that they manage and also provide read scalability and availability. As mentioned previously, at any point in time, one of the Replication Nodes in the shard is designated as the master, whereas the other nodes are designated as replicas. The master node can serve read as well as write requests; the replicas can only serve read requests. Replication Nodes are hosted on Storage Nodes (physical or virtual machines).

Conceptually, the Oracle NoSQL Database Client Driver is analogous to an ODBC or JDBC driver (used in relational database systems) in that it is linked into the application program and manages the interaction between the application and the Replication Nodes. Each Client Driver is "aware" of all the shards in the system and maintains a list of network addresses and port numbers for each Replication Node. It establishes a network connection to a Replication Node when it has to communicate with the node.

In addition to hosting one or more Replication Nodes, each Storage Node also runs a Storage Node Agent that is responsible for administering and managing the Replication Nodes on that Storage Node. Each Storage Node Agent interacts with the Administration Console; the Administration Console provides a unified management and administration view of the system.

Figure 3-1 illustrates the various components of a Oracle NoSQL Database with a single shard. Note that although only a single shard and single Client Driver is depicted, a typical system will have many shards and Client Drivers. Also note that the number of clients is unrelated to the number of shards in the system. For example, a large production application that manages many terabytes of data may have a few hundred shards and many client instances of the application program.

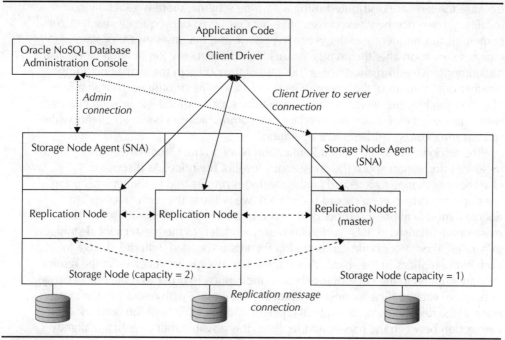

FIGURE 3-1. *Description of the various components in an Oracle NoSQL Database deployment*

Intelligent Client Driver

Unlike some other systems, Oracle NoSQL Database does not have a central repository that maintains the state information for all the nodes in the server because this would create a single point of failure as well as a single point of contention ("hotspot") in the system. Instead, each Client Driver maintains information about the mapping of keys to shards so that it can route a request for a specified key to the appropriate shard. Keys are mapped to shards using a hash function, described later. The mapping of keys to shards is relatively static and only changes when the number of shards is changed (for example, in order to add more capacity to the system).

The Client Driver also keeps track of the state of each Replication Node in every shard, including information about which node is currently the master, which nodes are replicas, and which nodes are offline at any given moment. Rather than using dedicated status messages for tracking state information, every Replication Node includes information about its state in the response messages that are sent to the Client Driver. After the state of a node changes, the next interaction between a Client Driver and the node will inform the Client Driver of that state change. Thus, each client learns about server node state changes independent of other clients.

Because the keys are distributed using a hashing scheme, there is generally no locality of reference between consecutive data requests; consequently, each client communicates frequently with every server node and becomes aware of state changes very soon after the change occurs. Of course, every Replication Node also has authoritative information about the state of the nodes in the shard (including whether one or more of the nodes in its shard are online or offline). Thus, if a new client connects to the server, it can discover the state of all the Replication Nodes as well. This design eliminates the need for any communication between clients while still ensuring correct and efficient operation.

The response message from a Replication Node to the Client Driver also includes information about the consistency level of the node. As discussed elsewhere, a change to a record (at the master) is propagated to the replicas using log shipping. Whenever a record is changed (we will use the term "change" to denote a modification, insertion, or deletion of a record in the database) on the master node in a shard, it is written (as described later) to the master's local storage; in parallel, the master node sends the log records associated with the change to each of the replicas in the shard. When these log records are received at the replica, they are applied to the copy of the data on the replica in order to reflect this change. In essence, each replica is constantly playing "catch-up" with respect to the master node. Thus, depending on the rate of changes and the latency of the network connection between the master and replicas, it is possible that a replica is slightly out of date with respect to the master because the log records have still not been received or applied on the replica side. Of course, if there are few or no modifications to the data, then each replica will be as current as the master.

Each log record is identified with a unique and monotonically increasing *log sequence number* (*LSN* for short). For the purposes of this discussion, it is easiest to think of an LSN as an integer, although, in reality, an LSN often includes additional information such as the log file ID and other internal information. Because LSNs are monotonically increasing and unique, the log record for the most recent change at any point in time will have the highest LSN. For example, if records A, B, and C are changed in that time sequence (C is changed most recently), the LSN for the change associated with record C will be higher than the LSN for the change to record B, which in turn, will be higher than the LSN for the change to record A.

Whenever a Replication Node sends a response to the Client Driver, it includes the highest LSN of its log in the response message. Consequently, each Client Driver is able to track the highest LSN for each Replication Node in each shard. In particular, for each shard, the client is aware whether a replica has the same or lower LSN than the master node; if the replica's LSN is lower than that of the master node, it is also aware of the "lag" between the master and the Replication Node. Because LSNs increase monotonically in time when records are modified, inserted, or deleted, LSNs can also serve as a proxy for the time at which a record was changed. Oracle NoSQL Database keeps track of the association between the time and the LSN of a change to a record. Thus, if a replica lags behind the master node, it is possible to infer the *time lag* between the replica and the master as well as the *LSN lag*. Obviously, a replica's LSN can never be higher than the LSN of the master.

An application can specify the degree of consistency required for every read operation. In particular, the application can choose between the following options: *any* (don't care how current the record is); *time-based* (okay to read a record that's out of date by no more than the specified time interval); *LSN-based*, also known as *version-based* (okay to read a record that is out of date by no more than the specified LSN interval); or absolute (read the most current version of the record). By keeping track of the consistency level for each Replication Node as discussed above, the Client Driver can route a read request to the most appropriate node, thus improving the efficiency and read scalability of the system. If the application requests absolute consistency, then the Client Driver will route the request to the master. On the other hand, if the application can tolerate a lower level of consistency, the Client Driver can route the request to one of the replicas that satisfies the consistency constraints of the request, thereby distributing the work among all the members of a shard. Also, keep in mind that because the master node is constantly sending new log records to the replicas and the replicas are as constantly applying the log updates, the Client Driver's knowledge of the lag between the master and replica is a pessimistic estimate. If the application requests a lower level of consistency, it is possible that the Replication Node will have a more current version of the record by the time the Client Driver sends the read request to the Replication Node. This is okay because the application sees a more recent version of the record than it was willing to accept.

For each node in the cluster, the Client Driver also keeps track of the number of currently active requests to each Replication Node. This information is used by the Client Driver as a heuristic to route a read request to a Replication Node with the lightest load, if more than one Replication Node can satisfy the read consistency constraints of the operation. Thus, the Client Driver plays a very important role in ensuring that application requests are served efficiently with a single message exchange.

The client's ability to track the consistency level and load for each node in the cluster becomes particularly important in a distributed datacenter scenario when the server nodes can be located in multiple geographic locations with differing network latencies. The following table summarizes the kind of information that the Client Driver maintains, and how it uses that information in order to deliver superior performance.

Information	Benefit
Mapping of keys to shards, including the partition map (partition maps are explained in more detail later).	Enables the Client Driver to route the request to the correct shard.

Information	Benefit
Online or offline state of each node in the cluster.	Enables the Client Driver to avoid sending useless requests to offline nodes.
For each node in each shard, maintain information about the current LSN lag as well as the current time lag.	Enables the driver to route the request to the appropriate node (master or replica) depending on the read consistency level specified by the application.
For each node in the cluster, maintain information about the number of active network connections from between the client and the Replication Node.	If more than one node satisfies the read consistency constraints of the application request, enables the driver to route the request to the node with the lowest load, thus providing the fastest response to the application.

Shards, Storage, and Network Topology

Each shard is set up as a Berkeley DB High Availability system; each shard has a master node and some number of replicas (typically, it is recommended that each shard have at least three Replication Nodes). Nodes within a shard are tightly coupled. Each member of the shard tracks the status (online or offline) of the other members in the shard. The master sends new log records to each of the replicas in response to update activity, and replicas send acknowledgments to the master. During periods of low update activity, heartbeat messages to monitor the state (offline or online) of the nodes in a shard are exchanged between members of a shard. If one of the nodes in a shard goes offline, the remaining nodes participate in an election in order to ensure that there is a unique master node in the shard.

Under normal circumstances, there are only two kinds of network interactions in a Oracle NoSQL Database system: client-server messages and messages between the members of a shard for replication and high availability. Shards never communicate with each other, except during data redistribution operations (discussed later). This is a critical aspect of the architecture because it allows the system to scale linearly as more shards are added (horizontal scalability). Oracle NoSQL Database has been tested on clusters of a few hundred nodes and demonstrated near linear scalability.

Replication Nodes run on Storage Nodes; a Storage Node is the physical or virtual machine that runs the Replication Node software. Although the architecture does not preclude the use of virtual machines, it is generally recommended that Oracle NoSQL Database be deployed on physical hardware, especially when the application is sensitive to performance and latency for data access. Virtualization software can also make it difficult to identify and troubleshoot performance problems in the system.

Oracle NoSQL Database does not require that all the Storage Nodes be identical in terms of processing power, memory, or storage capacity. Similarly, the network connections between the clients and Replication Nodes as well as the network connections between nodes in a shard can have varying characteristics and latencies. Because Oracle NoSQL Database is designed to be a cost-effective solution for managing huge volumes of data, in a typical deployment, the total amount of memory available on all the Storage Nodes in the cluster is likely to be much smaller than the amount of data being managed (on disk). Further, though Oracle NoSQL Database has an excellent buffer manager, there is unlikely to be locality of reference in a typical Oracle NoSQL Database application (because major keys are hash partitioned across shards). Thus, an application's request for data will most often incur one or more disk accesses in order to fetch the required records. Consequently, the throughput of a node is limited by the IO bandwidth of the storage device to which it is connected. For this reason, direct-attached storage is preferred over SAN or NAS storage for Oracle NoSQL Database deployments because the throughput and latency of direct-attached storage is more predictable than other storage alternatives. For extremely high throughput and low latency deployments, it is possible to use solid-state disks (SSD) or flash as the storage device. Results of performance tests of Oracle NoSQL Database have demonstrated that it can deliver over 30 times better throughput and latency using SSD or flash storage devices as compared to hard disk storage devices. (Yahoo! Cloud Serving Benchmark, http://labs.yahoo.com/news/yahoo-cloud-serving-benchmark/, was used to measure the performance of NoSQL Database.)

Oracle NoSQL Database does not require that all hardware in the cluster be identical. Some Storage Nodes can have more processing and storage capacity than others. Most often, this can happen when a Storage Node is replaced or when additional Storage Nodes are added to a cluster in production. When a new Storage Node is configured, it is necessary to specify the *capacity* for the Storage Node. The capacity of a Storage Node indicates the maximum number of Replication Nodes that can run concurrently on the Storage Node. Although processing capacity and memory are also important considerations, the available IO bandwidth is the most important consideration from a performance point of view. As mentioned earlier, throughput and latency of IO operations limit the throughput that a node can deliver. If two Replication Nodes share the same disk for storage, then only half of the available IO bandwidth is available to each Replication Node. Consequently, for hard disk–based systems, it is generally sufficient to set the capacity of the Storage Node to be equal to the number of attached disks. For example, if the Storage Node has multiple processors, large amounts of memory, and 10 disks, the administrator would specify the capacity for that Storage Node as 10. If a "small" machine with just one disk is being used, the capacity would be set to 1.

The recommendation for choosing the capacity of the Storage Node to be equal to the number of disks attached to the node applies primarily to hard disk–based deployments. Solid state storage (SSD) generally provides much more IO bandwidth and much lower latency as compared to hard disks Generally, it is sufficient to set the capacity to 1 for SSD-based deployments.

Proper selection of the capacity of each Storage Node ensures that the machine is utilized optimally. The capacity parameter can also be used to manage the amount of data that a single shard manages. For example, if the Storage Node has five disks attached to it and the capacity is set to 5, then each Replication Node will be assigned to a single disk. On the other hand, if the capacity is set to 1, then the Replication Node associated with this Storage Node will use the cumulative capacity of all five disks in order to manage the data, assuming that the disks are configured as a single logical storage volume using RAID or other techniques. Because each node within a shard manages the same subset of data, the amount of data that a shard can manage is limited by the Replication Node that has the least amount of storage associated with it.

If a Storage Node is configured with a capacity greater than 1, then it will host multiple Replication Nodes. In such a scenario, Oracle NoSQL Database ensures that each Storage Node hosts the same number of master nodes for the cluster. Because a Replication Node failure (cluster transition) can cause a new master to be elected, it is possible that at any given point in time, a Storage Node might have a disproportionate number of master nodes. The Oracle NoSQL Database administrator software periodically checks each Storage Node to determine whether it has a disproportionate number of master nodes. If that is the case, the Oracle NoSQL Database administrator agent will move some masters from the overloaded Storage Node to one of the other Storage Nodes in order to evenly distribute the number of masters among the Storage Nodes.

This is important for two reasons. Because the Storage Node (usually, a physical machine) is the unit of failure, if a Storage Node with a disproportionately high number of master nodes goes down, it will trigger master elections in multiple shards. Because an election requires additional processing, this will temporarily increase the response time for user operations on those shards until new masters have been elected. Although it is not possible to eliminate the overhead of elections, keeping the master nodes evenly distributed among the Storage Nodes ensures that only a few shards are impacted (momentarily) if the Storage Node fails. The other reason for distributing the masters evenly across all the Storage Nodes is that a master node has to do more work than a replica because it has to send log records to replicas for every change. By distributing masters evenly across the Storage Nodes, Oracle NoSQL Database ensures efficient utilization of the available hardware and better performance overall. Figure 3-2 illustrates this scenario.

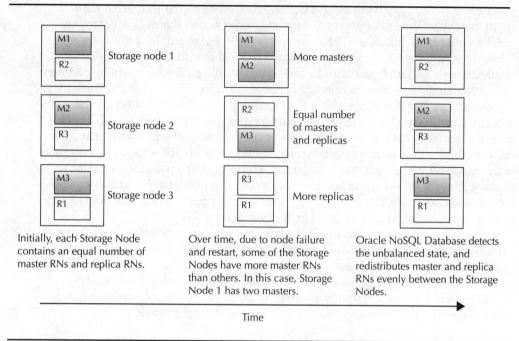

M1	
R2	Storage node 1

Initially, each Storage Node contains an equal number of master RNs and replica RNs.

Over time, due to node failure and restart, some of the Storage Nodes have more master RNs than others. In this case, Storage Node 1 has two masters.

Oracle NoSQL Database detects the unbalanced state, and redistributes master and replica RNs evenly between the Storage Nodes.

Time

FIGURE 3-2. *Maintaining an equal number of master and replica nodes on each Storage Node*

Hashing, Partitions, Data Distribution

As discussed earlier, Oracle NoSQL Database is a sharded, key-value, client-server system. Each distinct key (major key) is associated with exactly one shard. Oracle NoSQL Database uses a two-stage, hash-based algorithm in order to assign a key-value pair to a shard. We begin with a description of this mechanism. The reasons for the two-stage hash distribution will become clearer in the following discussion.

The major key for a key-value pair is a Java *string*. The Client Driver hashes the major key using an MD5-based hash function in order to determine a hash bucket. Oracle NoSQL Database uses the term *partition* to denote a hash bucket. The number of partitions is fixed (static hashing) and defined by the system administrator when a new Oracle NoSQL Database store is created. We recommend that the number of partitions be significantly larger than the maximum number of shards the system is expected to have over its lifetime. For example, if the system administrator determined that the system would have no more than 10 shards over its lifetime, then it would be reasonable to set the number of partitions to be 100 (or 1,000). The number of partitions is the absolute upper bound on the number of shards the system can have.

Oracle NoSQL Database assigns equal-sized *sets* of partitions to each shard, such that the total number of partitions managed by all the shards is equal to the total number of partitions (configuration parameter). For example, if the system is configured to have 100 partitions distributed over 10 shards, then Oracle NoSQL Database will assign 10 partitions to each shard. Partitions are identified by *partition IDs*. Information about the mapping of partitions to shards is stored in the Replication Nodes and propagated to the Client Driver when a new client connects to the system. Each Client Driver maintains a *partition map*, which contains the association between partition IDs and shards (it contains some additional information that will be described later). The mapping between partitions and shards is relatively static and can change only when the number of shards is changed. The two-stage algorithm isolates the logical association between keys to partitions from the physical association of partitions to storage. This ensures that a change in the number of shards does require that each key be rehashed and stored in the right shard.

Let us look at a specific example to understand how partitions are used. Assume that the system administrator has configured the system with two shards and 10 partitions. Oracle NoSQL Database might choose to assign the first five partitions to shard 1 and the remaining five partitions to shard 2, as illustrated in Figure 3-3. This assignment of partitions to shards is stored in the server nodes and loaded into the Client Driver's *partition map* when the client connects to the server.

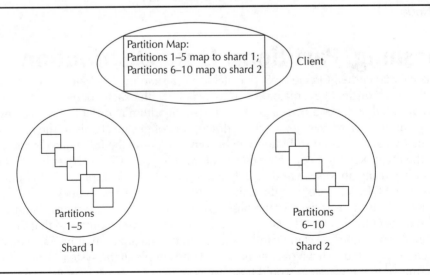

FIGURE 3-3. *Partition map for a system with two shards and 10 partitions*

For each API request, the Client Driver hashes the major key of the record to determine the partition ID. Then, it looks up the partition map to determine which shard the partition belongs to. Once the shard that owns the key has been determined, the Client Driver uses consistency and latency information (described earlier) in order to route the request to the appropriate node within the proper shard.

Changing the Number of Shards

Let us now examine what happens when the system administrator adds more Storage Nodes to the cluster in response to growing volumes of data. Continuing our previous example, assume that the system administrator adds enough hardware to accommodate one more shard to the cluster and initiates a data redistribution operation.

A partition is the unit of data movement and redistribution. When a new shard is added to the cluster, Oracle NoSQL Database moves some of the partitions from existing shards to the newly available shard in order to redistribute data evenly among the total number of shards in the system. In this example, Oracle NoSQL Database will redistribute partitions such that two shards manage three partitions each, and one shard manages four partitions. This data redistribution is referred to as *partition migration*. Figure 3-4 illustrates the new configuration of the system. A redistribution operation always moves some partitions from every existing shard; in other words, every existing shard contributes some partitions to the newly created shards.

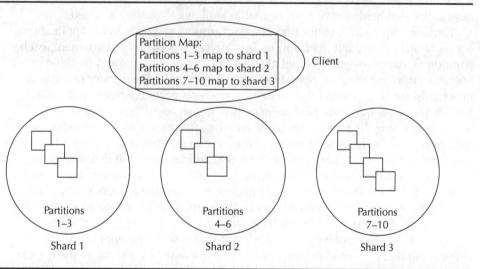

FIGURE 3-4. *Partition map after adding a shard*

Because keys are hashed across the available partitions, it is possible that some partitions are larger than others. During the redistribution operation, Oracle NoSQL Database moves partitions such that each shard manages approximately equal amounts of data. This ensures that each shard handles the same workload, assuming that the application's data access pattern is evenly distributed across the entire key space. Keep in mind that this even redistribution of partitions is aimed at ensuring that each shard (not Storage Node) manages roughly the same amount of data. As described earlier, it is quite possible that the newly allocated hardware might have different capacity than the hardware for the original set of shards. In that case, some Storage Nodes will manage more data than others. Although this does not affect correct behavior of the system, it is important for the system administrator to understand the performance implications of having nodes with differing capacity.

Another aspect of data redistribution related to the replication factor of the system is worth mentioning. The replication factor of an Oracle NoSQL Database store defines the number of replicas that each shard has. Every shard within a Oracle NoSQL Database store must have the same replication factor. When new hardware is added to the Oracle NoSQL Database cluster, the system determines how many new shards can be added. For example, if the replication factor of the existing system is three, and additional hardware with a cumulative capacity of nine is added, then three new shards will be created. On the other hand, if the cumulative capacity of the additional hardware is not a multiple of the replication factor, then some capacity will be left unused. In the extreme case, if there is insufficient capacity to host even a single new shard, then Oracle NoSQL Database will not redistribute the data; the newly allocated hardware will not be usable until more capacity is added.

Partition migration is performed as a background, online activity; application access continues without interruption. In a typical production environment, each partition manages several hundred gigabytes of data. Consequently, partition migration is a long duration operation. After the system administrator provisions new hardware and specifies the capacity of each new Storage Node, Oracle NoSQL Database *migration planner* generates a *plan* for orchestrating partition movement. Using the replication factor and the information about the capacity of each new Storage Node, the planner computes the number of new shards that will be added to the system. For each partition that will be moved, it determines the source and destination shards. This step takes partition sizes into account in order to ensure that each shard manages approximately the same amount of data in the final configuration (larger cluster). Finally, it determines the Storage Node that will host each Replication Node for each new shard.

There is an important issue in this last step that is worth mentioning, which is easily illustrated with an example. Assume that the replication factor of the Oracle NoSQL Database store is 3, and one additional machine, with a capacity of 3 has been provisioned by the system administrator. Obviously, after data migration is complete, the new configuration should have one additional shard. However, the question is: Where should the Replication Nodes for the new shard be placed? Because a Storage Node (typically a physical machine) is also the unit of failure, it is important that the Replication Nodes for each new shard be placed on different physical machines in order to avoid the loss of an entire shard if a Storage Node fails. Depending on the placement of Replication Nodes in the existing cluster, it may be necessary to *move* some of the existing Replication Nodes to the new hardware and then use this freed-up capacity to host some of the newly created Replication Nodes.

Before beginning the process of partition redistribution, the migration planner determines whether such a move is required. If some Replication Nodes need to be moved from one Storage Node to another, that movement is initiated first, before partitions are redistributed. Figure 3-5 illustrates this scenario.

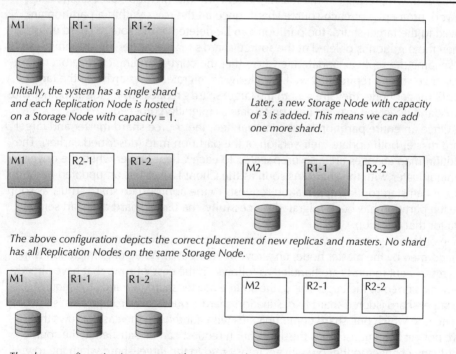

Initially, the system has a single shard and each Replication Node is hosted on a Storage Node with capacity = 1.

Later, a new Storage Node with capacity of 3 is added. This means we can add one more shard.

The above configuration depicts the correct placement of new replicas and masters. No shard has all Replication Nodes on the same Storage Node.

The above configuration is ncorrect with respect to placement of Replication Nodes for the new shard. Shard 2 has all replication nodes on the same Storage Node. If that Storage Node is lost, the entire shard will become unavailable.

FIGURE 3-5. *Proper placement of Replication Nodes for a newly added shard*

As is evident, partition migration is a complex and time-consuming process; consequently, only one partition migration plan can be active at any given time. Once the migration plan has been computed, each shard is informed about its role in the migration; in addition, the plan is persistently stored in the administrator console.

During the migration process, it is important that normal user activity proceed without disruption. At any given moment during a partition migration, some rows in the partition will still be on the original shard, other rows will be in transit, and the rest of the rows will have been transferred to the new shard. Further, the application might update rows that are actively involved in the partition migration process. Oracle NoSQL Database ensures uninterrupted user activity during a migration as follows.

To simplify the coordination and execution of partition migration, only master nodes participate directly in the migration process. Note that partition migration cannot be implemented using the log shipping mechanism used for keeping replicas updated and current with respect to the master node. Partition migration uses a different network protocol. For each source shard, once all the rows within a partition are moved to the target shard, the partition can be deleted at the source shard (master). When the partition is deleted at the source shard's master node, log shipping (used for keeping the replicas updated) ensures that the corresponding change occurs on the source shard's replicas as well. Similarly, as migrated rows arrive at the target shard's master node, they are sent to the target shard's replicas using log shipping. Thus, source and target replicas are kept up-to-date as migration proceeds.

Once an entire partition has been migrated, the source shard master and target shard master both update their version of the partition map (described earlier). The partition map changes are also propagated to each Client Driver when the driver communicates with the shard. As soon as the Client Driver has an updated partition map, it can start routing application requests to the appropriate shard. Thus, as soon as each partition has been migrated successfully, the target shard can start serving data for that partition.

In order to preserve correctness and uninterrupted application operation, migration is performed by the master node, on a row-by-row basis. While data migration is in progress, client requests are handled as follows. In the case of rows that have already been transferred to the target shard, the source master shard forwards the request to the target shard (source shard to destination shard request forwarding). This is the only situation in which one shard communicates with another. In the case of rows that have not yet been transferred, the application request can be satisfied at the source shard; any changes to the row will get transferred to the target shard when the row migrates. Finally, for rows that are actively being transferred, the source shard applies the change and also forwards the request to the target shard. Changes are idempotent; consequently, reapplying a change more than once doesn't affect the correctness of the update operation. This algorithm ensures that application data access continues uninterrupted during the migration process.

Although partition redistribution is an atomic operation, it cannot be undone. If the system administrator wishes to reduce the number of shards in the system, the administrator indicates that some hardware needs to be removed from the cluster. This initiates a partition transfer operation that *increases the number* of partitions per shard, consequently shrinking the total number of shards in the system. Once the transfer is complete, the machines that no longer manage data can be physically removed from the system.

Changing the Replication Factor

Oracle NoSQL Database supports another kind of data movement operation that serves a very different purpose as compared to the data redistribution mentioned earlier. In some scenarios, it is desirable to change (typically increase) the replication factor of the cluster. Increasing the replication factor improves availability as well as read scalability. Availability improves because the increased redundancy implies higher tolerance to hardware and Replication Node failures. Read scalability improves because read requests can be shared by the additional replicas. For example, during peak business periods (for example, in the holiday season), it may be desirable to provide higher read scalability, especially if the workload is predominantly read-only. Note that each replica requires some additional work on the master node to keep it updated. Consequently, if the workload is update-heavy, then increasing the replication factor to a very high value might potentially affect update performance adversely. In the case of update-intensive workloads, it is better to add more shards to the system, rather than increasing the replication factor.

Another common reason for increasing the replication factor is to expand the Oracle NoSQL Database store to multiple datacenters. For example, the Oracle NoSQL Database store might be initially set up in a single datacenter in one geographic location. At a later point in time, the system administrator might elect to improve availability by having some of the nodes located at a geographically remote location with independent failure characteristics. This can easily be achieved by provisioning the new hardware capacity at the new datacenter and increasing the replication factor of the original system. Note that Oracle NoSQL Database enforces the rule that each shard must have the same replication factor. Consequently, increasing the replication factor can only be achieved if the newly provisioned capacity is a multiple of the number of shards. For example, assume you have a 10-shard system with a replication factor of 3 in datacenter A. You now want to add another set of replicas in datacenter B. The system administrator would provision new hardware in datacenter B such that there are 10 new Storage Nodes, each with a capacity of 1. After this is done, the system administrator can invoke the command to increase the replication factor. Once the command is invoked, Oracle NoSQL Database will associate each new Storage Node in datacenter B with one of the existing shards in the system. After this is done, each shard begins the process of populating the new Replication Node (on the newly assigned Storage Node) in order to increase the replication factor; consequently, the database is now accessible at both datacenters.

The mechanism for increasing the replication factor is similar to resurrecting a failed replica, except that increasing the replication factor applies to all the shards in the cluster. Also, similar to partition migration, increasing the replication factor is a long duration operation. The planner first verifies that there is sufficient additional capacity to increase the replication factor. It then assigns a new (empty) Replication Node from the newly allocated capacity to each shard. Each shard adds the new node to the known list of members and then begins the process of bringing the new Replication Node up-to-date with respect to the master, using Berkeley DB Java Edition's restore and recover mechanisms. A snapshot of the data on the master node is used as a "backup" copy. This backup is restored on the new replica either by transferring the backup over the network (network restore) or by some other means (for example, physically transporting a copy of the backups from one location to another). Once the restore operation is complete, the replica needs to replay all the transactions that have occurred since the time of the backup, in order to become "current" with respect to the master. The master node in each shard sends its new replica the log records that the replica needs in order to catch-up with the master. This is the same log shipping mechanism that is used in order to keep replicas updated during normal operation of the system.

Considerations for Multiple Datacenters

As mentioned previously, Oracle NoSQL Database allows the system administrator to distribute the Storage Nodes across datacenters, possibly in geographically separate locations. This is commonly done to guard against disasters as well as to provide low latency read access to data from diverse locations.

Usually, variable network latency and network bandwidth between nodes is the most obvious impact on system operation in a multi-datacenter scenario. Let us consider a few typical ways in which nodes might be geographically distributed and some usage patterns and implications for read and write access. In the following paragraphs, we discuss the behavior in the context of a single shard to simplify the explanation; of course, in reality, an Oracle NoSQL Database deployment will consist of multiple shards and the same arguments apply to all shards in a typical, multi-shard deployment.

We will use a simple, three-datacenter scenario to explain some of the concepts and trade-offs involved. Consider an organization that has three datacenters, one located in San Francisco, the other in Arizona, and a third in China. For the purposes of this example, assume that the San Francisco datacenter and the Arizona datacenter are connected by a low-latency high-bandwidth network, whereas the China datacenter is connected to the other datacenters with a high-latency, low-bandwidth network connection.

Oracle NoSQL Database is designed to be a highly available system with no single point of failure. Thus, from an application's perspective, it is important that a change to a record (at a master node) be propagated to at least one other replica before the transaction can be considered durable. In the preceding example datacenter topology, if the master node is located in either the San Francisco or the Arizona datacenter, then a change at the master can be quickly propagated to another datacenter that is connected to the master node's datacenter via a low latency network, thus resulting in low-latency update transactions. On the other hand, if the master node is located in China, then it will take longer for the change to be propagated to one of the replicas in the United States, which will result in high-latency update transactions. If availability and low latency are important from the application's perspective, it is important to have low network latency between the master and at least one replica. Conversely, if the network latency between the nodes comprising each shard is high, then the application has to be willing to accept high-latency update operations (if durability and availability of data are important) or be willing to accept some data loss in the event of a node (or network) failure.

If the master node is in San Francisco, the loss of one datacenter (either the Arizona datacenter or the China datacenter) does not affect the correctness or availability of the system since there is a replica that can be used to make updates impervious to a single point of failure. However, if both the Arizona and China replicas are lost, then the datacenter with the master node (San Francisco in this example) will continue to serve read requests, but will not permit write requests because there is no way to make the changes durable cluster-wide.

Consider a different scenario. If the master node is in San Francisco and the San Francisco datacenter is lost, then the replica in Arizona will most likely be elected as master. This can be explained as follows. Because the Arizona datacenter is connected to the San Francisco datacenter by a low latency network, changes at the master will be propagated to the Arizona datacenter sooner than they are propagated to China. Consequently, the Arizona datacenter is more likely to have received the latest changes. As discussed earlier, the election protocol attempts to select the most current replica as the new master should an existing master fail. Again, loss of the master node does not affect either read availability or write availability of the system. Thus, Oracle NoSQL Database is able to provide availability for read and write requests under several (but not all) conditions of datacenter loss. Note that if the San Francisco datacenter is lost and the mastership is transferred to the Arizona datacenter, then the master in Arizona has to propagate changes over a high latency link to the node in China. Consequently, update transactions might experience higher latency unless the application chooses not to wait for acknowledgments from replicas (`acknowledgment = NONE`).

From the application perspective, it is desirable that requests be served as quickly as possible. In the preceding scenario, a client in the United States is likely to have a low-latency network connection to the U.S. datacenters and can get read requests satisfied by either the San Francisco or the Arizona datacenter, especially if it specifies stringent read consistency requirements. On the other hand, a client in China that specifies stringent read consistency requirements for reads will have the read operation served by one of the nodes in the United States. On the other hand, if the client in China can relax the consistency requirements to allow for high network latency, those requests can be served by the replica in China (this assumes that the client in China also has a high-latency network connection to the U.S. datacenters).

In all cases, write requests must be served by the master node (in the San Francisco datacenter in our example). This suggests that the client in China will have to incur high latency writes. If writes are relatively infrequent, or if the application can tolerate high latency writes (for example, if the writes are during an interactive user session that involves user think time), then the high latency writes are usually not a problem.

In other cases, client applications may require low latency writes to a subset of the data but read access to all the data. For example, if the application manages user profile data, then the client running in China will most likely prefer to have low latency write access to the user profiles of Chinese residents. In such scenarios, the application can create two Oracle NoSQL Database repositories, with each store potentially having the Replication Nodes at different datacenters for availability reasons. Obviously, the two repositories don't share any data. If we continue with our earlier example, the repository for the Chinese residents might have the master node hosted in the China datacenter, whereas the repository for the U.S. residents might have the master node hosted in the United States (either in San Francisco or Arizona). In order to service a user request, the *application* needs to determine which repository can serve the data and route the request appropriately. Figure 3-6 illustrates this scenario.

The preceding discussion is not exhaustive; it is meant to highlight some of the application design issues that the developer and system administrator need to keep in mind when they distribute Oracle NoSQL Database Storage Nodes over multiple datacenters. The application designer needs to make a trade-off between client to server network latency and read consistency requirements. Besides unexpected events such as natural disasters, scheduled maintenance as well as network outages can cause a datacenter to go offline. The system administrator needs to understand the behavior of the distributed system when one or more datacenters go off-line so that these maintenance activities can be planned and executed correctly without disrupting availability of the Oracle NoSQL Database service.

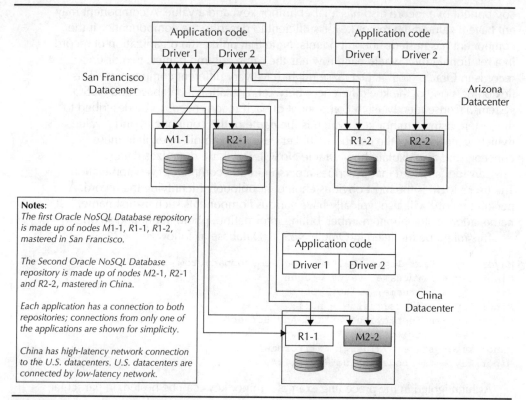

FIGURE 3-6.   *Federated configuration over multiple datacenters with differing network latencies*

Storing Records and the Flexible Data Model

Let us now examine how Oracle NoSQL Database stores records in the database. As mentioned in Chapter 2, Oracle NoSQL Database supports the notion of major and minor keys. The major key describes the globally unique identifier for a record. Conceptually, a minor key describes a specific *component* of the record. In the discussion that follows, we use the term *record* to describe a logical entity being represented in the database; we use the term *key-value pair* to describe a component of the record. A record generally comprises one or more key-value pairs. A specific record is identified by the *value* of its major key; in other words, the major key is simply the label (or name) for the unique identifier for a record. Similarly, a specific component of a record also has a label (minor key) and a value. A component may not have a value if the minor key is sufficient to describe the component or if the component has nested subcomponents. Note that unlike the organization of records in a relational table, where each row has the same column names, two distinct records in Oracle NoSQL Database might have very different components. (This flexibility is one of the key differences between a relational database and NoSQL systems.) Consequently, each component of each record needs to be described to the system using a minor key (which is the *name* of the component) and a value (which is the *value* of the component). Let's use an example to explain these concepts and also explain how Oracle NoSQL Database organizes data.

Consider a record that describes a person in an ecommerce web application. The user's login is the most obvious choice for uniquely identifying the record. A person's record will also typically have various components such as first name, last name, address, telephone number, billing information, photograph, and so on.

This might be modeled in Oracle NoSQL Database as follows:

```
Major key = User_login; Value = doe@acmecompany.com
Minor key = Firstname; value = John
Minor key = Lastname; value = Doe
Minor key = address; value = null;
Minor key = street; value = "123 Any Street"
Minor key = city; value = "Any Town"
Minor key = state; value = "California"
Minor key = ZIP code; value = "11111"
```

As highlighted in the preceding example, minor keys can be nested. In particular, the minor keys `street`, `city`, `state`, and `ZIP code` are nested under the minor key `address`.

From a storage point of view, the multiple components of a specific record are stored as individual Berkeley DB key-value pairs, with the guarantee that all these key-value pairs are stored in the same shard. This is illustrated in the following table. A key-value pair (component) is identified by its fully qualified key, which contains the `name` of the major key (for example, User_login) as well as the `value` of the major key (for example, doe@acmecompany.com) plus the ordered list of names of the minor keys. The `value` of the major key (doe@acmecompany.com in this example) is included as part of the fully qualified key.

Fully Qualified Key for Lookups	Value
/User_login/{doe@acmecompany.com}/-/	
/User_login/{doe@acmecompany.com}/-/Firstname/	John
/User_login/{doe@acmecompany.com}/-Lastname/	Doe
/User_login/{doe@acmecompany.com}/-/address/	

Fully Qualified Key for Lookups	Value
/User_login/{doe@acmecompany.com}/-/address/street/	123 Any Street
/User_login/{doe@acmecompany.com}/-/address/city/	Any Town
/User_login/{doe@acmecompany.com}/-/address/state/	California
/User_login/{doe@acmecompany.com}/-/address/ZIP code/	11111

This organization allows the user to access the entire user record—the `multi_get()` API call has to be used for this purpose—or specific components of the record very conveniently and efficiently. This is particularly important when the record contains some components that are large in size (for example, images, documents, or video content). The large content can be retrieved only if needed, thus improving network utilization and response time for the request.

Oracle NoSQL Database uses various key compression techniques (for example, Prefix compression) for the B-tree index. This ensures optimal utilization of memory and efficient retrieval of one or more key-value pairs of a specific record.

Oracle NoSQL Database also supports the notion of ordered iteration on the minor keys within a record (unique major key). For example, consider a record that is used to store the transaction history for a particular user. In this case, the most natural way to organize this content is to use the user's ID as the major key and then create a new key-value pair for each transaction that is indexed by the date and timestamp of the transaction. The table that follows illustrates how this information might be organized.

Fully Qualified Key for Lookups	Value
/User_login/{doe@acmecompany.com}/-/	
/User_login/{doe@acmecompany.com}/-/Firstname/	John
/User_login/{doe@acmecompany.com}/-Lastname/	Doe
/User_login/{doe@acmecompany.com}/-/address/	
/User_login/{doe@acmecompany.com}/-/address/street/	123 Any Street
/User_login/{doe@acmecompany.com}/-/address/city/	Any Town
/User_login/{doe@acmecompany.com}/-/address/state/	California
/User_login/{doe@acmecompany.com}/-/address/ZIP code/	11111
/User_login/{doe@oracle/com}/-/transaction_history 20130101/	Purchase car for $23,000.00
/User_login/{doe@oracle/com}/-/transaction_history /20130201/	Purchase laptop for $599.00
/User_login/{doe@oracle/com}/-/transaction_ history/20130301/	Sell old desktop in garage sale for $10.00

In the preceding example, the application developer creates a new minor key for each month with the format "`transaction_ history <year month day>`." This particular choice of format ensures that the internal sort order of the index matches the expected sort order. Note that the value for a minor key can contain information about one or more transactions (specified as a byte array); Oracle NoSQL Database does not impose any restriction on the contents of the value. The ordered iteration feature of the Oracle NoSQL Database API provides for a convenient way to retrieve the transaction history for reporting or analysis purposes. Oracle NoSQL Database also supports range queries, thus enabling the application to retrieve only a subset of the data.

Oracle NoSQL Database can also store information as JSON records using Avro schemas. The same information could be alternately stored as follows:

```
{
    "type" : "record",
    "name" : "userInfo",
    "namespace" : "my.example",
    "fields" : [{"First_name" : "firstname",
            "type" : "string",
            "default" : "NONE"},
            {"Last_name" : "lastname",
            "type" : "string",
            "default" : "NONE"},
            {"name" : "address",
            "type" : "record",
            "fields": [
                {"name" : "street",
                "type" : "string",
                "default" : "NONE"},
                {"name" : "city",
                "type" : "string",
                "default" : "NONE"},
                {"name" : "state",
                "type" : "string",
                "default" : "NONE"},
                {"name" : "zipcode",
                "type" : "string",
                "default" : "NONE"}]
        ]
}
```

Oracle NoSQL Database provides a very flexible storage paradigm for managing information. Over 15 years of experience with Berkeley DB has clearly demonstrated that the key-value paradigm directly supports several data models and can be easily used as the basis for modeling other data models such as XML. Oracle NoSQL Database's key-value paradigm can easily be used to model relational data structures.

It can also be used to manage Java objects, hierarchical data structures, nested data structures, JSON data, XML data, sparse tables, and so on. Oracle NoSQL Database can also be used as a repository for RDF graph data. This modeling flexibility simplifies the task of the application developer because it allows the developer to model the data in a manner most convenient to the application. Further, it is very easy for the application developer to evolve the data model; changes can be incorporated easily without having to unload and reload existing data.

Log-Structured Storage

Berkeley DB Java edition uses log-structured storage in order to organize data on disk. This has significant implications for the performance as well as maintenance and manageability of the system. Let us examine the storage and performance implications of log-structured storage in some detail. It is useful to contrast log-structured storage organization with a conventional "update-in-place" architecture that is common to several popular database systems, including the Oracle database.

For disk-based database systems, I/O is generally the performance bottleneck; hard disk is the slowest component in the system. Log-structured storage was invented in the early 1990s based on the observation that data access latency and throughput can be dramatically improved by replacing random I/O operations with sequential I/O operations. Performing random I/O is a lot more expensive than performing sequential I/O; magnetic disks incur rotational latency (delay until the required sector is under the disk head) and seek latency (radial movement of the disk head) in order to read or write a specific sector on disk. A random I/O involves seek latency as well as rotational latency in order to find the required sector. On the other hand, sequential I/O does not require a seek operation; consequently, it is possible to perform many more I/Os per second.

In a conventional update-in-place database architecture, the storage is organized as fixed-size *pages* or *blocks*. Pages contain individual records; if a record is larger than a page, the record is stored as a sequence of fragments where each fragment fits on a page. Figure 3-7 illustrates this page-based organization. Whenever a record needs to be modified, the corresponding page is read into memory, the appropriate changes are made, and the page is written back to the same location. This is why this architecture is referred to as update-in-place. When new records have to be added, the system either finds available space on existing pages or allocates new pages to store the new records. In order to manage disk space efficiently, the database system will typically look for free space on existing pages first before allocating new pages on disk. This can potentially cause multiple random I/Os on disk.

In contrast, log-structured architecture is an append-only architecture. The database is organized as a single logical log file on disk. The log file contains all the data including metadata such as indices. When a new record is inserted, it is

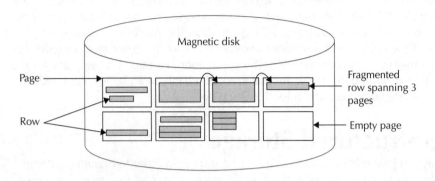

FIGURE 3-7. *Conventional "update-in-place" on-disk organization of data records*

appended to the end of the log. If an existing record is changed, a new version of the record is created and appended to the end of the log instead of changing the existing copy of the record. Thus, every change results in a new version of the record being created rather than the record being updated in place. Of course, indices and other related structures have to be updated in order to reflect the new position of the new version of the record on disk. This means that during normal processing, all changes (inserts, updates, and deletes) are written to the end of the log. Consequently, I/O performance is optimal, and this results in the best performance for the system.

When a record is updated, the previous version of the record is no longer needed and can be garbage collected. Berkeley DB Java Edition includes a garbage collection process called the *cleaner*. The cleaner is responsible for reclaiming the space associated with obsolete versions of records. The cleaner runs in the background, looking for obsolete records in the log file, and compacts the log file by moving current records to the end of the log and reclaiming space on disk. Keep in mind that the cleaner process does perform random I/O on disk. However, the cleaner I/O activity proceeds in the background with minimal interference with the I/O activity that is associated with transactions. In other words, the cleaner I/O activity is not in the critical path of the transaction.

Although log cleaning is a background activity, it is important to optimize the operation of the cleaner process so that it does not interfere with the overall performance of the system. Berkeley DB Java Edition has been tuned extensively in order to optimize the cleaner to deliver excellent steady-state performance of the system. Figure 3-8 illustrates log-structured storage as well as the cleaner. Because of Berkeley DB Java Edition's log-structured storage architecture, Oracle NoSQL Database is very well suited for update, insert, and delete operations. Because NoSQL systems are often used to capture data at high throughput, the log-structured architecture is ideally suited for insert-heavy workloads.

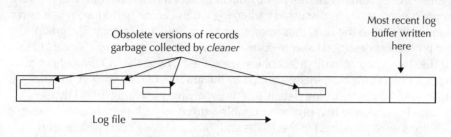

FIGURE 3-8. *Log-structured storage organization*

Log-structured storage has important implications for the amount of disk that is used by the system. In a conventional update-in-place architecture, the amount of storage used does not change when there is a lot of update (but not insert or delete) activity in the system. In contrast, in a log-structured storage architecture, updates result in new versions of records being created, consequently increasing the amount of storage required. Although the cleaner will reclaim this space shortly, in the steady-state, the amount of storage required by log-structured storage architectures is more than the amount of storage required by conventional update in-place architectures. It is possible to garbage collect more aggressively but that can result in suboptimal overall performance.

Since Oracle NoSQL Database is a highly available system, each record is replicated and stored more than once (on the replicas). It is important to keep the storage requirements of log-structured storage-based systems in mind when sizing the system for the application workload. This additional storage requirement is a small price to pay in order to achieve excellent performance and high availability for today's demanding workloads. Several modern NoSQL systems also use log-structured storage, with the trade-off of higher storage costs for high performance and availability.

Durability

In a conventional database system, a transaction's changes are made permanent by writing those changes to disk. A transaction cannot be declared complete (committed) until its changes are written to durable storage. In order to improve performance, database systems use the *write-ahead-log* protocol (to minimize I/O in the critical path of the user operation) and the *group commit* protocol (to improve the efficiency of log writes). The write-ahead protocol is an optimization technique that requires that only the log records associated with the changes be written to disk before the transaction can be declared complete. The changes to the records can be propagated to the disk lazily (these I/O operations are not in the critical path of the transaction). This is a very significant optimization: As discussed earlier, log writes can be performed much faster than random writes to the disk, thus improving throughput and latency. The group commit protocol is designed to write several log records as a group in a single I/O to the log file. The group commit protocol leverages the fact that the I/O throughput of writing to a disk is only marginally affected by the amount of data written. In other words, writing 100 bytes of log data is just as expensive as writing 1,000 bytes of log data. Together, the two protocols enable extremely high performance. These optimizations were pioneered in the 1970s and '80s, and have been widely used ever since.

Oracle NoSQL Database is also a highly available system. In order to ensure shard-wide durability, it is important to make the changes durable on the master node, as well as propagate the changes to the replicas before the transaction can be declared as complete. When a transaction is ready to be committed, Oracle NoSQL Database does the following (in parallel):

■ Write the transaction changes to the log file on the master node

■ Send messages containing the log records to the replicas

There are various options for these two operations that enable different degrees of durability and performance. In the most stringent scenario, it is necessary to propagate the changes to disk locally (on the master) as well as on each of the replicas in the shard. This ensures that the changes are durable not only on the master node, but on each of the replica nodes as well. A failure of one of the nodes in the shard does not impact the durability of the transaction because the change has been made durable on all copies.

Conversely, if the application has less stringent durability requirements, it may be sufficient to send the changes to the replicas but not wait for the changes to be propagated to disk before acknowledging completion of the transaction. The rationale for this kind of durability is as follows. Assuming that the failure of one of the nodes in the shard doesn't cause the failure of another node (failure independence) and assuming a reliable network, at least one of the nodes in the shard will have the latest set of changes; consequently, the transaction's changes can be considered durable and permanent.

In the context of writing the log records to disk, there are three possibilities to consider:

■ *Write the log record to the log buffer.* In this case, if the thread executing the transaction fails, the changes are contained in the log buffer. The log buffer will be written to disk shortly. This is the least expensive option because it does not involve any file system `write()` calls.

■ *Write the log buffer to the file system.* In this case, even if the process fails (but not the operating system), the changes will be written to disk asynchronously. This option is more expensive than the former because it involves a file system `write()` call, which copies the log buffer to operating system memory.

■ *Write the log buffer to disk (file system `fsync()` call).* This ensures that the changes are permanently written to disk. Even if the processor fails, the disk will have a record of the changes. This is the most expensive option because it involves a synchronous I/O to disk.

Note that these options for writing log records to disk are available at the master node as well as the replicas.

In the context of sending messages to the replicas, there are a few possibilities to consider as well:

■ The master can send messages to all the replicas but not wait for acknowledgment. In this case, the assumption is that messages will eventually propagate the replicas.

■ The master can send messages to all the replicas, and wait for an acknowledgment from a majority of the replicas. In this case, the master node needs to ensure that the majority of the replicas have received the changes.

■ The master can send messages to all the replicas and wait for an acknowledgment from all the replicas. This ensures that all the replicas have, in fact, received the changes.

The replicas can either acknowledge the message after writing the change message to the log buffer, or after writing the log buffer to the operating system, or after writing the log buffer to disk (`fsync`). Figure 3-9 illustrates the possible choices in the system.

From this description, it is clear that the user has a wide range of possibilities to choose from in order to determine what defines the commit of a transaction. Oracle NoSQL Database allows the user to specify the degree of durability (I/O semantics as well as response semantics) for master and replica nodes along the dimensions described earlier in order to decide what constitutes durability of a transaction. For example, the user might choose to declare a transaction as committed when the log buffer has been the written to the operating system on the master node and the master has received acknowledgments from a majority of the replicas in the system (even though the replicas have not written those log records to their local disk). The user might also choose to declare that a transaction is committed only when the master node as well as all the replicas have written the changes durably to disk and

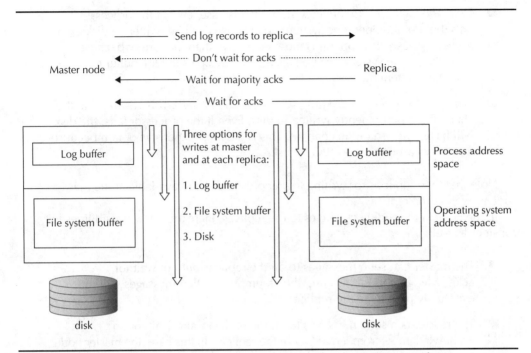

FIGURE 3-9. *Durability choices for a transaction in Oracle NoSQL Database*

acknowledged receipt of the messages. The former option provides good durability guarantees (assuming independent failure modes of replica nodes) and also provides excellent performance and throughput for transaction processing. The latter option provides the strictest durability guarantees but is also the most expensive in terms of performance and throughput.

This flexibility in choosing the degree of durability on a per-transaction basis is crucial from an application designer point of view. The developer can make an intelligent trade-off between performance and degree of durability for update operations without compromising the integrity of the overall system.

ACID Transactions and Distributed Transactions

Distributed database systems have been in existence for over three decades; these systems pioneered many features like sharding, high availability, distributed query optimization, and the two-phase commit protocol for distributed transactions. A distributed database system stores subsets of data in multiple data managers (called *resource managers* in distributed transaction terminology). In a distributed database system, a transaction will often operate upon data stored in multiple resource managers. The two-phase commit protocol is used to ensure common agreement (commit or abort) of the transaction between multiple resource managers.

Here's a brief and simplified description of the two-phase commit protocol. At the start of a distributed transaction, the *transaction coordinator* (the entity responsible for managing distributed transactions) initiates a new *global* transaction, which is associated with a globally unique *transaction ID*. During the execution of the transaction, the transaction ID is included in the messages that are sent to the resource managers that are involved in the distributed transaction. Each resource manager is responsible for making changes to the data that it manages. Each resource manager uses a sub-transaction in order to perform these local changes; it also associates the sub-transaction identifier with the global transaction ID that was passed to it by the coordinator.

When a distributed transaction is ready to commit, the transaction coordinator sends *prepare-to-commit* messages to all the resource managers participating in the transaction. Upon receiving the message, each resource manager determines whether they can commit the local sub-transaction. If they can, they write a *ready-to-commit* log record to the local log and respond with a *ready-to-commit* message to the coordinator. Once a resource manager has agreed to commit their sub-transaction, they cannot change this decision later on. However, if they receive an "abort" message from the coordinator, they must abort the local sub-transaction. The coordinator waits until they have received responses from all the resource managers participating in the distributed transaction. If all the resource managers respond positively (i.e., all of them respond with a ready-to-commit message), then the coordinator sends a *commit* message to all participants. Upon receiving the message, each participating resource manager commits the local sub-transaction and responds with a *done* message.

If at least one of the participating resource managers responds to the prepare-to-commit request with a *cannot-commit* message, then the coordinator sends an *abort* message to all participants. Thus, the two-phase commit protocol ensures that all resource managers participating in the distributed transaction record the same outcome for the transaction. The protocol is called the two-phase protocol because it has two distinct phases—the prepare phase and the commit phase. It is also a blocking protocol because the coordinator has to wait for responses from all participants.

From this description, it is obvious that the two-phase commit protocol is a pretty expensive protocol in terms of message exchanges. It also adds significant latency to the transaction because it is a blocking protocol. Further, the transaction coordinator is a single point of failure and also a hotspot because every distributed transaction needs to communicate with the coordinator. For all these reasons, almost all the modern NoSQL systems, including Oracle NoSQL Database, avoid using the two-phase commit protocol by not supporting distributed transaction capability. These new systems are intended to handle huge and unpredictable volumes of data and transactions in a cost-effective manner. Hence, they make the trade-off in favor of performance and simplicity, rather than functionality. Note that an application can still change a set of records in multiple different shards; in all likelihood, barring unexpected problems or failures, all the changes will be performed as expected. However, there is no mechanism (such as two-phase commit) to guarantee the atomicity of updates to a set of records stored in multiple shards.

As we have already discussed, Oracle NoSQL Database provides transactional semantics only for single-shard operations. Multi-shard operations such as scans do not support transactional semantics. For the vast majority of NoSQL applications, the performance, simplicity, and scalability benefits of single-shard transactions far outweigh the potential benefits of distributed transactions.

Summary

Oracle NoSQL Database is a highly scalable distributed key-value store. Oracle NoSQL Database has demonstrated linear scalability on clusters of a few hundred nodes. Recent YCSB (Yahoo! Cloud Serving Benchmark) testing has demonstrated performance of 1.25 million operations per second on a 15-node commodity cluster with a workload of 95 percent reads and 5 percent writes.

Oracle NoSQL Database supports ACID transactional semantics, but also allows the application developer to intelligently trade off durability for performance. There is no single point of failure or contention in the architecture. The system is resilient to single points of failure and is designed to deliver uninterrupted service in production for long periods of time. Oracle NoSQL Database is an enterprise-grade NoSQL system for modern big data applications.

CHAPTER
4

Oracle NoSQL Database Installation and Configuration

Prior to deploying Oracle NoSQL Database, it is imperative that a right-sized database topology is architected using the best practices of sizing Oracle NoSQL databases that satisfies the availability, reliability, and performance requirements as set forth by the Oracle NoSQL Database application. The total number of Storage Nodes and their respective hardware configurations, such as CPU, memory, and disks, must be defined by now. Otherwise, poorly sized systems are prone to performance and stability issues when subjected to production workloads. Please refer to Chapter 8 for the best practices of sizing Oracle NoSQL Database deployments.

The Oracle NoSQL Database deployment is typically a two-phase process. The first phase comprises the steps to install the Oracle NoSQL Database software on the individual Storage Nodes and starts the required processes. If your intention was only to use *KVLite*, you are done after this phase and may continue with developing your applications. KVLite is a single node and non-distributed version of Oracle NoSQL Database suitable for development and learning purposes. Further details on KVLite and application development are provided in Chapter 5.

The steps outlined in the second phase build a *distributed* and *clustered* version of Oracle NoSQL Database using a set of Storage Nodes. A distributed version is essential for achieving high availability, scalability, reliability, and performance requirements—the key characteristics of an enterprise-grade production system.

Oracle NoSQL Database Installation

Oracle NoSQL Database installation in itself is a simple process and can be completed very quickly, but the steps that occur before the installation may take most of your time. Verifying the installation prerequisites such as the hardware, network, and operating system is essential for ensuring a successful and, more important, stable installation. Furthermore, the operating system must be configured with the appropriate set of packages that are required by the Oracle NoSQL Database software. Hence, you must ensure that all Storage Nodes of the key-value store satisfy the following requirements:

- **Operating system**   Oracle Linux and Oracle Solaris are the officially supported operating systems for Oracle NoSQL Database. It may be true that Oracle NoSQL Database, as a Java application, can run on any platform that supports a Java Virtual Machine (JVM), but the chances of running into issues on unsupported platforms are much higher as Oracle Corporation tests its software products only on supported platforms. If you run into issues, you need to reproduce the problem on a supported platform before Oracle support can investigate and analyze the root cause. Therefore, it is very important to ensure that the underlying operating system (OS) is fully supported by Oracle.

- **Clock synchronization** A distributed computing cluster, such as the Oracle NoSQL Database cluster, requires the system clocks of individual Storage Nodes to be synchronized with a global time clock. This is essential to ensure inter-node communications between processes running on different Storage Nodes have the same understanding of time. The clock *drift* (time difference) between all the nodes in the cluster should ideally be close to zero. NTP (Network Time Protocol) is a reliable mechanism for synchronizing time between multiple nodes and readily available on many OS installations, including Oracle Linux and Oracle Solaris. As a best practice, ensure that NTP is set on all the Storage Nodes with an optimal synchronization interval, thereby reducing the clock drift to as close to zero as possible.

- **Java** Ensure that Java SE 6 (JDK 1.6.0 u25) or later is installed on the Storage Nodes. Otherwise, install the correct version of Java from Oracle's download site (http://www.oracle.com/technetwork/java/javase/downloads/index.html). You may use the `java -version` command to check the version of Java installed on the system.

- **File system for KVHOME and KVROOT** *KVHOME* is the file system location storing the Oracle NoSQL Database *software binaries* and *KVROOT* is the location for storing Oracle NoSQL Database configuration files and also serves as the default location for key-value pair *data*. Identify the directories on the file system to be used for these locations and ensure that they have enough space to hold their contents. It is recommended that you have both these locations on the local file system and not on a shared file system such as the Network File System (NFS), as sharing of I/O resources by multiple applications often leads to contention issues.

- **Network ports** The Storage Nodes and Replication Nodes of the key-value store communicate with each other using the TCP/IP protocol over Ethernet ports. Ensure that enough ports are available across all the Storage Nodes, and that the ports are free and unallocated and not blocked by network firewalls. The port numbers are user configurable and set during the initial configuration of Oracle NoSQL Database. Further details on assigning network ports are discussed later in this chapter.

NOTE
If you were to use the integration features of Oracle NoSQL Database such as the integration with Hadoop, Oracle Loader for Hadoop, and the Oracle 11gR2 Database via database external tables, you would require an installation of Oracle NoSQL database software on those systems as well.

Download Oracle NoSQL Database Software

The Oracle NoSQL Database software comes in two editions, the Community Edition (CE) and the Enterprise Edition (EE). The Enterprise Edition includes all features of the Community Edition, plus a few additional features related to the integration of NoSQL with other products, such as the Oracle Database and Oracle Event Processing. The EE also provides access to enterprise-level Oracle Support. Refer to Chapter 2 for further details on CE vs. EE.

No matter what edition you choose to install, the steps for installation and configuration do not deviate much. The Enterprise Edition may require additional steps to configure the integration-specific features, but those steps are covered later in the book.

You may download the Oracle NoSQL Database Community Edition and the Enterprise Edition from the Oracle Technology Network, and to suit your needs, you have an option of downloading a Tar or a Zip archive.

NOTE
Oracle NoSQL Database Community Edition is preinstalled on the Oracle Big Data Appliance (BDA) and configured during the BDA deployment process upon the customer's request.

Software Installation

By now you must have picked the directory locations for KVHOME, KVROOT, and the Oracle NoSQL Database *data* directory (unless using KVROOT as the default) on each Storage Node. Although it is not an absolute requirement, it is preferred that you have both KVHOME and Oracle NoSQL Database data directories on a local file system instead of a shared file system such as NFS. For KVHOME, this ensures that patching and upgrading of the software are done in a rolling fashion and with minimal downtime, and moreover, eliminate a single point of failure as one set of binaries is shared across all nodes. Using a local file system for the data directory ensures that the disks are dedicated solely for NoSQL, thereby eliminating unforeseen IO bottlenecks that may be introduced by other applications.

NOTE
KVROOT is the default location for storing Oracle NoSQL Database data and can be overwritten by using the –storagedir parameter of makebootconfig. Refer to the section "Create the Boot Configuration" for further details.

You must also ensure that KVHOME and Oracle NoSQL Database data are located in separate directories, and are consistent (that is, follow the same paths) across all the Storage Nodes in the key-value store by following standard naming conventions. This is a recommended best practice for avoiding configuration errors and helps with easier manageability. Also ensure that there is enough space allocated by the OS for these locations. The Oracle NoSQL Database data directory requires much more space than KVHOME as it stores the application key-value pair data. KVHOME, on the other hand, requires less than 50MB of disk space (for the current 11gR2 release).

NOTE
You do need superuser privileges to install Oracle NoSQL Database. The installation can be performed as a regular OS user.

Once you have downloaded the software, copy the Zip archive to all the Storage Nodes and move them to the root directory of KVHOME (the mount point or the parent folder of the intended KVHOME). Extract the package contents using the appropriate unzip utilities (gunzip followed by tar for *.gz and unzip for *.zip), and when the extraction completes, the KVHOME directory is created automatically. Repeat this process on all Storage Nodes, and once the extraction succeeds on all the nodes, you have completed the Oracle NoSQL Database software installation. The installation process is really that simple; there are no screens or parameters to configure.

The following example outlines the steps to install Oracle NoSQL Database version 2.0.39 Enterprise Edition using a *.gz file. The root directory of KVHOME used in the example is /opt/kvhomes, and at the end of the installation, KVHOME is created as /opt/kvhomes/kv-2.0.39.

```
$ cd /u01/kvhomes
$ gunzip kv-ee-2.0.39.tar.gz
$ tar xvf kv-ee-2.0.39.tar
$ ls -F /u01/kvhomes/kv-2.0.39
build.xml  doc/  examples/  exttab/  lib/  LICENSE.txt  README.txt
```

The actual packages and directories created in KVHOME depend upon the release, version, and the Oracle NoSQL Database edition (CE or EE). The KVHOME directory itself depends on the release and the version and typically follows the convention kv-M.N.O, where M is the software release, and N and O the major and minor release numbers, respectively. This naming scheme ensures that future upgrades do not overwrite existing installations and that previous installations can easily be identified.

Now that the installation is complete, you may quickly verify the installation by running a supplied test application called `kvclient.jar`, which is a part of the Oracle NoSQL Database software. The `kvclient.jar` application prints the current release and version of the Oracle NoSQL Database software on the screen. You may run `kvclient.jar` from one of the nodes (but ideally on all nodes) and ensure that the output you get follows the format of `version.M.N.O`, where the version is 11gR2 for the current release. The following example illustrates the use of `kvclient.jar`:

```
$ java -jar /u01/kvhomes/kv-2.0.39/lib/kvclient.jar
11gR2.2.0.39
```

Oracle NoSQL Database Administration Service

The Oracle NoSQL Database Administration Service is a process that runs on the Storage Nodes, and is in charge of a variety of administration activities on the Oracle NoSQL Database, such as instance startup/shutdown, initial configuration, ongoing modifications to the configuration, and monitoring system performance, without the need for manually writing complex scripts and commands. The Administration Service is also responsible for collecting and maintaining database performance statistics, and also for logging important system events, and thereby assisting with online monitoring and helping tune database performance. The Administration Service internally uses a database called the *Administration Database* to store configuration and monitoring data.

NOTE
The Administration Database under the covers uses a key-value store.

The availability of the Administration Service is critical to performing maintenance operations on the key-value store; therefore, it is important to have multiple Administration Services deployed across the store to ensure high availability. The best practice is to have a minimum of three Administration Services so at least one service is predicted to be available in a given time. The availability of the Administration Service is not to be confused with the availability of Oracle NoSQL Database itself, as normal database activities such as reads, writes, and replication occur without the intervention of the Administration Service.

The Administration Service is accessible from a command line interface called the *Administration CLI* or *CLI*, and a web-based console called the *Web Administration Console*.

Administration Command Line Interface (CLI)

The Administration CLI supports all administration activities on the key-value store. To start the Administration CLI, execute the `runadmin` class of `kvstore.jar`. The runadmin interacts with the Administration Service and provides the CLI prompt (the `kv->` prompt). However, when you are configuring the key-value store for the first time, you do not have any Administration Services running, but you still need to start the CLI and to configure other parameters, for example the key-value store name. It seems like a catch-22, and the solution to that is to use the built-in Administration Service of the Storage Node Agent process called the Bootstrap Administration Service. A default Administration Database gets created by the Bootstrap Administration Service and later, when the Administration Service gets deployed by the CLI commands, the final set of Administration Services gets created and the Bootstrap Administration Service is stopped and no longer used.

The Bootstrap Administration Service is automatically started upon starting the Storage Node Agent process when the administration port is specified in the boot configuration file (boot configuration is discussed next). Therefore, you need to ensure that the Storage Node Agent service is started prior to executing `runadmin` because `runadmin` communicates with the SNA using the registry port.

The CLI can be invoked mainly in three modes: an interactive mode, a single command mode, and a script mode. The *interactive mode* is most commonly used and is the only mode that provides a command prompt (the `kv->` prompt). Users input commands at the prompt, one at a time, and the commands are executed in the background (although they may run in the foreground using the `-wait` flag). The following is an example of starting the CLI using `runadmin` to access the Storage Node Agent on `node01` with the registry port `5000`:

```
java -jar KVHOME/lib/kvstore.jar runadmin -host node01 -port 5000
kv->
```

The *single command mode*, on the other hand, runs a single command directly at the OS command prompt while invoking the CLI. It passes the CLI command as a parameter to `runadmin`. Once the single CLI command completes its execution, the control is returned back to the OS. If the command completes successfully, the exit code returned to the OS is 0, and if it encounters an error, the exit code is a value other than 0. The general usage of invoking the CLI in the single command mode is as follows:

```
java -jar KVHOME/lib/kvstore.jar runadmin
-host <hostname> -port <port> [single command and arguments]
```

where `<hostname>` and `<port>` are the SNA hostname and the registry port, respectively.

Last, the *script mode* is very similar to the single command mode, but it runs a script containing multiple CLI commands instead of running only a single CLI command. With the script mode, it becomes easy to automate repetitive tasks, or run tasks in a batch mode, without requiring direct supervision of an administrator. As with the single command mode, the control returns to the OS prompt once the script completes. The script file is specified using the `load -file` switch when invoking `runadmin`. The following is a typical example of CLI in script mode:

```
java -jar KVHOME/lib/kvstore.jar runadmin
-host <hostname> -port <port> load -file <path-to-script>
```

The configuration steps in this chapter are mainly performed using the interactive mode. The CLI allows a number of commands, and some commands may even have subcommands. Commands are also grouped by the specific set of functions they perform; for example, the `show` command displays the state of the key-value store and its components, whereas the `ddl` command manipulates key-value store schemas. You may use the `help` command to discover all commands allowed by the CLI, or append a `-help` flag to a specific command to display its usage syntax. For a complete listing of all CLI commands, refer to the *Oracle NoSQL Database Administration Guide* provided by Oracle. Only the important CLI commands that get you through the configuration steps are covered in this chapter.

Web Administration Console

Besides the Administration CLI, the *Web Administration Console* can also be used to administer the Oracle NoSQL Database. The current release of the Web Administration Console supports mainly read-only type administration activities such as browsing the key-value store topology, monitoring plan executions, and browsing at the cluster-wide log file; however, it does not support activities related to the store configuration or modification. These are the tasks well handled by the Administration CLI.

The Web Administration Console is part of the Administration Services and uses a port to listen for HTTP requests from web clients, called the *Administration Port*. To access the Web Administration Console, point an HTML-based web interface to the host running the Administration Service and specify the Administration Port. For instance, you would use the URL `http://node01:5001` to access the Web Administration Console with the Administration Service running on `node01` and listening to port `5001`.

Create the Boot Configuration

So far, you only have the Oracle NoSQL Database software installed on the Storage Nodes. The next step is to perform a few additional tasks, such as specifying the network ports for Storage Node Agents (SNAs), the Web Administration Console and replication ports, and the KVROOT location to store the configuration files and, optionally, the data files. Although these tasks are related to configuration, they are still part of the first phase and are required to be completed before starting the main configuration steps, which is mainly focused on building a distributed cluster of Oracle NoSQL Database.

The Storage Node Agent (SNA) process and Administration Service utilize a configuration file at startup for setting up the network ports and other initialization parameters. This configuration file is also referred to as the "boot config" file and is located in the KVROOT directory with a default name of `config.xml`. For a freshly installed Storage Node, the boot config file does not exist, and needs to be created manually using the `makebootconfig` utility. The `makebootconfig` utility has the following the syntax:

```
java -jar KVHOME/lib/kvstore.jar makebootconfig [-verbose]
-root <rootDirectory> -host <hostname> -hahostname <hostname>
-harange <startPort,endPort> -port <port> [-admin <adminPort>]
[-config <configFile>][-storagedir <path>] [-capacity <n_rep_nodes>]
[-num_cpus <ncpus>][-memory_mb <memory_mb>]
[-servicerange <startPort,endPort>]
[-mgmt {snmp|jmx|none}] [-pollport <snmp poll port>]
[-traphost <snmp trap/notification hostname>]
[-trapport <snmp trap/notification port>]
```

The following are the details on the commonly used parameters of `makebootconfig`. It is a good idea to ensure that you have this information before creating the initial boot configuration.

- **`-root <rootDirectory>`**   This is the KVROOT location that stores the configuration files and, optionally, the key-value pair data (unless using the `-storagedir` clause to overwrite data storage location). If using KVROOT to store data, ensure that the disk space is large enough to accommodate the key-value pairs destined for the Storage Node. The storage location should also guarantee the I/O performance to satisfy the application requirements. The examples in this book assume that the KVROOT directory is built on `/u02/kvroot` on each Storage Node.

- **`-port <port>`**   Each Storage Node runs a Storage Node Agent (SNA) process to facilitate communications between other SNA processes and the client applications. The SNA listens to a *registry port* specified using the `-port` parameter. The registry port typically used in the examples is 5000.

NOTE
All ports required for Oracle NoSQL Database should be unallocated and unused by other applications, and not blocked by network firewalls. Ensure this is true on all the servers that are part of the Oracle NoSQL Database cluster.

■ **-admin <adminPort>** This is the port used by the Administration Service to listen for HTTP connections from web clients, also called the *Administration Port*. For initial configuration, use this option only on the first Storage Node to configure the Bootstrap Administration Service. Once the database is fully deployed, configure multiple Administration Services for HA and ensure that they all use the same Administration Port. Otherwise, it becomes difficult for users to identify the port of the next healthy Administration Service when the Storage Node running the primary fails. The Administration Port typically used in the examples is 5001.

■ **-harange <startPort, endPort>** Each Storage Node requires a set of ports (specified using a range, called the *HA Range* ports) to be used by the Replication Nodes and Administration Services for facilitating the replication of user data (key-value pairs). The SNA internally manages these ports and reserves one for the Administration Service and one for each Replication Node (RN) hosted by the Storage Node (SN). If there are multiple RNs per SN (yes, this is possible, as discussed in the corresponding note), then you need to ensure that the range specified has enough ports that are equal to the maximum number of RNs that the SN may ever host, plus one for the Administration Service, as there could be at most one Administration Service per SN. The ports are specified as a range using "startPort, endPort." The examples in this book use "5010, 5020" as the HA Range ports.

NOTE
Multiple Replication Nodes can be configured per Storage Node. Although this is not recommended as a best practice, in certain cases where there is ample CPU, memory, and I/O resources on the physical server, it could be justified.

■ **-servicerange <startPort, endPort>** The Storage and Replication Node services internally initiate Java-based RMI calls across the nodes in the cluster (separate from data replication operations). Using the -servicerange flag, you may specify a second range of free ports to be used specifically for such RMI invocations. If -servicerange is not used, the RMI ports are randomly allocated, thereby making it difficult for network administrators to configure firewall rules. This parameter is useful when there is a network firewall configured between the clients and the Storage Nodes and it restricts access to specific ports. Using this parameter forces RMI calls over a predefined range of ports upon which firewall rules can be proactively defined.

- **SNMP configuration**   You could optionally configure SNMP monitoring tools (such as Oracle Enterprise Manager or other third-party SNMP- or JMX-based tools) to capture critical events and alerts that arise within the Oracle NoSQL Database cluster. For this to occur, the critical events need to be propagated outside the Oracle NoSQL Database processes and memory structures through the built-in SNMP/JMX agent (specified using the `-mgmt` flag) via an *SNMP port* (specified using the `-pollPort` flag) to communicate with an external SNMP management system (specified using `-traphost` and `-trapport`).

- **`-num_cpus <ncpus>`**   This parameter is used when you have multiple Replication Nodes on a Storage Node. The `-num_cpus` specifies the total number of processors on the server available to all the Replication Nodes so the CPU resources can be appropriately allocated. This value defaults to 0, in which case the OS is queried to get the number of processors on the machine. The best practice, however, is to not default it to 0 because there is a chance that the user installing Oracle NoSQL Database may not have access to OS utilities such as `/proc/cpuinfo` (for Linux) as the file is typically owned by root, which may result in the query failing.

- **`-memory_mb <memory_mb>`**   The Replication Node cache and heap sizes are set accordingly with the total memory available on the server. Use this parameter to specify the total memory on the server in megabytes. If not specified, it defaults to 0. This makes the system query the OS to get the actual value but only when Oracle Hotspot JVM is used. The best practice is to follow the same guidelines mentioned earlier and specify the total memory using this flag instead of relying on the operating system. This value becomes even more important when the Storage Node hosts multiple Replication Nodes and the system needs to effectively manage the memory between multiple Replication Nodes.

- **`-hahostname <hostname>`**   This flag is used for specifying a separate network interface for routing replication traffic. This comes in handy when segregating client requests from internal replication traffic within the Replication Nodes. If `-hahostname` is not set, it defaults to the hostname specified using the `-host` flag.

- **`-capacity <capacity>`**   This parameter is optional and, when set, specifies the total number of Replication Nodes a Storage Node can support. Capacity is set to values greater than 1 usually when the Storage Node has sufficient disk, CPU, and memory, and can support multiple Replication Nodes.

- **-storagedir <path>** This parameter is used to override the default
Oracle NoSQL Database data directory for the Replication Node. As a best
practice, always specify –storagedir instead of defaulting to KVROOT,
and decouple the Oracle NoSQL Database configuration data location
with the key-value pair data. When multiple Replication Nodes are to be
configured per Storage Node, use this parameter along with the -capacity
parameter. If –storagedir is not specified and you have specified
–capacity greater than 1, the data storage directory for each Replication
Node gets created under the KVROOT directory with default names. You
may use this parameter multiple times in the command to specify multiple
directories, one each per Replication Node, not to exceed the -capacity
parameter. For example, if the Storage Node houses eight disks, you would
specify –capacity 8 and have eight -storagedir arguments, one per
each Replication Node.

Once you have obtained the preceding information, proceed with creating
the boot config file, as shown in the following example. The example calls the
makebootconfig command with /u02/kvroot as the KVROOT, the SNA
running on port 5000, the Administration Service running on port 5001, the range
for harange ports as 5010–5020, and the capacity of 1.

```
$> mkdir -p /u02/kvroot
$> java -jar /u01/kvhomes/kv-2.0.39/lib/kvstore.jar makebootconfig
   -root /u02/kvroot \
   -host <hostname> \
   -port 5000 \
   -admin 5001 \
   -harange 5010,5020 \
   -capacity 1 \
   -num_cpus 0 \
   -memory_mb 0
```

The next step is to start the Oracle NoSQL Database Storage Node agent (SNA)
processes on each of the Oracle NoSQL Database nodes. As mentioned earlier, the
SNA automatically starts the Bootstrap Administration Service if the -admin
parameter is specified at the time of the creation of the boot config file. You can use
the start utility to start SNA processes, and also remember to start the SNA on all
Storage Nodes that will be used to configure the Oracle NoSQL Database in the
next section.

The following example starts the SNA process using /u02/kvroot as the
KVROOT:

```
$> nohup java -jar /u02/kvroot/lib/kvstore.jar start -root /u02/kvroot &
```

NOTE
It is important to run the start *command in the background and preferably use* nohup *to avoid process hang-ups. Also, you should configure the nodes to start the SNA process automatically at boot time, using OS startup utilities such as* init.d *for Linux.*

Perform Sanity Checks

It is important to test the installation before proceeding with the configuration steps. There are several ways to perform sanity checks on the Storage Nodes and ensure that the nodes are running the required services and are void of any setup- and installation-related issues. The tests that you may perform at this stage should ensure that the host, operating system, and the Oracle NoSQL Database software processes are alive and healthy.

Use the JVM process status tool (jps) to check the Java processes running on the host. The SNA Agent process, the Administration Service, and the Replication Nodes will each have a Java process that runs on the operating system and should be visible on the output. At a minimum, you should see the Storage Node Agent process running with the name ManagedService and a class of RepNode, and if you have configured the Administration Service, you should see a second ManagedService process with a class of Admin. You may also see a kvstore.jar process if you have configured a distributed key-value store and a kvlite.jar process if you have started the KVLite database.

At the OS command prompt, run jps -m, as shown here:

```
$> jps -m
5705 kvstore.jar start -root /u02/nosql/kvroot
5945 ManagedService -root /u02/nosql/kvroot/movielite/sn1 -store

    movielite -class RepNode -service rg1-rn1
5757 ManagedService -root /u02/nosql/kvroot -class Admin -service

    BootstrapAdmin.5000 -config config.xml
25478 Jps -m
```

Further sanity checks are performed after the configuration steps in the next section are complete.

Oracle NoSQL Database Configuration

After completing the installation steps, Oracle NoSQL Database needs to be configured before it can be accessed by client applications, unless you plan on using only KVLite, in which case the configuration is already complete and you may proceed to Chapter 5 and start developing Oracle NoSQL Database applications.

Prior to understanding the configuration process, it is important to understand *plans* as they are used quite frequently during the initial configuration.

Plans

Plans are a set of commands that perform a series of predefined administrative tasks on the Oracle NoSQL Database cluster. Plans encapsulate multiple operations that may query or modify the state of the key-value store; interact with the key-value store Administration Service, the Storage Nodes, or the Replication Nodes; issue requests that require modifications to store parameters; or simply look up Storage Node configuration parameters. Plans can sometimes be long-running operations and may touch every Storage Node in the cluster, or sometimes run on specific Storage Nodes and complete very quickly.

Plans are created and executed by using the `plan` command from the Administration CLI. The `plan` command takes in a `subcommand` as the input parameter, which is a prebuilt administrative operation to be performed on the Storage Nodes. All subcommands are preprogrammed to perform documented and specific actions. For example, there are subcommands to create a datacenter and a Storage Node, and to reconfigure the parameters on a Replication Node. Examples of commonly used subcommands are

- **deploy-datacenter**   Deploys a datacenter to the key-value store

- **deploy-sn**   Deploys a Storage Node to a specific host in a datacenter

- **deploy-admin**   Deploys the Administration Service on a Storage Node

- **execute**   Executes a previously created plan

When a `plan` subcommand gets executed, the Administration Service stores the subcommand in the Administration Database and assigns an integer, internally referred to as the `plan_id`. You may list all available plans created in the system by using the `plan` command without arguments. For a complete list of all subcommands, you may use `help plan`, as shown in the following example:

```
kv-> plan
kv-> help plan
```

Plans are executed using the `plan` command from the Administration CLI. By default, the `plan` command runs asynchronously in the background and the prompt returns immediately. You may optionally use the `-wait` flag to make the plan run synchronously, in which case the command line prompt will only return after the plan completes. The following example illustrates the use of the `plan` command with the `-wait` flag:

```
kv-> plan deploy-datacenter -name "Dallas" -rf 3 -wait
Executed plan 1, waiting for completion...
Plan 1 ended successfully
```

The `plan wait` command (not the same as the `plan` command with the `-wait` flag) can be used to wait until the specified plan completes, or for a specified time period. The `-last` flag refers to the most recent plan that was created. The complete syntax for the `plan wait` command is

```
kv-> plan wait -id <id> | -last [-seconds <timeout in seconds>]
```

You can also create plans and defer their execution by using the optional `-noexecute` flag. The `-noexecute` flag saves the plan in the system and returns the `plan_id`. The plan can be executed later as required by using the `plan execute -id <id>` command.

The `-wait` and `-noexecute` options, when coupled with the `plan wait` command, provide the capability to program multiple plan executions using scripts. Using these flags, you can run a series of interdependent plans by ensuring that the current plan completes before the next plan is started. Moreover, you can capture the return code of the `plan` command within the script and take appropriate actions. Furthermore, you can also save plans and run them multiple times by retrieving them from a list of stored plans. By using these powerful options available for the `plan` command, the administrators can build a complex set of batch scripts that can be scheduled to run automatically and virtually unattended.

Configuration Steps

Finally, it's time to run the configuration steps. After all configuration steps are completed, a *set* of Storage Nodes is configured to act and work as one distributed cluster of the key-value store. The key value store is built in accordance with the topology you require, and contains the appropriate number of shards and Replication Nodes that you have identified as part of the capacity planning and sizing activity.

Before proceeding with the configuration steps, ensure that the individual Storage Node Agent (SNA) processes have started on all the Storage Nodes. If you followed the post-install steps from the installation section of this chapter, the SNA processes should already have been started.

The key-value store configuration process comprises the following steps:

1. Start the Administration CLI.

2. Name the key-value store.

3. Create a datacenter.

4. Deploy the first Storage Node.

5. Create an Administration Service.

6. Create a Storage Node Pool.

7. Create the remaining Storage Nodes.

8. Create and deploy Replication Nodes.

Start the Administration CLI

The configuration steps are performed using the Administration CLI. Prior to invoking the CLI, select the Storage Node that would serve as the primary administration node during the configuration process, and also the node that holds the master copy of the Administration Database. The Administration Database stores critical data about the key-value store and its topology, and ensuring its availability is important for the proper functioning of the Oracle NoSQL Database. By default, the first Storage Node you would ever connect to using the Administration CLI becomes the primary administration node (and the only node, until other Administration Services are added).

It is important to note that *all* steps for the configuration of the key-value store should be run on the *same* Storage Node. The Storage Nodes cannot be switched in the middle of the configuration. If that happens for any reason, you will have to start over by manually cleaning up an incomplete configuration.

Log in to the Storage Node you have identified as being the primary administration node. Start the CLI by invoking `runadmin`, as shown in the following example:

```
> java -jar KVHOME/lib/kvstore.jar runadmin -port 5000 -host node01
kv->
```

The CLI invocation assumes that the Storage Node `node01` is configured with the Storage Node Agent to listen on port `5000`, known as the registry port. Also, KVHOME is the directory where Oracle NoSQL Database software is installed.

NOTE
The configuration steps described next can also be coded into a script file and run collectively by passing the file using the `-script` flag of CLI. This is very helpful for avoiding typos and when running the configuration on multiple environments.

Name the Key-Value Store

One of the first attributes you will configure is the name for the key-value store. The name you choose should be suitable to the key-value store function, application, and/or contents. The key-value store name is used to build a directory path on the file system, under which subdirectories will be created to store the actual key-value pairs. Therefore, syntactically speaking, any name would be valid as long as it is allowed by the operating system for naming directories. The valid characters supported for a key-value store name are alphanumeric characters, a minus sign (–), an underscore (_), and a period (.).

At the `kv->` prompt, use the `configure -name` command to name the store. This command takes in the store name as a parameter (the only parameter) and ensures that the name is syntactically valid and allowed by the system. Otherwise, an error is flagged. In the example shown here, a key-value store is given the name `movieDBstore`:

```
kv-> configure -name movieDBstore
```

Create a Datacenter

Conceptually speaking, a *datacenter* is referred to as the facility that houses computer equipment and related infrastructure such as network, storage, and power, usually all components residing in one location. In the context of Oracle NoSQL Database, however, a datacenter is simply a set of Storage Nodes that are part of the key-value store and may be geographically distributed. The current release of Oracle NoSQL Database allows only *one* datacenter per key-value store. In future releases, the concept of multiple datacenters may be introduced to indicate physically separate entities that could be utilized by Oracle NoSQL Database to enhance its high availability and recoverability.

The replication factor for the key-value store can be set only at the datacenter level. Determining the appropriate replication factor is very important as the availability and recoverability of the store depends on it. The command used to create the datacenter is also used to define the replication factor.

Use the `plan deploy-datacenter` command to create the datacenter and define the replication factor. The command takes in a datacenter name via the `-name` input parameter and the replication factor via the `-rf` parameter. In the example that follows, a datacenter named `Dallas` is created with a replication factor of 3. The `plan` command returns the plan number and the status of its execution. The `-wait` flag is used to indicate that the prompt should wait for the command to finish before accepting further input.

```
kv-> plan deploy-datacenter -name "Dallas" -rf 3 -wait
Executed plan 1, waiting for completion...
Plan 1 ended successfully
```

Alternatively, if you do not specify the `-wait` option, you may check the status of the `plan` command by using `show plans`:

```
kv-> show plans
1 Deploy DC SUCCEEDED
```

Deploy the First Storage Node

You need to add the very first Storage Node to the key-value store. Although you have already connected to a Storage Node and started the SNA service, it has not been added to the key-value store. This step is a prerequisite for creating the Administration Service.

Run the `plan deploy-sn` command to add the Storage Node to the key-value store. This command takes in the datacenter ID as the input, which is obtained by the `show topology` command. The example provided here indicates that `dc1` is the datacenter ID of the `Dallas` datacenter:

```
kv-> show topology
store=movieDBstore  numPartitions=0  sequence=1
dc=[dc1]  name=Dallas  repfactor=3
```

Now that you have the datacenter ID, run `plan deploy-sn` and add the Storage Node `node01` with the registry port of `5000` to the datacenter ID `dc1`, as shown in the following example:

```
kv-> plan deploy-sn -dc dc1 -host node01 -port 5000 -wait
Executed plan 2, waiting for completion...
Plan 2 ended successfully
```

Create the Administration Service

The Administration Service is in charge of maintaining the Administration Database and providing a Web-based Administration Console. The step after creating the first Storage Node is to create the Administration Service using the `plan deploy-admin` command. This command requires the Storage Node ID (obtained from the topology command, as shown in the next example) and the HTTP port number of the Administration Service. As you may recall, the administration port number is used to route HTTP traffic to the Web-based Administration Console. The following example deploys the Administration Service on Storage Node ID `sn1` with the administration port of `5001`.

```
kv-> show topology
store=movieDBstore  numPartitions=0  sequence=1
dc=[dc1]  name=Dallas  repfactor=3
sn=[sn1]  dc=dc1  node01:5000  capacity=1  RUNNING

kv-> plan deploy-admin -sn sn1 -port 5001 -wait
Executed plan 3, waiting for completion...
Plan 3 ended successfully
```

NOTE
You may run the `show topology` *command at each step to show the progress of the configuration process.*

After a successful execution of the `plan deploy-admin` command, you would have a single Administration Service deployed in the key-value store. This is sufficient for you to continue with the remaining configuration steps, but later on, you should configure additional nodes to run the Administration Service to ensure that the service is available when failures occur.

Create a Storage Node Pool

A Storage Node Pool is a logical grouping of all the Storage Nodes that are present in the key-value store. Storage Nodes are associated with pools in order to facilitate optimal distribution of resources, especially when the Storage Nodes are added or removed from the key-value store.

Once you have created the Administration Service, create a Storage Node Pool using the `pool create` command. The command requires only the pool `name` as the input and is run only once at pool creation time. Next, add the Storage Nodes to the pool using the `pool join` command. You would run the `pool join` command on all the Storage Nodes, including the Storage Node you have created earlier. The `pool join` command associates a Storage Node to the pool and requires the pool name and Storage Node ID as the input.

The following example illustrates the CLI commands to be run for this step:

```
kv-> pool create -name movieDBpool
kv-> show topology
store=movieDBpool  numPartitions=0 sequence=2
  dc=[dc1] name=Dallas repFactor=3
  sn=[sn1]  dc=dc1 node01:5000 capacity=1 RUNNING
kv-> pool join -name movieDBpool -sn sn1
Added Storage Node(s) [sn1] to pool movieDBpool
```

Create the Remaining Storage Nodes

So far, you have created only one Storage Node and joined it to the Storage Node Pool. Although, technically speaking, a single node key-value store is allowed by the system (with a replication factor of one), it does not provide the high availability typically required for production deployments. Therefore, you need to deploy additional Storage Nodes to the key-value store and add them to the Storage Node Pool.

Use the `plan deploy-sn` command to deploy the Storage Node to the cluster and the `pool join` command to add the Storage Node to the Storage Node Pool, as you have done in the earlier step. Remember to repeat these commands on all Storage Nodes that you have identified to be a part of the key-value store.

The following example illustrates the addition of Storage Node 02 and Storage Node 03 to the key-value store.

```
kv-> plan deploy-sn -dc dc1 -host node02 -port 5000 -wait
kv-> show topology
kv-> pool join -name movieDBpool -sn sn2
kv-> plan deploy-sn -dc dc1 -host node03 -port 5000 -wait
kv-> pool join -name movieDBpool -sn sn3
....
```

In the preceding example, observe that `show topology` was run immediately after `deploy-sn` to obtain the Storage Node ID of the node just deployed. The ID is used by the `pool join` command for adding the Storage Node to the pool. But if you notice, the Administration Service allocates Storage Node IDs in a sequential manner. For instance, if the Storage Node that was just created has an ID of 5, then the next Storage Node that you create will be allocated an ID of 6. Therefore, you can always predict the Storage Node ID of the node you have just deployed by incrementing the ID of the previous Storage Node by one—which means you can directly run `deploy-sn` without the need to run `show topology`. Note that this is only true as long as only one CLI session is used to run the `deploy-sn` commands.

NOTE
Now that you have deployed all the Storage Nodes in the cluster, you may now create multiple Administration Services to ensure high availability.

Create and Deploy Replication Nodes

The last step in the configuration process is to create and deploy the Replication Nodes on all the Storage Nodes in the key-value store. Although there is not a direct command to create a Replication Node, you would create and deploy a *topology*, and this in turn would create and deploy the correct set of Replication Nodes on the Storage Nodes.

The `topology create` command is used to create the topology and it requires the topology name, Storage Node Pool, and the total number of partitions as the input. The *topology name* is a unique name that you define to identify the topology; the *Storage Node Pool* is the name of the Storage Node Pool you created earlier; and the *total number of partitions* is obtained by undergoing a capacity planning and sizing exercise (refer to Chapter 8 for further details). The total number of partitions is a static parameter and cannot be altered once it is set, so make sure that the number you provide here is more than the maximum number of shards that you would ever expect your key-value store to grow in its lifetime.

The `topology create` command will automatically create an appropriate number of shards and Replication Nodes based upon the number of Storage Nodes and the replication factor. The number of shards in the key-value store is calculated by dividing the total number of Storage Nodes by the replication factor of the datacenter, and the number of partitions per shard is calculated by dividing the total number of partitions provided by the total number of shards.

Finally, deploy the topology on the Storage Nodes by using the `plan deploy-topology`. The command requires the topology name, and upon its completion, it starts the Replication Node processes on all the Storage Nodes.

The following example illustrates the use of `topology create` and `deploy-topology` commands:

```
kv-> topology create -name movietopo -pool movieDBpool -partitions 300
kv-> plan deploy-topology -name movietopo -wait
Executed plan 6, waiting for completion...
Plan 6 ended successfully
```

The key-value store is fully installed and configured once the preceding commands are successfully completed.

Automating the Configuration Steps

Up to this point, you have run the configuration steps by creating and executing plans using the interactive command line interface of `runadmin`: the `kv->` prompt. In some cases, you would need to automate the configuration steps. Perhaps, you will be building test and development environments repeatedly, or you need to avoid potential typographical errors introduced at the command line, or simply run the configuration unattended during off-hours.

There are two ways to run the Administration CLI commands directly at the OS prompt. The first method uses the `load -file` flag at the time of executing `runadmin` to specify a script file containing a sequence of CLI commands. For example, you may create a script named `moviedeploy.kvs` with the following contents:

```
configure -name movieDBstore
plan deploy-datacenter -name Dallas -rf 3 -wait
plan deploy-sn -dcname Dallas -host node01 -port 5000 -wait
plan deploy-admin -sn sn1 -port 5001 -wait
```

Execute the preceding script by issuing the following command using the `load -file` flag:

```
java -jar kvstore.jar runadmin -host node01 -port 5000 \

    load -file moviedeploy.kvs
```

Second, you could run a single CLI command at the OS prompt by specifying the CLI command directly at the prompt, and thereby providing the capability to run multiple CLI commands by running multiple OS commands. The following example of a shell script illustrates the use of this method. Notice that each invocation of `runadmin` would start a separate instance.

```
#!/bin/sh
HOST=node01
PORT=5000
HTTPPORT=5001
KVADMIN="java -jar lib/kvstore.jar runadmin -host $HOST -port $PORT"

# Each of the following CLI command below starts a new instance of runAdmin
$KVADMIN configure -name moviestore
$KVADMIN plan deploy-datacenter -name Dallas -rf 3 -wait
$KVADMIN plan deploy-sn -dcname Dallas -host $HOST -port $PORT -wait
$KVADMIN plan deploy-admin -sn sn1 -port $HTTPPORT -wait
```

NOTE
On UNIX systems, you can also use a here document as a method of scripting CLI commands at the OS command prompt or within UNIX shell scripts. The here document provides a mechanism for streaming input strings to a command. Refer to your UNIX scripting guide for further details.

Verifying the Deployment

Several methods are available to test the sanity of the newly built key-value store—mainly, the Web Administration Console, the Administration CLI, the supplied sample programs, and finally the `ping` command provided by the SNA. You can always program your own verification method, but the ones outlined here are quick and readily available, and also quite effective.

Verification Using the Web Administration Console and CLI

The Web Administration Console and the CLI can both be used to validate the key-value store topology and observe the plan execution results. If using the Web Administration Console, point your browser to the machine and port running the Administration Service. For instance, if you used a host named `node01` and listening on port `5001` for HTTP requests, point to the URL `http://node01:5001` to launch the Web Administration Console.

The landing page shown is normally the topology section of the interface, as depicted in Figure 4-1 (if not, just click the topology link). The Topology section

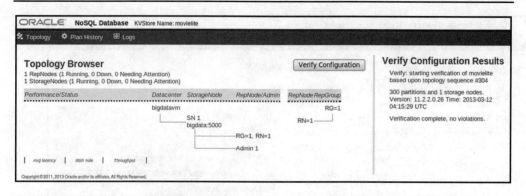

FIGURE 4-1. *Topology Browser*

displays the details of the key-value store topology and the current status of its components. Ensure that the datacenter, Storage Node, Replication Node, and Administration Node information is correctly displayed and processes have RUNNING status.

Verify Configuration is the function of the web-based console that verifies the topology using an internal topology sequence and alerts you about potential violations. Click the Verify Configuration button and observe the output, as shown in Figure 4-2. The verification step should inform you that the store is currently in RUNNING state and has no violations.

As shown in Figure 4-3, you may click Plan History and observe the list of plans that were run in the process of configuring the store, along with their respective status. Observe that the output is very similar to the show plans CLI command.

Alternatively, you may also use the Administration CLI for verifying the configuration. At the CLI prompt, run the show plans and show topology commands, as shown in the following example. The commands should display the

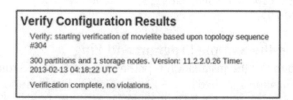

FIGURE 4-2. *Verify Configuration*

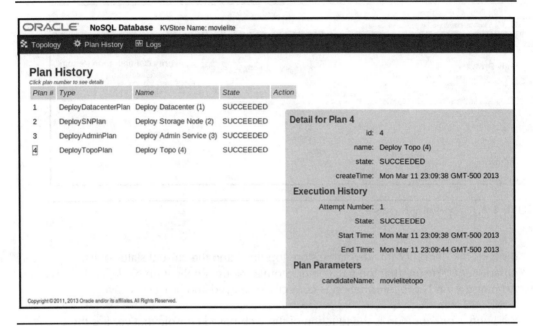

FIGURE 4-3. *Plan History*

status of SUCCEEDED for the plan executions and the status of RUNNING for SNA
and Administration Services.

```
kv-> show plans
     1 Deploy Datacenter (1)     SUCCEEDED
     2 Deploy Storage Node (2)   SUCCEEDED
     3 Deploy Admin Service (3)  SUCCEEDED
     4 Deploy Topo (4)           SUCCEEDED
kv-> show topology
store=movielite  numPartitions=300 sequence=304
  dc=[dc1] name=bigdatavm repFactor=1
  sn=[sn1]  dc=dc1 bigdata:5000 capacity=1 RUNNING
    [rg1-rn1] RUNNING
```

Verification Using the Sample Program and Ping

The best method to test the installation is perhaps to compile and run the sample
Hello World application supplied by the Oracle NoSQL Database software
installation. Running the sample application exercises various software libraries of
the installation and ensures the connectivity to the key-value store is fully functional.

The sample program outputs the string `Hello Big Data World` on the screen, if things work as expected.

The sample application is located in the `KVHOME/examples/hello` directory. The following example illustrates the steps for running this application:

```
# cd to KVHOME
$> cd /u01/kvhome/kv-2.0.39

# Compile the sample Hello World Application
$> javac -g -cp lib/kvclient.jar:examples examples/hello/*.java

# Run the Application. Substitute the <hostname>, <port> and <kvstore>
with your settings
$> java -cp lib/kvclient.jar:examples hello.HelloBigDataWorld \
-host <hostname> -port <port> -store <kvstore>
```

You may also run the `ping` command of `kvstore.jar` from the OS prompt. Remember that this command was also run prior to starting the configuration process and, at that time, it output only the version of Oracle NoSQL Database. But now it should output the status of your Oracle NoSQL Database topology, quite similar to the Verify Topology tool of the Web Administration Console. The following example shows the output from a successful execution of the `ping` command:

```
$ java -jar /u02/nosql/kv-2.0.26/lib/kvstore.jar ping -port 5000 -host node01

Pinging components of store movielite based upon topology sequence #304
movielite comprises 300 partitions and 1 Storage Nodes
Storage Node [sn1] on bigdata:5000

Datacenter: bigdatavm [dc1]

Status: RUNNING   Ver: 11gR2.2.0.26 2013-01-28 12:19:21 UTC

Build id: 99ef986805a3
  Rep Node [rg1-rn1] Status: RUNNING, MASTER at

  sequence number: 611 haPort: 5011
```

Summary

In this chapter, you have learned to install and configure a production-grade deployment of Oracle NoSQL Database. Although the actual installation steps are quite simple, to the extent that it's merely a matter of running `unzip` or a `tar` command, the activities that occur both prior to and after the installation process are quite essential, and need to be well planned. This is not only to ensure a successful installation, but also to ensure that the installed software operates at the optimal performance levels and provides the right levels of availability and reliability.

Therefore, the installation of enterprise-grade software should be treated like a mini-project. The project would comprise multiple phases such as planning, implementation, testing, and go-live, not to mention resource allocations that go alongside to manage and execute the project. The instructions outlined in this chapter and in Chapter 8 will help ensure that the Oracle NoSQL Database deployed in the datacenter is fully stable, sized to provide the right capacity, and delivers extreme performance.

CHAPTER
5

Getting Started
with Oracle NoSQL
Database Development

I n preceding chapters, we have covered the details surrounding distributed computing concepts, the architecture of Oracle NoSQL Database, and how Oracle NoSQL Database is installed in production environments. In this chapter, we begin to discuss how applications are developed on top of Oracle NoSQL Database. It is important to note up front that application development utilizing a distributed NoSQL database requires the application developer to carefully consider some very important questions, as the answers to these questions will lead directly to how the application will interact with NoSQL Database. More specifically, the following questions should be considered during the application design process:

- What are the latency requirements for the application? Does the application execute according to a service level agreement in which strict latency requirements must be met?

- How tolerant will the application be to inconsistent data? Are there portions of the application that can operate successfully on data that may not be the most recent copy?

- What kind of transactions will be needed in the application? Are there pieces of the application functionality that will need ACID transactions? Can ACID behavior be relaxed for portions of the application in exchange for increased throughput and lower latencies?

- How should the data be modeled in Oracle NoSQL Database such that the expected queries against this data can be satisfied easily and efficiently?

Application developers should think carefully about how to finesse the trade-offs between application throughput, latency, availability, and consistency. These are core concepts in developing successful applications on Oracle NoSQL Database and should be utilized to drive the choice of which API is appropriate for a given task. More specifically, the application designer is strongly encouraged to examine each part of the functional requirements of the application and decide what the trade-offs will be, and then choose the right Oracle NoSQL Database API to deliver on those trade-offs.

Of course, there are other issues to be considered during any application design phase such as threading model, class association, and algorithm design, but these types of questions will not be addressed in the context of this chapter.

Developing on KVLite

It is highly advisable to begin the application development process on top of KVLite, as this implementation of Oracle NoSQL Database provides all of the programmatic API functionality in an extremely simple and easy-to-use package. Once a sufficient level of comfort has been attained with the Oracle NoSQL Database APIs and modeling the key space, the development process should be moved to a clustered deployment of Oracle NoSQL Database. KVLite is a lightweight version of the NoSQL database server that runs on a single node, has a single replication group, and is packaged inside of the `kvstore.jar` file located in the lib folder in the KVHOME directory.

KVLite can be launched using the following command:

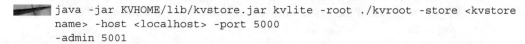

```
java -jar KVHOME/lib/kvstore.jar kvlite -root ./kvroot -store <kvstore
name> -host <localhost> -port 5000
-admin 5001
```

When you start KVLite successfully, it will either create a new store or open an existing store if it was started previously.

The different parameters to use with the KVLite command line utility are as follows:

- **-admin**   If this option is specified, the admin thread that is spawned will listen on the specified port. This will provide a listener for launching the admin command line user interface. This defaults to port 5001 if not specified.

- **-help**   Displays a description of the command line parameters.

- **-host**   This option specifies the name of the host on which KVLite is running. The DNS registered hostname should be used if the desire is to connect to the KVLite instance from another computer.

- **-logging**   Turns on Java application logging. The log files are placed in the examples directory in your Oracle NoSQL Database distribution.

- **-port**   Identifies the port on which the KVLite is listening for client connections.

- **-root**   Identifies the path of the Oracle NoSQL Database home directory. In the case of KVLite, the database files of the store are located here. The directory has to be present, and if the database files are not present, they will be created.

- **-store**   Identifies the name of the store. This option should be used *only* if you are creating a new store.

NOTE
KVLite can be stopped simply by performing a CTRL-C
in the shell where the KVLite instance was launched.

The APIs for Oracle NoSQL Database can roughly be broken down into the following high-level categories:

- **Writing data** The capability to insert key-value pairs. Several variants exist for the programmer to be able to put a key-value pair into the store. These include

  - **Vanilla put** Store a simple key-value pair, regardless of whether the key exists or not. If the key already exists in the store, the value will be overwritten.

  - **Put if not exists** Only insert the key-value pair if the key does not already exist in the store.

  - **Put if exists** Only insert the key-value pair if the key already exists in the store, effectively overwriting the value associated with the key.

- **Reading data** Reading from Oracle NoSQL Database is further broken down into the following sets of operations:

  - **Read single value** Given a key, the value associated with the key is returned.

  - **Read multiple values** Given a partial key prefix, call key-value pairs that begin with the supplied prefix will be returned. The programmer can further specify that the return occur as a fully materialized set or as a non-materialized iterator. Furthermore, the programmer may specify a range of keys (essentially a "between clause" for those familiar with SQL) to restrict the results being qualified.

- **Deleting data** Given a key, delete the record associated with that key. As with the put methods, several variants of the delete method exist:

  - **Vanilla delete** Delete a simple key-value pair, regardless of whether the key exists or not. If the key exists in the store, the key and the value will be deleted. If the key does not exist in the store, no action will be taken by this method; however, it will return false to the caller.

  - **Delete by version check** Delete only the key-value pair if the version of the key-value pair matches the supplied version.

  - **Multi-delete** Given a parent key, subrange, and depth, this method will delete the descendant key-value pairs associated with the parent key.

- **Mixed operations** The Oracle NoSQL Database API contains a method for the programmer to specify a collection of mixed write and delete operations along with an associated collection of key-value pairs. This enables ACID transactions across multiple operations, with the caveat that each key in the collection must share the same major path.

A Basic Hello World Program

As an initial exercise, we examine the program `HelloToNoSQLDB`, which is a very simple piece of code that writes a single key-value pair and then reads the value associated with the key. Note that this coding example and the examples that follow in subsequent chapters in this book presume a cursory level of knowledge around the Java programming language. The primary APIs of the Oracle NoSQL Database are written in Java, and any programmer that will interact with these APIs must know the Java programming language. Oracle NoSQL Database also publishes APIs written in the C programming language, but the programming examples in this book focus on Java.

The code for our simple example is as follows:

```
package helloNOSQL;

import oracle.kv.KVStore;
import oracle.kv.KVStoreConfig;
import oracle.kv.KVStoreFactory;
import oracle.kv.Key;
import oracle.kv.Value;
import oracle.kv.ValueVersion;
```

We've decided to place our code in a package entitled `helloNOSQL`. Although packages in Java are not mandatory, it's always a good idea to package your code in a namespace that makes it easy for others to find your functionality and potentially reuse your code. Also note that we have imported all of the classes that we will use in this example from the `oracle.kv` package. We have decided to call our class `HelloNOSQLWorld` and make this class public so that anyone can access it. Note the private key-value store instance variable that will act as our main handle to communicate with Oracle NoSQL Database.

```
public class HelloNOSQLWorld {

    private final KVStore store;
```

To run our program and to test it, we need a simple main method, which in our case is simply creating an instance of the `HelloNOSQLWorld` class and then calling the `runExample` method on that instance:

```
public static void main(String args[]) {
    try {
        HelloNOSQLWorld example = new HelloNOSQLWorld (args);
```

```
        example.runExample();
    } catch (RuntimeException e) {
        e.printStackTrace();
    }
}
```

The constructor for our class that follows expects three arguments, which are needed to open the store and write to it. We have default values for storeName, hostName, and hostPort. If the user does not provide any command line parameters, the default parameters are used. However, the user has the choice of passing the values for a particular store located on a particular machine, which has been configured with a non-standard port. In the code that follows, we parse through the arguments and then see if one or more arguments are passed through the command line. If it is passed, then it overwrites the defaults.

```
/**
 * Parses command line args and opens the key-value store.
 */
HelloBigDataWorld(String[] argv) {

    String storeName = "kvstore";
    String hostName = "localhost";
    String hostPort = "5000";

    final int nArgs = argv.length;
    int argc = 0;

    while (argc < nArgs) {
        final String thisArg = argv[argc++];

        if (thisArg.equals("-store")) {
            if (argc < nArgs) {
                storeName = argv[argc++];
            } else {
                usage("-store requires an argument");
            }
        } else if (thisArg.equals("-host")) {
            if (argc < nArgs) {
                hostName = argv[argc++];
            } else {
                usage("-host requires an argument");
            }
        } else if (thisArg.equals("-port")) {
            if (argc < nArgs) {
                hostPort = argv[argc++];
            } else {
                usage("-port requires an argument");
            }
```

```
      } else {
          usage("Unknown argument: " + this);
  }
```

Once the arguments are successfully parsed, a `KVStoreConfig` object is instantiated using the command line parameters passed or the defaults. (Note that we have chosen default values for these parameters which are the same default values that KVLite uses.) These parameters are then used to obtain a handle to the key-value store by calling the `getStore` method on the `KVStoreFactory` class. Using this handle, we have access to all of the Oracle NoSQL Database API calls for manipulating data.

```
      store = KVStoreFactory.getStore
          (new KVStoreConfig(storeName, hostName + ":" + hostPort));
  }
```

The function below just prints out the ways in which this HelloNOSQLWorld class can be used.

```
  private void usage(String message) {
      System.out.println("\n" + message + "\n");
      System.out.println("usage: HelloBigDataWorld ");
      System.out.println("\t-store <instance name> (default: kvstore) " +
                          "-host <host name> (default: localhost) " +
                          "-port <port number> (default: 5000)");
      System.exit(1);
  }
```

The function `runExample` that follows will perform the operations of writing a simple record into the NoSQL Database and reading that record back out again. In this example, we insert a key-value pair with the key as the string `Hello` and the value as the string `NOSQL World`. The insert is performed by calling the `put` method on our store object. Note that to do this, we must first create an instance of an `oracle.kv.Key` object and an instance of an `oracle.kv.Value` object. In general, instances of `oracle.kv.Key` objects can be created from Java Strings and instances of `oracle.kv.Value` objects can be created from Java byte arrays. This is important to keep in mind as we begin discussing how to model keys and values in your application later in this chapter.

```
  /**
   * Performs example operations and closes the key-value store.
   */
  void runExample() {

      final String keyString = "/Hello";
      final String valueString = "NOSQL World!";
```

```
        store.put(Key.fromString(keyString),
Value.createValue(valueString.getBytes()));
    }
```

Now the next step is to obtain the value of the key we have stored to verify that we have successfully inserted the key-value pair into our store. To do this, we try to use the get method on the store handle. There are many variations of the put and get methods to insert and retrieve the key-value pairs into the store, but we use the simplest methods in this chapter as a way to start our quest into the programming world of Oracle NoSQL Database.

```
final ValueVersion valueVersion = store.get(Key.fromString(keyString));

System.out.println(keyString + " " +
                    new String(valueVersion.getValue().getValue()));

store.close();
    }
}
```

We complete this example code by closing the handle to Oracle NoSQL Database, cleaning up any resources that are allocated within this handle.

Before moving deeper into the Oracle NoSQL Database APIs and discussing more in-depth programmer topics, it is important to understand how to model the key space for your application.

How to Model Your Key Space

Now that you have seen a simple example of the Oracle NoSQL Database APIs and are familiar with the basic concept of key-value storage, we turn to the topic of key space modeling before moving on to more complex programming examples. As with any database, care must be taken to model the data for your application such that querying your data can be accomplished within the following constraints:

- **Correctness**   For applications that must exhibit transactional consistency or isolation, modeling the keys correctly to support this functionality is crucial.

- **Efficiency**   Most applications are concerned with retrieving data as fast as possible and using as few system resources as possible.

- **Extensibility**   If you're developing a production application, and you're lucky enough to have many users on your application, chances are that you will be asked to enhance your application by adding new functionality in subsequent releases. An extensible data model will afford you the ability to extend your application without entirely redesigning your data model.

- **Normalization** For most transaction processing applications, it is desirable to structure your data model such that queries may access the data by limiting or completely eliminating data duplication.

Keys in the Oracle NoSQL Database are bifurcated into two discrete parts:

- **Major component** The major component of a key denotes the shard that will contain the records for all of the minor keys that follow from a specific major key. This means that records that share the same combination of major key components are guaranteed to be in the same shard, which means they can be efficiently queried. In addition, records with identical major key components can participate in ACID transactions. Keys are distributed across the store by hashing on the key's major component.

- **Minor component** The minor key component of a key can be thought of as the shard local path to the record. Hashing the major component will point you to the shard that contains the data; using the minor component of the key will point you to the record in that shard.

The entire key, major plus minor components, must be unique in Oracle NoSQL Database.

Let's take an example application for the following key space modeling exercise. For this exercise, we choose a simple e-mail application. For this application, we have been given the following simple set of requirements:

1. Users must have the following folders available when they bring up the e-mail application:

   a. **Inbox** This is where e-mail messages arrive when delivered and must be managed as an ordered container by time.

   b. **Deleted folder** After a user clicks a delete control on a message, this folder must be populated with the message such that when a user clicks on the deleted folder, the message will be displayed in this folder. This folder must also be managed as an ordered container by time.

   c. **Sent folder** After a user clicks a send control on a message, this folder must be populated with the message such that when a user clicks on the Sent folder, the message will be displayed in this folder. Again, this folder must also be managed as an ordered container by time.

2. Users must have the ability to search the messages in any folder given a search term and a start and end date.

Given the requirements just stated, we choose to model the keys in the following manner:

```
/users/id/folders/-/inbox/date
/users/id/folders/-/deleted/date
/users/id/folders/-/sent/date
```

As a concrete example, consider a user with ID 34271 and the date 07/13/2013. The preceding three keys would then look like the following strings;

```
/users/34271/folders/-/inbox/20130713
/users/34271/folders/-/deleted/20130713
/users/34271/folders/-/sent/20130713
```

At this point you may be wondering why we chose to structure the keys for this application in this manner. Let's drill down and see what our rationale was for modeling the keys this way:

- **ACID transactions** In Oracle NoSQL Database, ACID transactions are only supported on a shard local basis. Remember that Oracle NoSQL will hash the major portion of the key, and all keys that have the same major path will hash to the same shard. Notice that we have structured the major path such that all of the mail folders for a single user contain the exact same major path, hashing to the same shard, and ultimately able to participate in ACID transactions. Hence, we have just satisfied requirements 1b and 1c simply by structuring our keys appropriately.

- **Extensibility** It will be trivial to add more folders as these requirements materialize. Let's say we get a subsequent requirement to support calendars for all e-mail users. We would simply add another key as /users/id/folders/-/ calendar/20130713.

- **Ordering in folders** Notice that all of the keys end with a string representation of a day that is formatted as YYYYMMDD. We chose this way to model our keys because Oracle NoSQL Database uses the natural sort order of the Java String class, and keys in Oracle NoSQL are simply instances of the Java String class. Hence, if we structure our dates in this manner, we can have Oracle NoSQL order the results of queries for us such that we may satisfy the ordering requirements for 1a, 1b, and 1c.

- **Searching folders** To support requirement 2, we will again make use of the modeling construct we devised by putting a string date format at the end of each key. This can be utilized in API calls to Oracle NoSQL to restrict the results that are returned; furthermore, this restriction can be supplied as a start and end range. To satisfy requirement 2, it's not realistic to build a key on every word contained in every e-mail. However, being able to restrict the number of e-mails by time and executing this restriction in the NoSQL cluster will be a good option for this application.

In short, having a solid understanding of how to model the keys in your application can go a long way to meeting your application requirements. As you will see in subsequent sections, knowledge of the APIs and how these relate to the data modeling exercise is important to being able to tie all of this together and will help you achieve a successful application implementation.

The Basics of Reading and Writing a Single Key-Value Pair

Now that we have discussed the basics of how to model a key space, the very first task the programmer faces is how to insert data into the Oracle NoSQL Database. Fortunately, the Oracle NoSQL Database API gives you a wide variety of options to tackle this task. There are several ways to write records into the key-value store depending on the complexity of the functional requirements that you are trying to address.

The code fragment that follows explores the different ways of creating a key and storing a value using the Oracle NoSQL Database APIs. In this example, we create a key that will be used to reference notepad data for a specific user; we choose a user with ID 34271. Note that in both examples, the minor portion of the key (the string after the dash) is optional. Also note the initialization of the KVStore object, which is created by calling the getStore method on the KVStoreFactory class. The KVStoreConfig is created using the name of the store we wish to connect to as well as one of the host computers in the Oracle NoSQL Database cluster and the port to contact on that host machine. This computer is used only as a bootstrap mechanism to retrieve the topology of the Oracle NoSQL Database cluster. All subsequent API calls will be routed to the appropriate machines in the cluster by the Oracle NoSQL Database driver.

```
String notePadKey = "/users/34271/folders/-/notepad";
 String valueString = "A test nodepad item that means nothing";
  KVStore store = KVStoreFactory.getStore
        (new KVStoreConfig("kvstore", aStoreHost + ":" + port)))

Key myKey = Key.fromString(notePadKey);

System.out.println(myKey.getFullPath());

System.out.println(myKey.toString());
```

```
Value myValue = Value.createValue(valueString.getBytes());

store.put(myKey,myValue);
```

In this example, the output of the System.out.println would look as follows:

```
[users, 34271, folders, notepad]
/users/34271/folders/-/notepad
```

In a real e-mail application, we would certainly not have the ability to statically declare a path that includes a user ID to a specific folder. This path would be materialized at run time based on the user that is currently logged in, and possibility some notion of that user's authorization to reach the specific folder (in this case, the notepad folder). An alternative to construct the key given these constraints is shown. In the code that follows, we presume that the user ID is returned by an application function that contains an `AuthorizationContext` class for retrieving the currently logged-in user:

```
ArrayList<String> majorList = new ArrayList<String>();
ArrayList<String> minorList = new ArrayList<String>();
int userId = AuthorizationContext.getCurrentUserId();

majorList.add("users");
majorList.add(userId);
majorList.add("folders");

minorList.add("notepad");

Key myKey = Key.createKey(majorList, minorList);
store.put(myKey,myValue);
```

Now let's take a look at how you would use the Oracle NoSQL Database API to read the contents of a user's notepad folder:

```
ValueVersion valueVersion = store.get(myKey);
String notePadContents = new String(valueVersion.getValue().
getValue());
```

Consistency and Durability from the Programmer's Perspective

In this section we introduce the concepts of durability (for writing data) and consistency (for reading data). As you will see, these are key concepts to writing successful applications on the Oracle NoSQL Database.

Durability

If you look up the term "durability" in the Merriam-Webster's dictionary, you find the following definition:

"Something that is able to exist for a long time without significant deterioration"

Translating this definition to the world of data storage, you can see the parallel to how long data can be stored on any particular media before it deteriorates, or even worse, completely disappears. You can think of durability as the storage of data in the memory of a single computer. The data will be durable until that computer fails or encounters a power outage. Alternatively, you can create a single copy or multiple copies of this data and place it in the memory of another computer or set of computers to gain confidence in the durability of the data; however, should there be a loss of power to all of the computers, the data is lost. You can take this definition several steps further by considering single or multiple copies of the data on disk, or you can increase the confidence in the data's durability by copying the data to computer memory or disks that reside in separate datacenters that are physically separated.

Oracle NoSQL Database codifies the notion of durability into a policy that can be set by the programmer for each API call that writes data to the store. The stricter the durability policy, the higher your level of confidence that the data can survive a media failure. In Oracle NoSQL Database, there are two distinct but related sets of durability policies:

- **Replica acknowledgment-based policies**   Acknowledgment-based policies define how strict the master should behave with respect to how many replicas respond successfully before the master considers the write committed and responds to the caller of the API. There are three flavors of the acknowledgment-based durability:

    - **ALL**   This is the most stringent and most durable acknowledgment-based policy and dictates that all replicas must acknowledge successful writes before the master will consider the transaction committed. From the programmer's perspective, one can think of this as synchronous replication as the caller of the API will wait until all replicas have written the data before the API call will return.

    - **SIMPLE_MAJORITY**   This is the next most stringent and is sometimes referred to as *quorum writes*. In this durability policy, the master will asynchronously replicate the data to all replicas and then wait for a successful response only from a majority, or quorum, of replicas before considering the transaction committed. For example, if there is a total of three nodes (a master and two replicas), the master need only wait for a single replica to respond before committing the transaction, as a total of two writes have occurred, making this a majority.

- **NONE**   This is the least stringent policy and from the programmer's perspective, this can be thought of as purely asynchronous replication. The master will write the data locally, send the data to the other replicas, and immediately consider the transaction committed without waiting for any responses from the replicas.

- **Synchronization-based policies**   Defines the basic guarantee that a write operation has been saved to persistent storage. High levels of synchronization offer a greater guarantee that the transaction is persistent to disk, but trade that guarantee for lower performance. There are three flavors of synchronization policies and these can be specified for master node as well as for non-master node writes:

  - **SYNC**   This is the most stringent level of durability and implies the most overhead from a performance perspective. Using this policy will force each node to flush the write to persistent storage before returning success. While this policy gives the programmer a very high level of confidence that a write will never be lost, it comes at a cost of performance.

  - **WRITE_NO_SYNC**   This is the next most stringent level of durability and will cause each node to make a system call that will write the data to the file system buffer cache, but not flush the data directly to persistent storage. The data will get flushed to persistent storage by the file system in an asynchronous fashion.

  - **NO_SYNC**   This is the least stringent level of durability and will cause each node to write the data to its memory cache. The data will be flushed to persistent storage either on a checkpoint or when the data gets evicted from the node's cache.

When choosing a durability and acknowledgment policy for any particular operation, it's important to think about several issues:

- **The type of data that is being stored**   If you're storing high-value operational data that is absolutely critical to the business and you cannot consider any trade-offs with respect to the confidence of durability and the latency of the API call, this should guide your choice of durability and acknowledgment option toward the more stringent durability choices. Our e-mail application discussed earlier is a good example of data that should be stored with a high confidence of durability, as this application does not have extreme SLAs for latency (single- or double-digit milliseconds) and users of our e-mail application expect zero data loss no matter what happens to the underlying systems. On the other hand, if the data is low value and non-critical, you should consider trading off the confidence of durability for lower latency.

- **The type of workflow being implemented** There are some workloads that dictate a very low latency service level agreement (SLA), and for these workloads you should consider a less stringent durability and acknowledgment policy, as this might be the right trade-off in order to achieve the SLAs on latency that are required. For example, in systems that service online display advertising, publishers of online content will require that ad servers return to the browsers in less than 75 milliseconds. This requirement, coupled with the fact that the writes in this workload are tracking consumer browsing behavior, indicates a perfect scenario for choosing a very low durability confidence setting in exchange for very low latency on write operations.

Your application requirements will dictate the strategy of the durability and acknowledgment policies used as a default setting in Oracle NoSQL as well as for specific API calls. The default durability policy can be set for the entire store in the KVStoreConfig class, and as you will see later in this chapter, this default configuration can also be overridden in each API call.

Consistency

While *durability* speaks to the resiliency of writing data to Oracle NoSQL Database, *consistency* speaks to the resiliency of reading data from Oracle NoSQL Database. More specifically, consistency refers to the ability for an application to read the most recent copy of data as it has been written to the store. Because a key-value store is typically composed of a cluster of computers (called nodes) that are working together in a distributed fashion, it is possible for a record to be written by the master node in a shard and then subsequently read from another node in the shard. Because there is a time lag between the time that a record is written to the master and the time it takes for the record to be transferred over the network to the other nodes in the shard, the record may not be consistent with the master if read from a node that has not yet received the most recent update from the master. The level of consistency that an application requires between records being read on any node in Oracle NoSQL Database is called the consistency policy. As with the durability and acknowledgment policies in Oracle NoSQL, the consistency policy gives the programmer a powerful tool to be able to trade off performance (lower latency/ higher throughput) for stringent consistency. There are four distinct consistency policies in Oracle NoSQL Database:

- **ABSOLUTE** This is the most stringent consistency policy and dictates that the read must be executed at the master node of the shard, thereby guaranteeing that the most recent committed version of the record is returned to the caller of the API. While using this policy gives the programmer a nice guarantee for the state of the read, it comes at a potential cost in system throughput as well as read latency. Using this policy will prevent the NoSQL Database driver from spreading the read load out across all of the nodes in the shard, thereby possibly overloading the master node and reducing overall system throughput as well as increasing the latency of reads in the system.

- **Time** This is the next most stringent consistency policy and, when supplied by the programmer along with a time ceiling X and time unit Y, specifies that the read can be performed against any node in the shard as long as that node's version of the record is no longer than X time units lag from the version of the record held at the master. The Oracle NoSQL Database driver is always topology-aware and can easily compute a heuristic for how far off any node is from its master in the shard. As an example of how one would use this policy, consider your e-mail application. Let's say you're reading the calendar for the current user. You could supply a time-based read, a ceiling of 500, and a unit of milliseconds, thereby specifying that you would be willing to utilize any node in the shard for this read as long as the record you're reading is no more than 500 milliseconds lagging from the master.

- **Version** This consistency policy is at least as stringent as the time-based consistency policy described previously, but can be utilized in a slightly different way. Version-based consistency allows the programmer to supply a version object to the read call and dictates to the Oracle NoSQL Database driver that it may read from any node that contains at least this version of data and greater. Versions in Oracle NoSQL Database are simply externalized notions of the underlying storage system's log sequence number, and each insert into the store will be tagged with a log sequence number, externalized through the APIs as an instance of a `Version` class. This policy is generally useful for those applications that maintain some state information about previously inserted or updated objects and can use the saved version information for these objects as an optimization hint to the Oracle NoSQL Database driver.

- **NONE_REQUIRED** This consistency policy tells the driver that it can read the record from any node that it thinks is the most optimal node to read from whether or not that node has data that is consistent with its master node. This policy thus places no constraints on the read and is the most optimal policy that can be used when reading records from Oracle NoSQL. This policy is quite useful for those workloads that have very strict latency SLAs and highly favor the ability to return something, even though it may be out of date within say, 10 or 15 milliseconds. Again, we see this type of requirement in the online display advertising world where publishers of online content have placed extremely tight latency restrictions on their ad serving providers. These providers are reading user behavioral data in an attempt to increase the probability that the user will actually click through an ad that is placed on the publisher's website.

The following code snippet illustrates how to set a default level of durability and consistency as well as how these defaults can be overridden at the individual API call. The first parameter defines the synchronization policy at the master node level, the second parameter defines the synchronization policy at the replication node level, and the third parameter configures the replication acknowledgment policy. Note that in the code snippet that follows, nothing is done with respect to exception handling from the API calls. This is an important topic for the programmer of any NoSQL-based application and will be covered in detail in Chapter 6.

```
            Durability defaultDurability = new Durability(
Durability.SyncPolicy.SYNC, // Master sync
Durability.SyncPolicy.NO_SYNC, // Replica sync
Durability.ReplicaAckPolicy.SIMPLE_MAJORITY);
            // Create an instance of the KVStoreConfig class by specifying the name
            // of our store and any machine:port in our cluster of nodes
KVStoreConfig conf = new KVStoreConfig("kvstore", "a_machine:5000");
conf.setDurability(defaultDurability);

conf.setConsistency(Consistency.NONE_REQUIRED);

            store = KVStoreFactory.getStore(conf);
```

The code snippet that follows will actually create a key-value pair and insert it into the key-value store based on a new durability policy, which will override the default one.

```
            majorList.add("users");
            majorList.add(userId);
            majorList.add("folders");

            minorList.add("notepad");
            Key myKey = Key.createKey(majorList, minorList);
            String content = "A test nodepad value";
            Value myValue = Value.createValue(st.getBytes());

            // Create durability policy to override the durability policy at the
            // configuration object level
            Durability durability = new Durability(Durability.SyncPolicy.NO_SYNC,
Durability.SyncPolicy.NO_SYNC, Durability.ReplicaAckPolicy.NONE);
            try {
                store.put(myKey, myValue, null, durability, 0, null);
            } catch (DurabilityException de) {
                de.printStackTrace();
            } catch (RequestTimeoutException re) {
                re.printStackTrace();
            }
```

```
// Override the default consistency policy and specify absolute
// consistency for reading back the record we just wrote
//
ValueVersion vv = store.get(myKey, Consistency.ABSOLUTE, 0, null);
```

Summary

There are many important things to consider when designing an application on top of Oracle NoSQL Database. We have covered issues from the modeling of the key space to the detail settings for durability and consistency, and each area denotes a set of critical design decisions for the programmer. Unlike applications built on top of traditional relational database systems, programmers approaching the design of applications on Oracle NoSQL Database are encouraged to think carefully about how their code will interact with the Oracle NoSQL APIs and how application requirements should drive the API level trade-off decisions that will be crucial to the overall performance and proper functioning of the application.

CHAPTER
6

Reading and Writing Data

I n the previous chapter, you were introduced to the application design process and the basics of what it takes to start developing applications on top of the Oracle NoSQL Database. In this chapter, you dig much deeper into the wide variety of APIs and the use cases that compel you to choose one form of an API over another. The Oracle NoSQL APIs give the programmer a wide variety of choices in terms of accessing data from the NoSQL store; this chapter covers the details on all of these variations. By the end of this chapter, you should feel confident that you have a solid basis for determining which specific APIs are the most suitable for your application needs and what trade-offs you are favoring by using that specific API.

Development Environment Setup

The sample code in this chapter and the next chapter have been developed using a setup involving the following components:

- **Eclipse**   Download Eclipse and create a Java project. You can see in Figure 6-1 that all the key-value store libraries are imported and ready for use.

- **NoSQL KVLite**   KVLite should be started and running. You can see a typical KVLite process running in Figure 6-2.

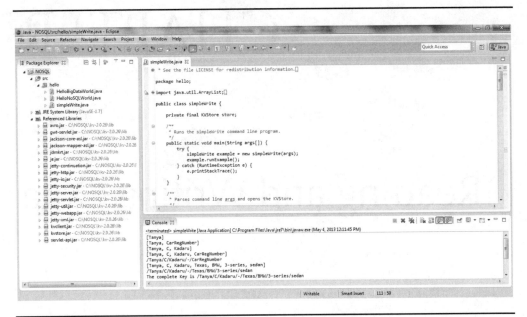

FIGURE 6-1.   *Example Eclipse IDE setup for NoSQL application development*

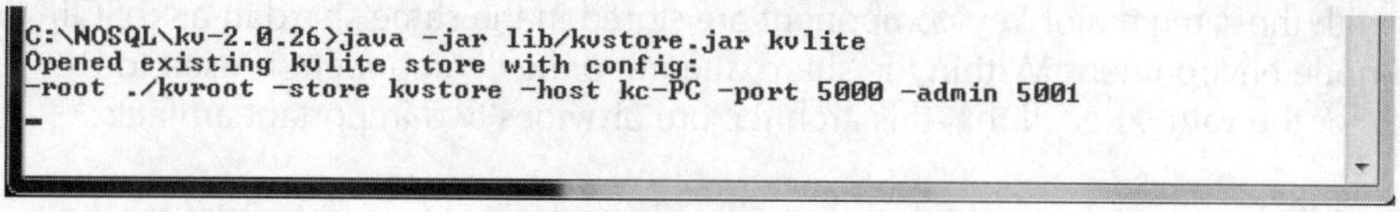
C:\NOSQL\kv-2.0.26>java -jar lib/kvstore.jar kvlite
Opened existing kvlite store with config:
-root ./kvroot -store kvstore -host kc-PC -port 5000 -admin 5001

FIGURE 6-2. *Screenshot of a running KVLite process*

- **Key-value store** Should be created and accessible on the machine running Eclipse and KVLite. Figure 6-3 shows where the key-value store is located on the Windows file system.

Writing Records

Writing records into Oracle NoSQL Database is as basic as an `insert` statement in a relational database and in many ways is simpler than the classic relational `insert` statement. There are several ways of writing records into the key-value store depending on the complexity of the business case you are trying to solve. The task of inserting or writing data into the key-value store starts from building the key itself. Recall that a key consists of two parts:

- **Major key component** Has to be a non-null single string or can have multiple parts.
- **Minor key component** Can be null or can have one or more parts.

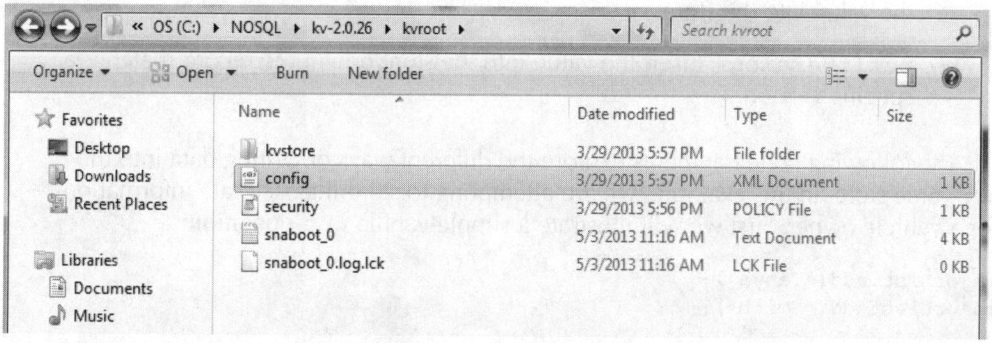
« OS (C:) ▸ NOSQL ▸ kv-2.0.26 ▸ kvroot ▸
Search kvroot
Organize
Open
Burn
New folder
Favorites
Desktop
Downloads
Recent Places
Libraries
Documents
Music
Name
Date modified
Type
Size
kvstore 3/29/2013 5:57 PM File folder
config 3/29/2013 5:57 PM XML Document 1 KB
security 3/29/2013 5:56 PM POLICY File 1 KB
snaboot_0 5/3/2013 11:16 AM Text Document 4 KB
snaboot_0.log.lck 5/3/2013 11:16 AM LCK File 0 KB

FIGURE 6-3. *Location of key-value store on the Windows file system*

The major and the minor keys together form the full key path. All the key value pairs with the same major key component are stored in the same shard in a NoSQL multi-node environment. Within the shard, the minor key component is used to search for the value. Recall that this architecture provides two important artifacts:

- **Efficient access** If all the values related to a major key component are stored in the same shard, the get operation can be performed in a single network I/O more efficiently.

- **ACID transactions** If one or more values contain the same major key component, they can be modified together in a single ACID-compliant transaction.

Basic API Functionality

There are several different APIs for writing records into the Oracle NoSQL Database and each type of API addresses slightly different requirements. In this section, we cover the details and present examples for the following APIs to write data:

- **Vanilla put** The easiest form of inserting records into the Oracle NoSQL Database. Simply takes a key and value.

- **putIfAbsent** A form of the classic atomic test and set operator. Will insert a key-value pair into Oracle NoSQL only if the key does not already exist in the store. The check for existence is made in a transactional fashion (obeying strict isolation semantics of the ACID properties), and as you will see later in this section, this provides the programmer with a unique set of capabilities.

- **putIfPresent** A form of the classic atomic test and set operator except that, in this case, the check is to ensure that the key exists before inserting the value into the store.

- **putIfVersion** Insert the value into the store only if the record matches a specific version.

The following code fragments explore the different ways of writing data into the key-value store. In this example, we are attempting to store license plate information for a vehicle owner. First we will illustrate a simple vanilla put operation:

```
majorList.add("Tanya");
majorList.add("Smith");

minorList.add("HONDA");
```

```
minorList.add("Accord");
minorList.add("20090213");

String valueString = "CY1R651";
Key myKey = Key.createKey(majorList, minorlist);
Value myVal = Value.createValue(valueString.getBytes());
store.put(myKey,myValue);
```

The putIfAbsent method gives you some unique capabilities that you can use to solve certain classes of synchronization problems in distributed systems. For example, let's say that you'd like to build a global sequence generator for your application that will generate globally unique ID values for every object that you wish to insert into the store for your application. In part of the algorithm, you'll choose the putIfAbsent method as it gives you an atomic way to test that no other callers in your distributed system have created the initial value of your ID generator while you're creating it. The code that follows illustrates the method that will return the current sequence number in the store, or if the sequence number does not yet exist, it will create it with an initial value of 1.

```
/**
 * Return the current value of the sequence number object or if it does
 * not exist, initialize it to 1 and return it.
 * Uses the atomic test and set operation of putIfAbsent to make sure
 * that no other processes are stomping on the sequence number while the
 * caller of this code is in there.
 **/
public ValueVersion getCurSeqNum() throws DBAccessException {
        //  Retrieve the current value of the global sequence number
        ValueVersion seq = db.getStore().get(Key.fromString(
           "/GlobalSeqNum"), Consistency.ABSOLUTE, 0, null);
        int currWaitMillis = 0;

        //  No one has created it yet, we'll go and create it now
        if (seq == null) {
            Value value = Value.fromByteArray(new byte[]{
                                        new Integer(1).byteValue()});
            while (seq == null) {
                try {
                    Version seqVersion = db.getStore().putIfAbsent(
                                                seqKey, value);
                    if (seqVersion == null) {
                        // Someone got here before us
                        seq = db.getStore().get(seqKey,
                                        Consistency.ABSOLUTE, 0, null);
                    } else {
                        /* We inserted it, wrap it up
                         * in ValueVersion class for return
                         */
```

```
                        seq = new ValueVersion(value, seqVersion);
                    }
            } catch (RequestTimeoutException e) {
                try {
                    if (currWaitMillis >= MAX_TIMEMOUT_WAIT_MILLIS) {
                        throw e;
                    }
                    Thread.currentThread().wait(TIMEMOUT_WAIT_MILLIS);
                    currWaitMillis += TIMEMOUT_WAIT_MILLIS;
                } catch (InterruptedException ie) {};
            }
        }

    }
    return(seq);
}
```

The putIfPresent method gives you a convenient way to test the key, ensure that it has not been deleted or that it does exist altogether, and then update its value, all in a single atomic call. This type of mechanism is extremely useful in applications that must utilize asynchronous processes. For example, it is very common in online advertising for ad servers to update the budget of a campaign asynchronously from the users that may be modifying the campaign. In such a scenario, utilizing the putIfPresent method can ensure that the ad server is updating a campaign that has not been deleted (or deactivated). It's a bit beyond the scope of this book to present the code for such an involved example as online display advertising. The example that follows gives the reader some indication of how this method may be used.

```
/**
 * Update the budget for a campaign only if that campaign still exists.
 *
 * @param campaignId - Key for the campaign to update
 * @param val - The value to replace the existing budget value (byte array
 *              representation of a Double).
 * @return true if successful, false otherwise
 */
public boolean updateCampaignBudget(Key campaignId, byte val[]) {

    Value upValue = Value.createValue(val);

    Version upVer = store.putIfPresent(campaignId, upValue);
    return(upVer == null ? false : true);
}
```

The putIfVersion method is useful for those application scenarios where some state can be saved in the client of Oracle NoSQL. This becomes interesting in distributed and concurrent programming as a way for programmers to ensure that no other processes (or threads) have updated a value since the last time it was seen by the current thread/process. In the example code that follows, we expand upon the previous example, which gets the current sequence number, and add the complete implementation for globally unique sequence number generation. Notice that a key part of the generation is utilizing putIfVersion.

```
/**
 * Generate and return the next value for the globally unique sequence number
 */
public int getNextSeq() throws RequestTimeoutException {
    // Get the current value of the sequence number
    ValueVersion curSeqNum = getCurSeqNum();
    Version v = null;
    Integer nextSeq = null;
    int currWaitMillis = 0;

    // Keep trying until we're successful or we time out
    while (v == null) {
        int newSeq = java.nio.ByteBuffer.wrap(
                            curSeqNum.getValue().toByteArray()).getInt();
        nextSeq = new Integer(newSeq++);
        Value newVal = Value.fromByteArray(new byte[]{nextSeq.byteValue()});

        try {
            v = db.getStore().putIfVersion(seqKey, newVal, curSeqNum.getVersion());
        } catch (RequestTimeoutException e) {
            try {
                if (currWaitMillis >= MAX_TIMEMOUT_WAIT_MILLIS) {
                    throw e;
                }
                Thread.currentThread().wait(TIMEMOUT_WAIT_MILLIS);
                currWaitMillis += TIMEMOUT_WAIT_MILLIS;
            } catch (InterruptedException ie) {};
        }
        // Someone got in there and incremented the sequence number
        // before we could. We'll have to try again.
        if (v == null) {
            curSeqNum = getCurSeqNum();
        }
    }
    return(nextSeq);
}
```

How to Specify Durability in Write API Calls

In Oracle NoSQL, durability may be specified for every API call that performs a write (either the key-value store's default durability is used or it is explicitly supplied by the programmer at an API call). Hence, the concept of durability is crucial for the programmer to understand and we revisit this concept within the context of the Oracle NoSQL write APIs. As stated in the previous chapter, a durability policy can be thought of as your level of confidence in the survival of a piece of data in the event of

Policy Name	Definition	Quality of Policy	In Case of Failure
All Replicas	Write to be completed on all nodes	Most secure	Any replica can be made as master.
No Replicas	Write to be completed only on master	Least secure	No copy to fall back upon.
Simple Majority	Write to be completed on a simple majority of nodes	Balanced	A node in a simple majority of nodes can be made as a master.

TABLE 6-1. *Acknowledgment-Based Policies*

catastrophic failures of hardware or software. As the durability policy gets stricter, the confidence level increases that the data survives. The two types of durability policies are reviewed in Tables 6-1 and 6-2.

How to Choose a Durability Policy Based on Real-Life Examples

The simple answer to how a durability policy is chosen is that it all depends on the application business use case you are trying to solve. When choosing a durability policy, the application developer should examine several issues and carefully consider the trade-offs. Generally speaking, the application developer will be trading off latency and throughput for increased confidence that the data will survive a failure. For example, there may be situations where latency SLAs of single-digit milliseconds are absolutely necessary, and to achieve this latency, the application developer is willing to use a durability policy that will favor latency

Policy Name	Quality	Where Is It Written
NO_SYNC	Fastest and least durable	In-memory cache
WRITE_NO_SYNC	Balanced	File system buffers after the in-memory cache
SYNC	Slowest and most durable	Storage

TABLE 6-2. *Synchronization-Based Policies*

over the confidence of data survival in the event of a hardware failure. We consider some real-world use cases in the following list that will shed some light on how to think about these trade-offs:

- **Online display advertising**   Technology providers in the online display advertising business are typically given very strict SLAs by publishers (website owners) when pages are loaded. These SLAs are usually in the low double-digit millisecond range (for example, 50 milliseconds). It is within these constraints that ad servers must deliver the right ad to the right user such that there is a high probability that a user will click the ad, thereby maximizing revenue for the ad server provider as well as for the publisher. This is a perfect use case for decreasing durability and trading off that decreased confidence to latency. Since the data in this case is being used to increase the probability of an event, it's not so critical if a few data points are lost in the event of a hardware or software failure.

- **Online social gaming sector**   There are use cases for in-game social interaction that require the server to know the locations of all players on a canvas as the players move around. In this case, the latency of the write operations are essential, as player movement must be perceived as real time by the game players while the movements must be stored and retrieved as the player moves around the canvas. This use case is also a good example of one in which you might choose to favor latency over the confidence of survival of player movement data.

- **Building a scalable e-mail service**   In the case of e-mail applications such as those provided by Google or Yahoo (similar to the example in the previous chapter), the data is critical and the acknowledgment-based policy that favors durability over latency would almost certainly be used.

So generally speaking, the synch policy along with the acknowledgment policy will have a large impact on latency and throughput. The SYNC policy will exhibit longer latencies compared to WRITE_NO_SYNC and NO_SYNC. Similarly in acknowledgment policies, ALL will exhibit longer latencies compared to others. Note that throughput as it relates to the overall latency of ongoing operations will also be negatively affected. The key point to understand here is that in general terms, the trade-off for a higher degree of confidence that the data will survive in the event of a catastrophic failure is latency and throughput of the application.

Now let's use an example similar to the one used in the previous chapter of storing the Inbox information for a mail provider to explain how the durability acknowledgment policies are used in the case of critical data. You can set the durability policy at a global level in the configuration object of the key-value store. However, we will override it and change it at an individual API call for the strictest form of durability policies as per our business requirement. The first parameter defines the synchronization policy at the master node, the second parameter defines the synchronization policy at the Replication Node, and the third parameter configures the replication acknowledgment policy.

In the current use, you use the key-value store to store the e-mail messages and their contents in different folders such as the Inbox, Deleted Items, and so on. The major key and the minor key are defined with key attributes such as date, time, from, and to information that bring uniqueness to it. The value is the actual e-mail text itself.

```
majorList.add("users");
majorList.add("12345");
majorList.add("folders");

inboxList.add("inbox");
inboxList.add("20130801");
inboxList.add("174510");
inboxList.add("From:Tanya");
inboxList.add("To:Jennifer");

Key inboxKey = Key.createKey(majorList, inboxList);

String st = "Hi Jennifer, Happy Birthday. Tanya";
Value emailText = Value.createValue(st.getBytes());
```

You store the e-mail content of one e-mail in the Inbox for a user using the strictest durability policy available and then print it back to the console.

```
Durability durability = new Durability(Durability.SyncPolicy.SYNC,
            Durability.SyncPolicy.SYNC, Durability.ReplicaAckPolicy.ALL);
try {
        store.put(inboxKey, emailText, null, durability, 0, null);
} catch (DurabilityException de) {
        de.printStackTrace();
} catch (RequestTimeoutException re) {
        re.printStackTrace();
}

ValueVersion vv = store.get(inboxKey, Consistency.ABSOLUTE, 0, null);
System.out
        .println("The email content for first email on 20130801 is "
                + inboxKey.toString()
                + " is "
                + new String(vv.getValue().getValue()));
```

The output of the code snippet will be as follows. The store is closed in the end for releasing resources.

```
The email content for first email on 20130801 is /users/12345/folders/-/
inbox/20130801/174510/From:Tanya/To:Jennifer is Hi Jennifer, Happy
Birthday. Tanya
```

Executing a Sequence of Operations

In the previous section, you saw an insert into the key-value store for storing the e-mail text into the Inbox folder. Now, assuming the user wants to delete the e-mail, you need to move the e-mail from the Inbox folder to the deleted items folder. This involves two separate operations of deleting the e-mail from the Inbox folder and adding it into the deleted items folder. Now if there is a catastrophic failure after the first operation happens, the data would be inconsistent because the e-mail would have been inserted into the deleted items folder and not deleted from the Inbox folder. This particular use case demands the facility to be able to execute a series of operations in an all-or-nothing fashion. Oracle NoSQL provides an API to perform a sequence of operations where all of the operations execute successfully or none of them will. This is defined as the atomicity property of ACID (Atomic, Consistent, Isolated, Durable) transactions in the RDBMS world. The key requirements and characteristics for this API in Oracle NoSQL are

- The operations are on the keys with the same major path components.

- They are on a list and they may not be executed in the order specified.

- All the operations should not be on the same key.

- All the operations are performed in isolation (not visible to other processes until all of the operations are 100 percent complete).

Now we'll illustrate the concept by continuing the preceding example. You insert this e-mail into the deleted Items folder and delete the e-mail from the Inbox folder. The steps followed in this process are

1. Get a handle to the operation factory, which helps create operations for the put method and the delete method.

2. The operations are added to a list.

3. The list is passed on to the execute method on the instance of KVStore.

4. Different exceptions are caught.

The operation factory handle is obtained and the array list is created to hold the list of operations.

```
OperationFactory of = store.getOperationFactory();
ArrayList<Operation> opList = new ArrayList<Operation>();
```

The key-value objects are created with unique elements identifying the e-mail to be added to the deleted Items folder and its content.

```
deletedList.add("deletedItems");
deletedList.add("20130801");
deletedList.add("174510");
deletedList.add("From:Tanya");
deletedList.add("To:Jennifer");

Key deletedItemsKey = Key.createKey(majorList, deletedList);
```

The operations are created based on the deletion and insertion. The first operation is a simple put because you are inserting the deleted e-mail into the deleted items folder. The second operation is the delete from the Inbox folder, so you create an operation based on the delete method. The operations are then added to the operations list. Once the operations list is ready, it is passed on to the execute method on the key-value store as a parameter.

```
opList.add(of.createPut(deletedItemsKey, emailText));
opList.add(of.createDelete(inboxKey));

try {
    store.execute(opList);
    } catch (OperationExecutionException oee) {
    } catch (DurabilityException de) {
    } catch (FaultException fe) {
    }
store.close();
```

Exception Handling for Write Operations

Creating highly available applications involves many subtle design and implementation details that should be considered. One of those important details is the proper handling of exceptions such that application failures are never or extremely rarely seen by the end user. Hence, most applications that exhibit this degree of availability are programmed to avoid throwing errors back to the application user. This type of "defensive" coding is also recommended when creating applications on Oracle NoSQL Database. Typically, programs will attempt to retry a failed operation up to a certain threshold before returning an error to the user. Thresholds may be defined as upper bounds on time, or as upper bounds on number of attempts, and your specific

Exception	Likely Cause	Possible Resolution
DurabilityException	The programmer has specified an acknowledgment policy other than `Durability` `.ReplicaAckPolicy` `.NONE`, and a quorum of replicas was not available to acknowledge receipt of the write.	1. A Replication Node may be temporarily unreachable and a retry may succeed. 2. As a fallback mechanism, the program may wish to retry the write operation with `Durability` `.ReplicaAckPolicy.NONE` if this level of durability is more acceptable than an application error.
OperationExecutionException	Thrown when one or more operations in a list has failed. This exception is only thrown from the `execute` method.	More than likely, a retry of this method will fail again as there is an offending operation in a list. It is possible, however, that a retry may succeed, as a transient error may have occurred on the specific operation that has failed. The `getFailedOperation` method on this exception class will return the specific operation that has failed.
RequestTimeoutException	This exception denotes an internal error with Oracle NoSQL Database.	It's possible that the error detected is a transient error and the operation can be retried.

TABLE 6-3.   *Exception Handling Guidelines for Writes*

choice should be driven by the business requirements of your application. Table 6-3 should be used as a guide to determine whether or not your code should consider re-try logic for a write operation that throws an exception.

Reading Records

Retrieving records from Oracle NoSQL Database is as basic as a `Select` statement in a RDBMS database. Fortunately, Oracle NoSQL Database equips the users with a lot of arrows in their quiver to retrieve records from the key-value store. It can be as simple as retrieving a single record from the key-value store or as complex as retrieving multiple records sharing common major keys. There is also a capability of filtering the data by setting the range on the result iterator. This is the equivalent of the frequently used where clause of the RDBMS world. Now that you have written some records into Oracle NoSQL Database in the previous section, let's read some of them.

Read One Record
or Multiple Records in Many Ways

This section explores reading records through an example of car ownership and the license plate information of county dwellers. You may need to interact with this data in a number of different ways, and we present some important methods. The following assumptions are made for these use cases:

- The key-value store is created and is open for use.

- The records are already written and present in the key-value store.

Simple Get Method

The sample code that follows reads one single record from the key-value store. You create a key that is structured with a major key component and a minor key component. The following lines create the major and minor key components as instantiations of an `ArrayList` class. Now you can search for the license plate number of a car registered in the state of Texas using the first name, last name, and the last four digits of the owner's Social Security number. The major key component and a minor key component are initialized in the following code, and then a key is created using them.

```
majorList.add("Tanya");
majorList.add("Smith");
majorList.add("1006");

minorList.add("Texas");
minorList.add("BMW");
minorList.add("3-series");
minorList.add("sedan");

Key myKey = Key.createKey(majorList,minorList);
```

Now you get the value associated with this key by running the simple `get` method on the store handle. For this code snippet, let's assume that a handle to the key-value store has been obtained after providing the `KVStoreConfig` object to the `KVStoreFactory`.

```
ValueVersion vv = store.get(myKey);

System.out.println("The license plate number of the car "+myKey
  .toString()+ " is "+new String(vv.getValue().getValue()));
```

The preceding snippet of code produces the following output:

```
The license plate number of the car /Tanya/Smith/1006/-/Texas/BMW/3-
series/sedan is CY1R651
```

MultiGet Method

In this use case, one person may own multiple automobiles with license plates from different states. You have seen that the major component stores the personal information such as name and Social Security number, and the minor component stores the automobile information such as state, model, and make. The minor component is defined in multiple levels and is similar to levels in a tree-like data structure. The number of levels of data to obtain is defined by the Depth parameter. The Depth parameter has four possible choices:

■ **Children only**   Only the immediate first-level children are selected.

■ **Descendants only**   All the children are selected irrespective of the depth, which means children, grandchildren, and so on are all selected.

■ **Parent and children**   Only the parent and the first-level children are selected.

■ **Parent and descendants**   All the children are selected, including the parent.

In the code snippet that follows, all the cars owned by this person are listed. To achieve this, you need to create a key with a major component and perform a multiGet operation on the store. Once again, you assume that a handle to the key-value store has been obtained after providing the KVStoreConfig object to the KVStoreFactory.

```
ArrayList<String> majorList = new ArrayList<String>();

majorList.add("Tanya");
majorList.add("Smith");
majorList.add("1006");

Key myKey = Key.createKey(majorList);
```

Now you declare a SortedMap of type Key and ValueVersion, which is used to store all the values obtained from the multiGet operation on the key-value store.

```
SortedMap<Key, ValueVersion> myRecords = null;

try {
myRecords = store.multiGet(myKey, null, Depth.PARENT_AND_DESCENDANTS);
          } catch (ConsistencyException ce) {
```

```
        // do something when the consistency guarantee was not met
    } catch (RequestTimeoutException re) {
        // do something when the operation was not completed within the
        // timeout value
    }
```

The KeyRange and the Depth parameters in the multiGet method call are optional. You specify the depth as PARENT_AND_DESCENDANTS so that you can list all the cars owned by the individual irrespective of model and the state where the license plate originated. You set KeyRange as null because you are not doing any additional filtering at this point. Notice that you are trying to catch the consistencyException and the RequestTimeoutException in the preceding code snippet. More details on exception handling are discussed later in this chapter. You iterate through the entries in the Sorted Map that you have obtained from the function call to the key-value store. The following statement prints out the registration plate information of all the cars owned by the individual.

```
for (Map.Entry<Key, ValueVersion> entry : myRecords.entrySet()) {
        System.out.println(entry.getKey().toString()+": "
                        +new String(entry.getValue().getValue()
                        .getValue()));
    }
```

The console output from this part of your code snippet will look something like this.

```
Output of MultiGet Method with depth - 'Parent and all descendants'
/Tanya/Smith/1006: CY1R651
/Tanya/Smith/1006/-/California/Ford/Mustang/convertible: 1224RED
/Tanya/Smith/1006/-/CarRegNumber: CY1R651
/Tanya/Smith/1006/-/NewYork/Mercedes/MClass/convertible: 122RED4
/Tanya/Smith/1006/-/Texas/BMW/3-series/sedan: CY1R651
/Tanya/Smith/1006/-/Texas/BMW/5-series/convertible: 1RED224
/Tanya/Smith/1006/-/Texas/BMW/7-series/coup: 12RED24
```

Notice that it shows all the entries in the key-value store which are matching the major key component.

MultiGet Method with Iterator

While using the multiGet methods, you do not know ahead of time how many records will be read from the key-value store for a particular major component. So this method is very useful in the scenario where the result may be too large to fit into the memory. The use of the iterator enables you to perform an ordered traversal while specifying how many records to fetch in one batch. This prevents high utilization of the available network bandwidth and also optimizes the number of network roundtrips.

There are two important differences in the method call that follows apart from the use of an iterator.

- **Direction** This parameter simply specifies the order in which the key-value pairs are returned. The three choices are forward, reverse, and unordered and they are self-explanatory.

- **KeyRange** This is a filter mechanism similar to the way a where clause operates in relational database systems, and it can be applied to the keys. The KeyRange was set to "Texas" in the example to filter the result set to get only those automobiles with Texas license plates. The KeyRange is a string that is applied to the minor key component in this example. The KeyRanges are string-based and they can be constructed in two ways:

  - KeyRange constructed with one string.

  - KeyRange constructed with a beginning string, ending string, and parameters indicating whether the beginning and the end strings are inclusive in the filter operation. This version of the API is used and explained in the Deleting Records section later in the chapter.

```
myKey = Key.createKey(majorList);
KeyRange kr = new KeyRange("Texas");

Iterator<KeyValueVersion> mgi =  store
  .multiGetIterator(Direction.REVERSE,4,myKey,kr,Depth
  .DESCENDANTS_ONLY,Consistency.ABSOLUTE,0,null);
System.out.println("Output of MultiGet Method using iterator
  with Depth- 'Descendants only'");

while (mgi.hasNext()) {

    KeyValueVersion kvvi = mgi.next();
    System.out.println("The key and Value are"
      +kvvi.getKey().toString() + "            " +new String(kvvi
      .getValue().getValue()));
}
```

Note that this snippet of code prints only three records compared to the seven in the previous example. The difference occurs because the result set is filtered by the KeyRange, and also occurs because we have changed the Depth to descendants only, which means that the parent record is not returned. The following is the final output printed to the console:

```
Output of MultiGet Method using iterator with Depth- 'Descendants only'
The key and Value are/Tanya/Smith/1006/-/Texas/BMW/7-series/coup
```

```
12RED24
The key and Value are/Tanya/Smith/1006/-/Texas/BMW/5-series/convertible
1RED224
The key and Value are/Tanya/Smith/1006/-/Texas/BMW/3-series/sedan
CY1R651
```

MultiGetKeys and MultiGetKeysIterator Methods

There are certain use cases where retrieving just the keys from Oracle NoSQL can address the use case while giving the programmer a more optimal solution than retrieving the fully materialized value. It's important to keep in mind that Oracle NoSQL Database will always attempt to cache the keys residing in the B-tree in memory, while values are never cached. Thus, it is always more optimal to request an in-memory B-tree scan to retrieve keys rather than performing I/O to retrieve values. You can see this type of key-only retrieval scenario in the relationship graph use case where object relationships can be modeled as keys only. This is extremely common in the social networking space, where many applications will have a use case to find "friends of friends" to a certain degree. For this type of use case, you can model these relationships in Oracle NoSQL Database as follows:

```
/users/id/friends/-/users/id
```

Furthermore, you can choose to model the display name of a user as follows:

```
/users/id/profile/-/display_name
```

The following are example friend keys:

```
/users/34271/-/users/67511
/users/34271/-/users/89757
/users/34271/-/users/37519
```

The following are examples of profile information for a user:

```
/users/34271/profile/-/Joe Palooka
/users/67511/profile/-/Sharon White
/users/89757/profile/-/Vincent Carillo
```

As you can see, you now have the ability to perform "friend of friend" type queries simply by retrieving keys only from Oracle NoSQL Database. The following code presents an example of how to retrieve the friends of Joe Palooka. More complex "degrees of separation" queries are left as an exercise for the reader.

```
ArrayList majorKey = new ArrayList();
ArrayList minorKey = new ArrayList();


    //  Create the key /users/34271/profile/-/Joe Palooka
    majorKey.add("users");
```

```
majorKey.add("34271");
majorKey.add("profile");
minorKey.add("Joe Palooka");
store.put(Key.createKey(majorKey, minorKey),
                        Value.createValue(new byte[]{}));

// Create the key /users/67511/profile/-/Sharon White
majorKey.clear();
minorKey.clear();
majorKey.add("users");
majorKey.add("67511");
majorKey.add("profile");
minorKey.add("Sharon White");
store.put(Key.createKey(majorKey, minorKey),
                        Value.createValue(new byte[]{}));

// Create the key /users/89757/profile/-/Vincent Carillo
majorKey.clear();
minorKey.clear();
majorKey.add("users");
majorKey.add("89757");
majorKey.add("profile");
minorKey.add("Vincent Carillo");
store.put(Key.createKey(majorKey, minorKey),
                        Value.createValue(new byte[]{}));

// Create key /users/34271/friends/-/users/67511
majorKey.clear();
minorKey.clear();
majorKey.add("users");
majorKey.add("34271");
majorKey.add("friends");
minorKey.add("users");
minorKey.add("67511");
store.put(Key.createKey(majorKey, minorKey),
                        Value.createValue(new byte[]{}));

// Create key /users/34271/friends/-/users/89757
minorKey.clear();
minorKey.add("users");
minorKey.add("89757");
store.put(Key.createKey(majorKey, minorKey),
                        Value.createValue(new byte[]{}));

// First we'll look up the keys that contain the IDs of Joe's
// friends
// Use a partial path and get everything underneath it
Key joePalooka = Key.fromString("/users/34271/friends");
```

```
        SortedSet<Key> friendsOfJoe = store.multiGetKeys(joePalooka, null,
                                Depth.DESCENDANTS_ONLY,
                                Consistency.NONE_REQUIRED, 0, null);

        Iterator<Key> friendsIterator = friendsOfJoe.iterator();

        System.out.println("Joe Palooka's friends:");

        while (friendsIterator.hasNext()) {
                // Now build a key for each item in the iterator so that
                // we can retrieve the display_name from the profile
             ArrayList<String> friendMajor = new ArrayList<String>();
             Iterator <String> i =
                        friendsIterator.next().getMinorPath().iterator();
             while (i.hasNext()) {
                friendMajor.add(i.next());
             }
             friendMajor.add("profile");

             Key friendKey = Key.createKey(friendMajor);
             Iterator<Key> friendNames = store.multiGetKeysIterator(
                        Direction.FORWARD, 10, friendKey, null, null);
             while (friendNames.hasNext()) {
                Key k = friendNames.next();
                System.out.println("\t"+ k.toString());
             }
        }

        // close the connection before we exit
         store.close();
        }
```

When executed, the preceding code will print the following to the console:

```
Joe Palooka's friends:

/users/67511/profile/-/Sharon%20White
/users/89757/profile/-/Vincent%20Carillo
```

Notice that spaces are printed using the standard URI encoding of %20.

StoreIterator to Print Everything in the Store
If your goal is to know about all the license plate information of all the cars of all the people stored in the key-value store, then use `storeIterator`.

```
Iterator<KeyValueVersion> it = store.storeIterator(Direction.UNORDERED,0);
System.out.println("In StoreIterator Method: Printing Everything ");
while (it.hasNext()) {
        KeyValueVersion kvvi = it.next();
```

```
System.out.println(new String(kvvi.getValue().getValue())+
                   "              " + kvvi.getKey().toString());
}
```

The storeIterator function on the key-value store gives you the capability to iterate through all the key-value pairs in the key-value store. Unlike other methods that retrieve key-value pairs from the store, however, the result of the storeIterator method is not transactional in nature. When using the storeIterator method, obtaining the records in batches helps minimize the network trips and can make large store scan operations more optimal. The following is a partial output of the preceding code snippet :

```
In StoreIterator Method: Printing Everything
AAA999            /Kiyara/K/Kadaru/-/Texas/Pontiac/Solstice/Convertible
CY1R651           /Tanya/Smith/1006
1224RED           /Tanya/Smith/1006/-/California/Ford/Mustang/convertible
CY1R651           /Tanya/Smith/1006/-/CarRegNumber
122RED4           /Tanya/Smith/1006/-/NewYork/Mercedes/MClass/convertible
CY1R651           /Tanya/Smith/1006/-/Texas/BMW/3-series/sedan
1RED224           /Tanya/Smith/1006/-/Texas/BMW/5-series/convertible
12RED24           /Tanya/Smith/1006/-/Texas/BMW/7-series/coup
..._Andy_Murray       /authorList
    ABCQWE9       /Swarna/K/Walker/-/NewYork/Chevrolet/Camaro/Convertible
```

Introduction to API for Enforcing Read Consistency

The cornerstone of any RDBMS system is its ability to enforce ACID properties; in particular, read consistency is an important property in the ACID quartet. Irrespective of how many nodes you have in a relational database, in which node you update a particular piece of data, and from which node you retrieve the same piece of data, users must always get the same consistent answer. In a distributed shared nothing system like Oracle NoSQL, consistency is typically defined as "eventual." This means that data on different nodes will eventually become consistent as changes to the data arrive at nodes across the cluster. Oracle NoSQL Database provides unique capabilities for the programmer to enforce different consistency policies based on the use cases that are being addressed.

Based on the knowledge obtained in the previous chapters of this book, you should now understand the multi-node architecture of the NoSQL database. Writes happen to the master node first and then get propagated to the other nodes in the shard. The change propagation is not instantaneous and the application may get different results while querying for the same data, depending on whether the query was satisfied by the master node or another node in the shard. The choice of which node will service that query can be influenced by the consistency policy that is utilized. If the system gets the copy of the data from the master node, then it can ensure that it is the most recent version of that piece of data because all the writes happen on the master node. If the system gets the data from a non-master node, then the data may or may not be the most recent. The different kinds of consistency policies supported by Oracle NoSQL Database are:

- **`Consistency.NONE_REQUIRED`**   Data can read from any node in the shard regardless of how recent the data is with respect to the master node in the shard.

- **`Consistency.Time`**   The amount of time that a replica is allowed to lag from the master. When using this policy, the application must supply an upper bound indicating the maximum amount of time that the application is willing to tolerate for the recency of data from a Replication Node.

- **`Consistency.Version`**   A consistency policy that ensures that the environment on a Replication Node is at least as current as denoted by the specified key-value pair version.

- **`Consistency.ABSOLUTE`**   Data will be read from the master node of the shard. Guarantees that the most recent committed transaction on a piece of data is returned to the caller.

There are important trade-offs to consider when utilizing the `ABSOLUTE` consistency policy. While this policy guarantees the most recent data, the cost for this policy is that all read requests will be routed to the single master node in the shard. This could significantly affect the throughput and latency of the shard as the master node could quickly become overwhelmed by servicing all of the write requests for the shard while servicing the entire set of read requests as well. Thus, great care should be taken to carefully examine the use case when considering the use of absolute consistency.

Using the `NONE_REQUIRED` consistency policy allows for fast reads and low latency because it reads from the replicas but sacrifices the guarantee of the recentness of the data. The time-based and version-based consistency policies also have the potential to achieve better performance than `ABSOLUTE` consistency by agreeing to read from the replicas, which do not guarantee the most recent data. The data read may fall behind the most recent data by some number of versions or some permissible time lag. Hence, it is clearly evident that there is a trade-off between the quality of the data and the latency of the reads from Oracle NoSQL Database. As a programmer, the kind of consistency policy to choose should be driven by the business requirements. Table 6-4 describes how different business requirements may translate to different consistency policies.

The configuration set at the configuration object level of a key-value store can be overridden by the setting at the individual API call. We illustrate this point in the

Business Requirement	Consistency Policy
Very fast web pages or low latency	`Consistency.NONE_REQUIRED`
Commodity low budget hardware for master node	`Consistency.NONE_REQUIRED`
Most recent data always needed	`Consistency.ABSOLUTE`
Fine to display data that is not recent by a few seconds if latency is low	Time-based consistency
Fine to display data that is not recent by a few updates if latency is low	Version-based consistency

TABLE 6-4. *Consistency Policy Guidelines*

following code snippet where the configuration setting at the Store Configuration object level is `NONE_REQUIRED`.

```
KVStoreConfig conf = new KVStoreConfig(storeName,hostname
            + ":" + hostPort);
        conf.setConsistency(Consistency.NONE_REQUIRED);

store = KVStoreFactory.getStore(conf);
```

At the individual operation level we set the consistency as `ABSOLUTE`.

```
majorList.add("Tanya");
majorList.add("Smith");
majorList.add("1006");


minorList.add("Texas");
minorList.add("BMW");
minorList.add("3-series");
minorList.add("sedan");
Key myKey = Key.createKey(majorList,minorList);

ValueVersion vv = store.get(myKey,Consistency.ABSOLUTE,0,null);
System.out.println("The license plate number of the car
with Absolute Consistency override at the statement level is
"+myKey.toString()+ " is "+new String(vv.getValue().getValue()));
```

Notice how the consistency policy is changed to `ABSOLUTE` at the statement level. The output of the code snippet is as follows:

```
The license plate number of the car with Absolute Consistency override at
the statement level is /Tanya/Smith/1006/-/Texas/BMW/3-series/sedan is
CY1R651
```

Timeouts in Oracle NoSQL

Applications that are concerned with latency as well as high availability need to place an upper limit on the amount of time that will be spent waiting for a response from Oracle NoSQL Database. Many types of issues that occur in distributed systems can cause a request to reach unacceptable response time limits. These issues may include the following:

- **Transient network load**   Network utilization may reach limits such that packet roundtrip latency causes unacceptable delays.

- **Excess load on spinning disks**   Disk access may be unacceptably delayed due to a high number of requests queued up for a particular spindle.

- **Transient garbage collection**   Even though Oracle NoSQL Database goes to great lengths to avoid JVM garbage collection, there may be rare occurrences where the Java garbage collector causes unacceptable response times.

The timeout and timeout unit parameters in the Oracle NoSQL APIs can be utilized by applications to place an upper limit on the amount of time that an application thread will wait for response from an API call. Oracle NoSQL makes a best effort not to exceed the specified limit. If the "get" operation cannot be performed with the required consistency in the specified time limit, then a `RequestTimeoutException` is thrown.

The methods on the key-value store that contain the timeout parameter can be broadly be classified as

- Get operations

- Delete and multi-delete operations

- Execute operations

- Put operations

- Store Iterator operations

There are two ways to specify the timeout parameters. They can be specified at the individual operation level as we did in the read operation previously, or they can be specified at the store level in the store configuration. The different kinds of timeouts that are specified at the store level are:

- **Default LOB timeout**   Default value associated during operations using the large object APIs.

- **Default open timeout**   Default value associated with opening sockets that are used to make key-value store requests.

- **Default read timeout** Default value associated with read at underlying sockets to make client requests.

- **Default request timeout** Default timeout associated with key-value store requests.

A shorter timeout value usually results in fast failure detection. The read timeout value should be greater than the request timeout. If the end user is fine waiting for 10 seconds for a request to complete, there is no reason to wait at the socket for only 5 seconds. In this case a socket read timeout will occur before the request time. The concept of a timeout in the context of time-based consistency is explained in detail in the next section.

Time-Based Consistency

Time-based consistency defines the upper bound on the lag of a data item between the timestamp of that data item at the Replication Node and the timestamp of that item at the master node. In order for time-based consistency policy to be effective, the clocks on all the nodes in the store must be synchronized using a protocol such as NTP. Let us explain this concept with a use case.

In this use case, you have three datacenters for a financial services application: one in New York City, one in Princeton, New Jersey, and one in Hartford, Connecticut. This is a consumer-oriented application that allows consumers to display their investment portfolios, perform research, edit properties of the portfolio, and finally, to perform trades that will update the contents of the portfolio. There are some key aspects to this application scenario that will drive the rest of this use case:

- **Mostly read-only** The majority of your consumer users will log into the application, look at their portfolio and positions, and then log out. Hence this workload is 95 percent reads and 5 percent writes.

- **Trade and edit properties** The only operations that affect the contents of the portfolio are trade executions and portfolio property updates.

In a situation in which a datacenter fails due to a disaster, the other datacenters will automatically serve read and write requests. During this time, the application is still able to service consumers, but response times to users would suffer because of a lack of capacity. Once the failed datacenter is brought back online, the Replication Nodes running in shards at this datacenter will begin to catch up to their master nodes running in one of the other datacenters. While these Replication Nodes are catching up to the master, they are operational and can service read requests, but these requests will be out of date with the master until the nodes can catch up in the replication stream. At this time, it might be advantageous for the application to use time-based consistency to increase service levels for users. The goal here is to lower response times by servicing as many reads as possible from the Replication Nodes that are coming online and catching up to the master. This may be acceptable, but only if the data being read is no more than a few minutes' lag from the master nodes because the probability of reading out-of-date updates is very low since the workload is 95 percent reads and 5 percent writes. An application may also specify a timeout parameter for time-based consistency operations. This is referred to as the *consistency timeout*, and is treated a bit differently than the operation timeout, which is an optional parameter to all Oracle NoSQL API calls. The key-value store client driver implements a read operation by choosing a node (usually a non-master) from the shard, and sending it a request. If the node cannot guarantee the desired consistency within the consistency timeout, it replies to the request with a failure status. If there is still time remaining within the operation timeout, the client driver picks another node and tries the request again (transparent to the application); otherwise a `ConsistencyException` is thrown.

The following example code snippet will set a store-wide default consistency policy to time-based consistency with a consistency timeout of 4 seconds.

```
Consistency.Time cTimePolicy = new Consistency.Time(2,
          TimeUnit.SECONDS, 4, TimeUnit.SECONDS);
conf.setConsistency(cTimePolicy);

store = KVStoreFactory.getStore(conf);
```

Version-Based Consistency

A key-value pair gets a version number assigned when it is first written to a key-value store. On every subsequent update to the key-value pair, the version gets updated and the version number increases. Remember that the writes are performed on the master node and the change is propagated to the Replication Nodes. There is a steady replication stream, which sends changes to the Replication Nodes from the master node. The same key-value pair present in the master and the replica can have different values because they may be at different versions and the replica may be lagging the master by one or more versions. Version-based consistency ensures that a read performed on a replica is at least as current as some previous write performed on the master node. This is ensured using the version of the piece of data. If the client driver cannot obtain the desired version from replica A, then it tries to read it from replica B, and so on and ultimately tries to read it at the master to accomplish the task in a predefined operation timeout period. If the client driver cannot read the desired version of the data within the specified time at a replica, it replies back with a failure status. Consistency timeout is the time the client driver is willing to wait at a particular replica before giving up and moving to the next replica. The client driver uses the consistency timeout as a norm for the time taken to service normal requests when the replica is healthy. If the replica cannot satisfy the request within that time frame, then it is safe to assume that something is wrong at that replica and that it should move on to the next replica. The operation timeout can be thought of as the maximum amount of time the client driver is willing to wait to obtain the piece of data across all the replicas. Thus, for the consistency timeout to be meaningful, it must be smaller than the operation timeout.

Let's use the portfolio application defined in the previous section as an example use case. When a user goes to the home page on the website, the portfolio is presented along with a variety of read-only information such as disclosures, stock research, company 10-k and options, and so on. The majority of the site is largely read-only, with rare updates occurring, but the portfolio section can exhibit writes that are more frequent than the other sections of the site. Thus, we've built-in a requirement that the application must service the portfolio section such that read will always return the latest committed writes, while the other sections of the site can read data in any state (because the state rarely, if ever, changes). When a read is performed, the reads are usually directed to the replicas and the replicas may contain stale data compared to the master node by a few versions. This is fine for the non-portfolio data but not for the portfolio information as per our requirements. As of yesterday, user Tanya Smith owns 500 shares of Facebook stock in her portfolio. Today, she executes a stock purchase order and now owns 1,000 shares. Immediately after the purchase, the website has to reflect the updated portfolio with the updated number of shares for accuracy. You cannot afford to just perform a simple read because the read activity might be directed to a replica and that can result in stale data being presented to the end user. This requirement can be implemented by using version-based consistency. Once the stock purchase is performed, a write happens to the master node and you obtain the version number of your newly updated key-value pair. Any subsequent reads performed by an application will use this version in conjunction with the version-based consistency policy. The following code snippets illustrate this use case.

```
ArrayList<String> majorList = new ArrayList<String>();
ArrayList<String> minorList = new ArrayList<String>();
majorList.add("Tanya");
majorList.add("Smith");
majorList.add("Stocks");

minorList.add("FB");
Key myKey = Key.createKey(majorList, minorList);

ValueVersion vv = store.get(myKey, null, 0, null);

System.out.println("The initial version of the KVPair from VV is "+vv
                   .getVersion().getVLSN());

System.out.println("Key indicating stocks is   "
```

```
        + myKey.toString()
        + " and value is "
        + new String(vv.getValue().getValue()));
```

The following is the console output of the preceding piece of code:

```
The initial version of the KVPair from VV is 12409
Key indicating stocks is /Tanya/Smith/Stocks/-/FB and value is 500
```

Now the stock portfolio update, triggered by a stock purchase, is performed in the following code. The recent version is also obtained along with the update.

```
String st1 = "1000";
Value myValue1 = Value.createValue(st1.getBytes());
Version currVersion = store.putIfPresent(myKey, myValue1);
System.out.println("Updated Version of the KVPair is "+currVersion
    .getVLSN());
```

The console output of the preceding piece of code is as follows:

```
Updated Version of the KVPair is 12409
```

Now let's create a version-based consistency policy based on the recent version obtained. You then perform a read operation based on the version-based consistency policy we created, and if the request cannot be satisfied, an exception is thrown.

```
try {
        Consistency.Version verCon = new Consistency.Version(currVersion,2,
        TimeUnit.SECONDS);
        vv = store.get(myKey, verCon, 0, null);
        System.out.println("The number of shares of FB stock read
                        with Version Consistency: "
                        + myKey.toString()
                        + " is "
                        + new String(vv.getValue().getValue()));
        System.out.println("The version of the obtained KVPair is
                        "+vv.getVersion().getVLSN());
} catch (ConsistencyException ce) {
        ce.printStackTrace();
}
store.close();
```

Console output is presented here so that you can better understand the example:

```
The number of shares of FB stock read with Version Consistency: /Tanya/
Smith/Stocks/-/FB is 1000
The version of the obtained KVPair is 12409
```

Exception Handling for Read Operations

As with write operations, proper exception handling is central to providing highly available applications. For read operations, this will typically involve retry operations during timeouts as well as varying the consistency policy, catching the consistency exception, and then tightening up the policy in a retry operation. You can think of this as a lever on optimistic reads such that the application may start with a version-based consistency policy and a consistency timeout setting to optimistically try a read at any given node in the shard. If this fails with a consistency exception, the application can back off and retry the operation using absolute consistency, which will guarantee the latest version of the data at the cost of placing more load on the master node of the shard. Table 6-5 illustrates the different exceptions thrown by the read APIs in Oracle NoSQL and presents the likely cause of each along with a possible resolution.

Deleting Records

There are many ways to delete records from the key-value store. The simplest way to delete is to delete a record based on a single key. Programmers can perform a `multiDelete` where the major key component of a key is provided and all the keys that match the major key component will be deleted. The following code

Exception	Likely Cause	Possible Resolution
ConsistencyException	The desired consistency constraint could not be satisfied at replicas in the shard within the supplied timeout.	Retrying the operation with absolute consistency is guaranteed to succeed. The application may want to retry again with the original consistency constraint, but this may be unsuccessful again.
FaultException	It's likely that an internal error occurred with one or more nodes in the NoSQL cluster.	A retry should be attempted, but may still fail. This error could indicate a possible transient network failure, hardware failure, or software failure in Oracle NoSQL Database.
RequestTimeoutException	The read could not be satisfied within the time constraint supplied to the API.	More than likely, the application has supplied this constraint as an upper bound on the time willing to wait for the read to complete and there's little recourse in this scenario.

TABLE 6-5. *Exception Handling Guidelines for Reads*

snippet demonstrates both ways of deleting the records. The major key components and the minor key component are initialized for a particular Key.

```
ArrayList<String> majorList = new ArrayList<String>();
ArrayList<String> minorList = new ArrayList<String>();

majorList.add("Tanya");
majorList.add("Smith");
majorList.add("1006");

minorList.add("Texas");
minorList.add("BMW");
minorList.add("3-series");
minorList.add("sedan");
```

The Key is created based on the major and minor components and the `delete` method is invoked on the store for this particular Key.

```
Key myKey = Key.createKey(majorList,minorList);

Boolean b = store.delete(myKey);

System.out.println("The single record was deleted and the boolean value
                    returned is "+b);
```

The output for the preceding code snippet is as follows:

```
The single record was deleted and the boolean value returned is true
```

Utilizing the `multiDelete` method in Oracle NoSQL, a programmer may delete an entire set of key/value pairs in one call. This may be extremely useful for certain programming tasks. Consider the e-mail application previously mentioned. Let's say that you would like to implement the "empty deleted folder" control, which will permanently delete all of a user's messages from the Deleted folder. The `multiDelete` method is a perfect choice for implementing this control as in a single call to the NoSQL cluster; you can delete all of the items in a user's Deleted folder. The following code gives an example of using `multiDelete` to permanently remove all of the messages from user 34271's Deleted folder.

The `KeyRange` and the `Depth` parameters are optional so you pass the null value.

```
myKey = Key.fromString(/users/34271/folders/-/deleted/");

int a = store.multiDelete(myKey, null, null);
store.close();
```

The preceding code snippet gives the following output. The return value is an integer indicating the number of records deleted from the key-value store. Note that there are seven entries at the time of reading the records in the key-value store for the user, and while we deleted one in the single delete function shown previously, the `multiDelete` operation deleted the rest of the six records in the key-value store.

```
The delete was done and the number of records deleted for us is 6
```

There are many use cases where you may wish to delete many records in a single API call but not all of the data under a major key. You may have to filter what you delete based on user-defined criteria. In the preceding e-mail application, let's say a user, Tanya Smith, wants to delete all the e-mail messages in the deleted folder received in the month of December. To accomplish this, you need to create a major key pointing to the deleted folder and then apply a key range to it. The data in the key-value store is stored in the format shown here. The `Key` is the location of the e-mail message with the major key defining the user and the minor key defining the folder, date, time, and the "to" information. The value in the key-value pair is the e-mail message.

```
/users/TanyaSmith/folders/-/deleted/20130101/174510/To:Jennifer:
   Hi Jennifer, This is the email number on 20130101. Thanks Tanya
/users/TanyaSmith/folders/-/ deleted /20130102/174510/To:Jennifer:
   Hi Jennifer, This is the email number on 20130102. Thanks Tanya
/users/TanyaSmith/folders/-/ deleted /20130103/174510/To:Jennifer:
   Hi Jennifer,
This is the email number on 20131224. Thanks Tanya
…..
…..
/users/TanyaSmith/folders/-/ deleted /20131225/174510/To:Jennifer:
   Hi Jennifer, This is the email number on 20131225. Thanks Tanya
/users/TanyaSmith/folders/-/ deleted /20131226/174510/To:Jennifer:
   Hi Jennifer, This is the email number on 20131226. Thanks Tanya
/users/TanyaSmith/folders/-/ deleted /20131227/174510/To:Jennifer:
   Hi Jennifer, This is the email number on 20131227. Thanks Tanya
```

You create the major key component and the minor key component as shown here:

```
majorList.add("users");
majorList.add("TanyaSmith");
majorList.add("folders");

minorList.add("deleted");

myKey = Key.createKey(majorList,minorList);
```

Now the `KeyRange` is constructed and passed as a parameter to the `multiDelete` function. The `KeyRange` defines a range of `String` values for the key components immediately following the last component of a parent key that is used in a multiple-key operation. In our example, the `KeyRange` is immediately applied after the key we constructed, which contains the major key component and a part of the minor key component. In terms of a tree structure, the range defines the parent key's immediate children that are selected by the multiple-key operation.

```
KeyRange kr = new KeyRange("20131201",true,"20131230",true);
```

The Boolean parameter after the lower range boundary and the upper range boundary indicates whether the lower or upper range is included or not.

```
int a = store.multiDelete(myKey, kr, Depth.PARENT_AND_DESCENDANTS);

System.out.println("The delete was done and the number of records
deleted for us is "+a);
```

The console output shows that 30 e-mails have been deleted.

```
The delete was done and the number of records deleted for us is 30
```

Updating Records Based on a Version

In this section, we illustrate the concept of updates in the key-value store. We also explain how updates can happen only if the key-value pair has not been updated from the last known version. Also, you can make sure you only insert a new key if the key is absent. To illustrate the concept, let's insert a new record (the license plate number of another vehicle) for the example person we are dealing with:

```
ArrayList<String> majorList = new ArrayList<String>();
ArrayList<String> minorList = new ArrayList<String>();

majorList.add("Tanya");
majorList.add("Smith");
majorList.add("1006");
minorList.add("Texas");
minorList.add("YAMAHA");
minorList.add("YZF999");
minorList.add("sportsBike");
Key myKey = Key.createKey(majorList, minorList);

String st = "YAH999";
String newSt = "YAH000";
Value myValue = Value.createValue(st.getBytes());
```

Use the `putIfAbsent` method, which inserts the new record only if it is not already present in the key-value store. When this code snippet is run for the first time, it inserts the record and returns a version. When the code snippet is run the second time, it does not get inserted because the record is already there and the version returned is NULL. In this case, an update happens.

```
Version ver = store.putIfAbsent(myKey, myValue);

if (ver == null) {

        ValueVersion vv = store.get(myKey);
        System.out.println("The current version of the Key is "
                            +vv.getVersion().getVLSN());
        System.out.println("The key and current value is "+myKey.toString()+"    "
                            +new String(vv.getValue().getValue()));

        Version newVer = store.putIfVersion(myKey,
                            Value.createValue(newSt.getBytes()), vv.getVersion());
        System.out.println("The version of the updated record is "
                            + newVer.getVersion());

        vv = store.get(myKey);
        System.out.println("The key and value of the updated record is "
            +myKey.toString() +"  "+ new String(vv.getValue().getValue()));

} else {
        System.out.println("The current version of the Key is "+ver.getVersion());
        System.out.println("The key and current value is "+myKey.toString()
                            +"    "+ new String(myValue.toByteArray()));

}
myKey = Key.createKey(majorList);

        store.close();
```

The version is printed along with the key and value of the record on different runs. The console output during the first run is as follows:

```
The current version of the Key is 742
The key and current value is /Tanya/C/Kadaru/-/Texas/YAMAHA/YZF999/
sportsBike
YAH999
```

The code is run a second time to update the license plate number of the bike. Note how the version gets changed, and also how the value gets changed. The console output during the second run is as follows.

```
The current version of the Key is 742
The key and current value is /Tanya/C/Kadaru/-/Texas/YAMAHA/YZF999/
sportsBike    YAH999
The version of the updated record is 744
The key and value of the updated record is /Tanya/C/Kadaru/-/Texas/
YAMAHA/YZF999/sportsBike    YAH000
```

Summary

Writing successful applications utilizing the Oracle NoSQL Database APIs involves careful consideration of many factors. Having a solid understanding of the functional requirements of the application and how to nuance consistency, durability, and exception handling to achieve these trade-offs can be the difference between an application that is always on, scales easily to meet demand, and maintains low response times, and an application that is wrought with data errors, scaling problems, and high response times. The examples and use cases presented in this chapter give the reader a good basis for making these important decisions about acceptable trade-offs.

CHAPTER 7

Advanced Programming Concepts: Avro Schemas and Bindings

In the preceding chapters, you learned about the various methods of retrieving and storing key-value pairs in Oracle NoSQL Database and discovered that a rich set of APIs exists to assist with building complex and distributed NoSQL Database applications. You also learned about the importance of modeling the key space, and that the modeling choices you make can either help you in addressing application requirements or hurt you.

Similarly, imposing a structure or a model on the value field of the key-value pair ensures that the data adheres to a standard format, thereby facilitating its exchange with other entities and helping optimize its storage footprint. In the examples presented in the previous chapter, the format of the value field of the key-value pair was a simple string and did not adhere to any specific structure or a predefined *schema*. Defining a schema on the value part ensures that the composition or the structure of data is known in advance, and can be understood when it is fetched or transmitted to other applications or software components.

In this chapter, we discuss *Avro schema*, an integral part of the Apache Avro framework, and the mechanism behind standardizing data serialization and exchange among different applications and/or software components.

NOTE
Defining Avro schemas on the key-value pair data in many ways is similar to defining XSD (XML Schema Definition) on XML data. The XSD ensures that the XML document conforms to a structure, as defined by the XSD.

Avro Schema

Before we talk about Avro schema, it makes sense to talk about Apache Avro, an Apache open source foundation project. Apache Avro (or just *Avro*) is a serialization framework built to facilitate data storage, retrieval, and exchange among multiple applications. Data serialization in the software industry is the process of encoding data into an efficient format (such as the binary format) so that it can be stored optimally on a persistent storage medium such as the hard disk, or exchanged efficiently between two applications over the network. Similarly, a deserialization is the reverse of serialization, in which the binary representation of data is taken from persistent storage and re-created in memory in the format that is efficient for processing by computer programs.

Another key component of Avro aside from serialization is the standardization of data exchange by defining a format on data using an *Avro schema*. The Avro schema defines a structure on the data, in a fashion similar to a database table structure or the structure of an XML document. When the data portion of the key-value pair is stored on disk, the schema is stored with it, and when the data is read, the schema is applied to ensure that the data conforms to the structure defined in the schema. When exchanging data between two applications, the schema would be known to both applications beforehand and the schema conformance on the data can be tested by the receiving application.

Oracle NoSQL Database supports the use of the Avro schema for the value part of the key-value pair. With the Avro schema, the value part is serialized in a space-efficient binary format and is prepended with an internal schema identifier. The schema identifier is very compact in size (occupying less than 4 bytes) and does not incur much overhead in storage. The identifier is used to refer to the schema definition, which is stored in an internal catalog called the Avro catalog. The association of the values to the Avro schema is made transparent to the application and the schema identifier is managed by the Avro bindings, which are discussed later in this chapter.

An Avro schema is represented using a JSON (JavaScript Object Notation) object, a lightweight data interchange format that is easy for both humans and machines to read, write, and understand. The following example illustrates a simple JSON object that stores user profiles for a social networking website.

```
{
    "type" : "record",
    "name" : "userProfiles",
    "namespace" : "com.user.profiles",
    "fields" : [
                {"name" : "FullName","type" : "string"},
                    {"name" : "UserName","type" : "string"}
                ]
}
```

Let's closely examine the different parts of the preceding JSON object:

■ **Type**   Specifies the "type" of the JSON record. At the top level of an Avro schema, it is mandatory that the type be of "record". It is also mandatory to define the type of an individual field, which can be either a complex (i.e., a record) or a primitive data type. We discuss complex and primitive data types later in the chapter.

■ **Name**   The name of the Avro schema being defined. The name can be alphanumeric and must begin with a character.

■ **Namespace**   The namespace is a high-level logical identifier of the Avro schema, and although it could be any alphanumeric value, it makes sense to use a name that identifies the application or the department that owns the Avro schema. The combination of name and the namespace used to define an Avro schema in the key-value store must be unique.

Primitive Types	Description
Null	Used when you want to define a field as having no value
Boolean	Binary value denoting true or false
Int	32-bit signed integer
Long	64-bit signed integer
Float	32-bit floating point number
Double	64-bit floating point number
Bytes	Sequence of 8-bit unsigned bytes
String	Unicode character sequence

TABLE 7-1.   *List of Primitive Types and Their Descriptions*

- **Fields**   These are the individual data elements that make up the JSON object. You may have multiple fields and each field can either be of a simple data type such as a string or an integer, or a complex data type such as a "record," which can be further made up of simple and complex data types.

Table 7-1 contains the complete list of primitive data types supported by Avro. In Apache Avro, you can also use complex types. Complex types are defined as follows:

- **Record**   Records contain some mandatory attributes such as name, type, and fields. They also contain optional attributes such as namespace, doc, and aliases. The mandatory attribute field record has multiple subfields:

  - **Name**   The name attribute at field level is mandatory. It begins with letters and can contain only letters and digits and is case-sensitive.

  - **Type**   Describes the type of a field, which is either a record or an embedded JSON Schema definition. The value of type in top-level schema definitions must be record.

  - **Fields**   Mandatory one or more occurrences describing the record as a whole.

The following optional attributes are provided:

- **Namespace**   Uniquely identifies a `record` type. The `namespace` and name attributes together must form a unique qualifier.

- **Doc**   Provides documentation about the record. It is stored with the schema and is accessible using the Avro API but it does not decrease the serialization efficiency in any way.

- **Alias**   Provides the ability to use an array of alternate names for the JSON record. You may optionally use aliases to map a writer's schema to the reader's. This facilitates schema evolution as well as processing disparate datasets.

- **Default**   Default value the field will take if no data is supplied.

- **Order**   An optional attribute. Possible values are `ascending`, `descending`, or `ignore`. Oracle NoSQL Database always ignores this property.

■ **Enum**   Used to enumerate different types and has similar attributes of name, `namespace`, `alias`, and `doc` as the `record` and the `field` objects do. However, there is a new attribute in enum called `symbols`, which stores all the values of the Enum as an array of names. `Symbols` is a mandatory attribute and the rest of the attributes behave in much the same way that `record` and `field` do.

```
{
  "type" : "enum",
  "name" : "userTypes",
  "namespace" : "com.user.profiles",
  "doc" : "These are the different user profiles",
  "symbols" : ["personUser", "smallBusinessUser", "LargeBusinessUser",
              "nonProfitBusinessUser"]
}
```

■ **Array**   The only attribute that the array type supports is the `items` attribute, which is mandatory. The `items` attribute identifies the type of the items in the array. In the example that follows, the items are typed as integers.

```
{"type": "array", "items": "int"}
```

- **Maps**   Behaves like an array with data as key-value pairs. The key has to be a string and the only attribute supported is `values`. In the example, the items are typed as strings.

  ```
  {"type": "map", "values": "string"}
  ```

- **Union**   Used to represent a field as something that can be more than one type. It is represented as a JSON `array`. A hypothetical use case requires a field to be a string or a null. Then the field is defined as a union, in which case it is represented as `["string", "null"]`. The following is a complete example:

  ```
  {
      "type": "record",
      "namespace": "com.user.profiles.user.address",
      "name": "Address",
      "fields": [
          { "name": "Address1", "type": ["string", "null"] },
          { "name": "Address2", "type": "string", "default" : "" },
          { "name": "City", "type": "string", "default" : "" },
          { "name": "State", "type": "string", "default" : "" }
      ]
  }
  ```

  The field `Address1` can be a string or a null value.

- **Fixed**   A `fixed` type is used to declare a field of fixed size (in bytes) that is used for storing binary data. The required attributes are `name` and `size`. The following is an example of a fixed object named `sampledata` with 200,000 bytes of size.

  ```
  {"type": "fixed", "name": "sampledata", "size": 200000}
  ```

Schema Evolution

Over time in any enterprise project, the schema requirements may change for a record, and you may have to add, delete, or modify the record fields contained in the schema. The modification of the schema over time because of the new requirements is termed *schema evolution*.

Consider a scenario in which data may have been written to the key-value store using one version of the schema; then the schema is modified to satisfy the new application requirements, and the data needs to be read again. Which schema do you think will be used for the read, the old schema or the new schema? Thankfully, Avro contains rich support for schema evolution via its specification of the writer schema (the schema used to store the value) and the reader schema (the schema used to read the value), thereby allowing multiple versions of the schema to coexist in the Avro catalog. The Avro catalog is a catalog of Avro schemas being used by the store.

Oracle NoSQL Database fully supports schema evolution by storing the unique ID of the schema at the time the record was written along with the record. Therefore, if you use the unique ID, it is possible to identify the schema that was used to write the record (writer schema), and all read operations on that record could be performed using the writer schema. The following sequence of events occurs when the application needs to store a value in the key-value store (the serialization process):

1. A version of the schema is chosen from the list of available schemas for the key-value store and it is called the "writer" schema.

2. A binding is created based on the schema chosen for the serialization process.

3. The `AvroBinding.toValue()` method is called to serialize the data.

4. The binary value gets written to the store along with the schema identifier.

The following sequence of events occurs when the application needs to read a value from the key-value store (the deserialization process):

1. The binary value is read from the store.

2. A client application chooses a schema from the list of available schemas and this schema is called the "reader" schema.

3. A binding is created based on the schema chosen to deserialize.

4. `AvroBinding.toObject()` is called to deserialize the data.

To further explain the concept of schema evolution, let's take a look at the previous JSON schema that was designed to store user profile information, and evolve it by adding a gender type, as shown in bold:

```
{
    "type" : "record",
    "name" : "facebookProfiles2",
    "namespace" : "com.facebook.profiles",
    "fields" : [  {"name" : "FullName","type" : "string"},
                  {"name" : "UserName","type" : "string"},
                  {"name" : "age","type" :"int","default":18},
                  {"name" : "gender","type" :"string","default":"unspecified"}
               ]
}
```

You should be familiar with the following two scenarios when a new field is added:

■ **Client uses old schema to write and new schema to read.** Because the field was written with the old schema, it could not have stored the new element (i.e., `gender`), so you use the default value of the new field (i.e., `unspecified`), and the read succeeds.

■ **Client uses new schema to write and old schema to read.** Because the new schema is used to write, the new field is also written to the key-value store; however, because the reader schema does not need this field, this field value is simply ignored when reading. It is important to note that when inserting values with the new schema, all field values *must* be supplied even though the new field has a default value. Default values are only used for readers.

Now, let's see what happens when you delete existing fields from the Avro schema. Consider that you have modified the JSON schema (again) from the previous example and removed the age field:

```
{
    "type" : "record",
    "name" : "facebookProfiles2",
    "namespace" : "com.facebook.profiles",
    "fields" : [  {"name" : "FullName","type" : "string"},
                   "name" : "UserName","type" : "string"},
                   "name" : "gender","type" :"string","default":"unspecified"}
               ]
}
```

You should be familiar with the following two scenarios when a field is deleted.

■ **Client uses old schema to write and new schema to read.** Because the deleted field is not present in the read request, the request is satisfied by dropping the deleted field and the data is returned.

■ **Client uses new schema to write and old schema to read.** In this case, the deleted field is not written to the key-value store, but the reader schema needs this field when reading so the default value (as defined by the old schema) is added and the read request is satisfied.

General Rules for Schema Evolution

There are a few general rules to follow when modifying schemas. From the previous example, you have seen that when adding a new mandatory field, it is best to provide a default value so that for applications reading an older version of data when the field did not exist alongside the new version of the schema when the field exists, the default value could be returned and the request still satisfied without an error.

There are a few modifications that you can safely perform and a few that will result in an error or rejection of the new schema. Removing, adding, or changing non-mandatory attributes of a field will typically not result in an error. The following are some examples of changes to non-mandatory attributes:

- A field's doc attribute is changed, added, or removed.

- A field's order attribute is changed, added, or removed.

- Field or type aliases are added or removed.

The following are some examples of modifications to the schemas that are permitted by the system:

- A field with a default value is added.

- A field that was previously defined with a default value is removed.

- A field's default value is added or changed.

- A non-union type may be changed to a union that contains only the original type, or vice versa.

The following are other best practices to follow so that you can avoid errors while adding the schema to the key-value store:

- Do not rename an existing field. Use an alias instead.

- While adding a new field, always provide a default value.

- Do not change a field's data type. If it has to be done, add a new field with the new data type.

Managing Avro Schemas

The Avro schemas may need to be managed on an ongoing basis. You can create or add a new schema, or modify, disable, or delete existing schemas. The following sections describe the basic commands for managing Avro schemas.

Create/Add a Schema

Now that you understand the different parts of an Avro schema and the ways of defining it, it's important to learn how to create it and use it in Oracle NoSQL Database to validate the "value" part of the key-value pair. The steps needed to accomplish that are:

1. Create the Avro schema (usually done in a text editor such as Notepad) and store it as a text file.

2. Add the Avro schema to the NoSQL data store.

3. Create a file called `userProfile-simple.avsc` with the simple schema that follows. We have intentionally inserted errors into the schema so we can explain the concept of debugging and adding the schemas.

    ```
    {
        "type" : "record",
        "name" : "userProfiles",
        "namespace" : "com.user.profiles",
        "fields" : [    {"name" : "FullName","type" : "string"},
                        {"name" : "UserName","type" : "string"},
                        {"name" : "age","type" :"int","default":"hello"}
    }
    ```

4. Make sure the key-value store (or KVLite) is running before executing the `runadmin` command. The `runadmin` command is used to start the CLI prompt in which you can run administration commands. Start the CLI by executing the following command:

    ```
    $>java -jar lib/kvstore.jar runadmin -port 5000 -host kc-PC
    kv->
    ```

5. Add the schema by using the `ddl add-schema` command, as shown here:

    ```
    kv-> ddl add-schema -file userProfile-simple.avsc
    ```

The preceding command results in the following error because there is a missing square bracket (]).

```
org.codehaus.jackson.JsonParseException: Unexpected close marker '}': expected ']'
(for ARRAY starting at [Source: java.io.StringReader@4a710a3e; line: 4, column: 37])
 at [Source: java.io.StringReader@4a710a3e; line: 8, column: 2]
```

You fix the error by adding the square bracket and then try to add the schema again.

```
kv-> ddl add-schema -file userProfile-simple.avsc
```

The schema was not added because one error and two warnings were detected.

To override warnings, specify -force. Errors cannot be overridden with -force.

This time you should see an error and two warnings. The error occurs because of a mismatch between the field type and the type of the default value assigned to it. The warnings result because of the missing default values on a few fields. Once the errors are fixed, only the warnings remain:

```
kv-> ddl add-schema -file userProfile-simple.avsc
```

The schema was not added because two warnings were detected.
To override the warnings, specify -force.

This may create some issues if your schema needs to evolve. If you have a strong business reason not to provide a default, then continue to add the schema by suppressing the warnings. To suppress these warnings and still add the schema, you need to use the -force option.

```
kv-> ddl add-schema -file userProfile-simple.avsc -force
```

6. Make sure your schema was successfully added by listing the available schemas. Even though the command prints all the schemas available in your key-value store, make sure that your schema was successfully added by listing the available schemas via the show schemas command.

```
kv-> show schemas
```

Change/Evolve a Schema
The process of modifying the schema is quite simple. You start by updating the schema definition file, and then run the CLI command to add the updated schema as a new

schema to the Avro catalog. The CLI command `ddl add-schema` is used with the `-evolve` flag.

The following example adds the gender type to the previous userProfiles schema. Start by opening the schema source file you used earlier for adding the first version of the schema, and then add a new field to make it look like the following:

```
{
    "type" : "record",
    "name" : "userProfiles",
    "namespace" : "com.user.profiles",
    "fields" : [ {"name" : "FullName","type" : "string"},
                 {"name" : "UserName","type" : "string"},
                 {"name" : "age","type" :"int","default":18},
                 {"name" : "gender","type" :"string","default":"unspecified"}
               ]
}
```

Now let's add the new schema to the key-value store by using the following command. Notice the option `-evolve`, which indicates that the same schema has evolved that was already present in the key-value store.

```
kv-> ddl add-schema -file userProfile-simple.avsc -evolve -force

Added schema: com.user.profiles.userProfiles.11
2 warnings were ignored.
```

To ensure that you have added a new version of the schema, run the `show schemas` command as follows:

```
kv-> show schemas
```

The preceding command should show that there are two versions of the same schema and that it has evolved.

Enable/Disable a Schema

There may be instances where a particular schema needs to be disabled because of an error in its definition of one or more fields. You can disable a schema as follows:

```
kv-> ddl disable-schema -name com.user.profiles.userProfiles.11

  Status updated to DISABLED
```

Show the List of All Schemas

After disabling the preceding schema because of the incorrect name, the name has been corrected and a new schema has been added. To show the list of all the available schemas, execute the following command:

```
kv-> show schemas
```

To list all the schemas, including the schemas that have been disabled in the previous steps, execute the following command:

```
kv-> show schemas -disabled
```

Avro Bindings

In the context of programming, a binding is defined as the technique of connecting two elements together. Avro bindings bind the schemas (that contain the structure of the data) to the data (the value part of the key-value pair). As you have already learned, the value part is stored in a space-efficient binary format in the key-value store. The Avro bindings are used during the storage (serialization) of Java objects into the space-efficient binary format and during the retrieval (deserialization) of the binary data into the computer's memory as Java objects. Avro bindings are stored in the Avro catalog in the key-value store along with the Avro schemas.

There are different types of Avro bindings and each type provides a different mechanism of handling the Avro data format. The data format itself does not change no matter what type of bindings are used. Also, whether or not you use Avro bindings for reading the key-value pairs, the APIs for performing CRUD (Create Update and Delete) operations do not change.

Oracle NoSQL Database provides four different kinds of Avro bindings:

- **Specific bindings**   A simple solution providing type safety and specifically designed for an Avro schema when the schemas are known ahead of time.

- **Generic bindings**   A binding solution without type safety and designed for situations when the schemas are not known ahead of time.

- **JSON bindings**   A binding solution suitable when interoperability with other applications in the web world involving JSON objects is desired.

- **Raw bindings**   An advanced binding solution that uses low-level Avro APIs for serializing and deserializing the data. `RawAvroBinding` specifies the Avro binary data as a byte array. It provides the least amount of safety and is the most difficult to use.

Attribute	Generic Binding	JSON Binding	Specific Binding
Value handled as	Generic record	JSON record	Specific record
Type safety handled	No	No	Yes
Need to know schemas at compile time	No	No	Yes
Need to know schemas at run time	Yes	Yes	No
Can be described in one phrase as	Simple and easy to use	Popular in the web world	Type safety

TABLE 7-2. *Key Attributes of Different Bindings*

Application architects choose to use a particular type of binding based on the characteristics of the real-world application. Table 7-2 compares the different aspects of the commonly used bindings and provides a reference to choose the right bindings based on the business use case.

The following methods may be used for retrieving specific, generic, and JSON bindings from the Avro catalog.

- **Single-schema binding** A single-schema binding provides type checking, which is considered a safe programming practice. In the case of specific binding, a single-schema binding provides compile-time type checking, and in the case of generic and JSON bindings, it provides runtime type checking.

- **Multiple-schema binding** A multi-schema binding is much more useful when reading key-value pairs of different types as it does not enforce type checking. All the different schemas that you may need to deal with in your application are added into the `HashMap`, which is a parameter that gets passed when obtaining the bindings from the catalog.

Records are read from the key-value store by first choosing the type of binding and then obtaining the binding using the single-schema or multi-schema binding methods. The type of the record that gets returned needs to be identified so that it can be displayed to the end user. If the key is built according to the application-specific knowledge and you know the type of value that it is going to hold, then you can use multi-schema bindings and the resulting records you obtain can be typecast based on knowledge of the application. If the keys are not built according to the application-specific knowledge, then it is safe to use a single-schema binding.

The type of the record returned from a query operation can be identified using the schema name or the class name of the returned object. The schema name can be used in the context of both generic and specific bindings, but the class name can only be used in the context of specific bindings because in the case of generic bindings the class name returned is always "generic record" irrespective of the schema name. If it is a specific record, you can typecast to that class and obtain the parameters using the specific getter and setter methods. If it is a generic record, then you get the individual values of properties based on strings and typecast them to the corresponding type to get the values.

Specific Bindings

Specific bindings can be defined as a binding solution designed individually for a specific schema in the key-value store. It is the easiest and safest binding to use among the different binding choices available. Specific bindings are used when the schemas are known ahead of time during application development or during compile time. The specific bindings make use of POJO (plain old Java objects) classes generated using Avro compiler tools that can be invoked from the Apache ANT build system. One or more POJO files are generated for every schema that you want to use the specific bindings for. The generated classes will have setter and getter methods for individual fields in the schema.

Programmatically, the specific bindings treat the value in the key-value pair as a specific record. Avro is relatively easy to use once the classes have been generated because you do not need to typecast the results, and you use the getter methods to get a particular value and setter methods to set a particular value for a field. The methods describe the fields (`first name`, `last name`, and so on) that you are setting and also specify the types (for example `int`, `string`, and so on) of the values. This provides type safety because you can only set a particular type of value into the method. The methods listed in Table 7-3 are the different ways of obtaining the specific bindings.

Binding Type	Method on Avro Catalog
Single-schema bindings	`AvroCatalog.getSpecificBinding()`
Multiple-schema binding	`AvroCatalog.getSpecificMultiBinding()`

TABLE 7-3. *Methods for Obtaining the Specific Bindings*

Generate Specific Java Files

You can generate the specific Java classes for the Avro schemas in different ways:

Directly Invoke the Avro-Tools Jar File   After manually downloading the avro-tools jar file, it can be directly invoked to generate code as follows:

```
java -jar /path/to/avro-tools-1.7.5.jar compile schema <schema file> <destination>
```

To generate the specific classes for your simple schema, run the following command:

```
java -jar C:/NOSQL/kv-2.0.26/bookExamples/avro/generate-specific-libs/
    avro-tools-1.6.3.jar compile schema ../userApps.avsc
```

Once the command is run, the schema is compiled and the required classes are generated in the destination folder using a directory structure that is based on the namespace of the schema.

Use a Build Tool such as ANT   You need to install a build tool such as ANT (version 1.6.0 or later) and create an ANT script file that will download the required jar files. The script then calls the SchemaTask tool, which is a Java class available through the avro-tools jar file; its namespace is `org.apache.avro.compiler.specific.SchemaTask`.

```
<target name="generate" depends="retrieve-libs">
  <taskdef name="schema"
           classname="org.apache.avro.compiler.specific.SchemaTask">
    <classpath refid="lib-classpath" />
  </taskdef>
  <schema destdir="${output.dir}" stringType="${stringType}">
    <fileset dir="${input.dir}">
      <include name="*.avsc" />
    </fileset>
  </schema>
</target>
```

The ANT script and the schema AVSC files are placed in the same directory, and the ANT script is invoked. Once you invoke the ANT tool, it uses the ANT script and picks up all the Avro script files in the local directory. It downloads many open source jar files, which are required for the specific binding creation. The jar files that are downloaded include the following:

- ANT
- Avro
- Avro compiler

- Avro tools
- Commons
- Jackson
- Snappy
- Velocity
- Sl4j

One Java class file per Avro schema is created if it defines a simple record. Multiple Java files are created for an Avro schema file if it defines embedded records. The tool creates the Java files in the same directory as the AVSC file when no namespace is used. Java files are created in the innermost directory of the specified namespace in the AVSC file if a namespace is used for the schemas.

NOTE
Use a build tool such as Maven that will download the required jars and invoke the avro-tools jar file. Note that if you are using the Avro Maven plugin, there is no need to manually invoke the schema compiler; the plugin automatically performs code generation on any .avsc files present in the configured source directory.

Specific Bindings Example

To illustrate the concept of specific bindings let's use the example of storing user profiles and usage data for trend analysis. You have already created the schema and also added it to the key-value store. You then generated the Java classes using the ANT-based Java class generation technique. Because this particular schema is based on a record with two more embedded records, a total of three Java POJOs will be created. The following high-level steps are performed in the sample program.

- Insert a simple key-value pair into the key-value store.
- The value is based on the Avro schema with the namespace
  `com.user.profiles.userProfilesDetailed.`
- Specific Bindings are used to insert and extract data from the key-value store

In the following code, the handle to the Avro catalog is obtained and a specific Avro binding based on our POJO is declared. You need to ensure that the Java class is imported into the eclipse project for it to be available to use.

```
final AvroCatalog catalog = store.getAvroCatalog();
final SpecificAvroBinding<userProfilesDetailed> sbinding;
sbinding = catalog.getSpecificBinding(com.user.profiles.userProfilesDetailed.class);
```

In the following code, an object of type `userProfilesDetailed` is created and the different variables are set using the setter methods you have in the generated Avro classes for the different properties.

```
userProfilesDetailed profileToInsert = new userProfilesDetailed();
profileInformation pi = new profileInformation();
usageInformationLastMonth ui = new usageInformationLastMonth();

userProfilesDetailed profileRead = new userProfilesDetailed();

pi.setAge(25);
pi.setEducation("Graduate");
pi.setPhone("469-525-6725");
pi.setProfession("Lawyer");

ui.setAvgNumberOfLikes(45);
ui.setAvgNumberOfLoginsPerDay(5);
ui.setAvgNumberOfMinutesSpentPerDay(130);
ui.setAvgNumberOfShares(3);
ui.setNumberOfPostingsOnWall(2);

profileToInsert.setUserName("tsmith");
profileToInsert.setFullName("TanyaSmith");
profileToInsert.setProfileDetails(pi);
profileToInsert.setUsageDetails(ui);
```

The user profile object created is serialized using `Binding.toValue()` so that it can be written to the key-value store. The serialized value is passed on as the `value` parameter for the store `put()` method. Let's assume here that a store handle and a key are already created:

```
Key myKey = Key.createKey("tsmith");
store.put(myKey, sbinding.toValue(profileToInsert));
```

Once inserted, you retrieve the key-value pair and read the content using the specific bindings you have created. You do not have to typecast values as you do in the case of generic bindings because you have specific getter functions for each property in the Avro schema.

```
vv = store.get(myKey);
if (vv != null) {
profileRead = sbinding.toObject(vv.getValue());
```

The value that is obtained from the get method is deserialized using the Binding.toObject() method. This returns a specific record of type userProfilesDetailed object. You do not have to typecast the values as you had to in generic bindings because you have specific getter functions for each of the properties of the Avro schema object.

```
System.out.println("The content read from the key-value store using specific bindings
    is the following:");
System.out.println("Facebook UserName:"+profileRead.getUserName());
System.out.println("Facebook user Full Name:"+profileRead.getFullName());
System.out.println("Facebook Avg Number of Likes in Last Month:"+profileRead
    .getUsageDetails().getAvgNumberOfLikes());
System.out.println("Facebook User Education Level:"+profileRead.getProfileDetails()
    .getEducation());
```

The following is the console output of the program:

```
The content read from the key-value store using specific bindings is the following:
Facebook UserName:tsmith
Facebook user Full Name:TanyaSmith
Facebook Avg Number of Likes in Last Month:45
Facebook User Education Level:Graduate
```

This concludes the sample program to help you understand the use of specific bindings for a single schema.

How to Manage Multiple Schemas in Case of Specific Bindings

In the previous section, you learned that specific bindings can be obtained from the key-value store catalog either for a single schema or for multiple schemas. Also, in the previous example, you obtained bindings for one class or schema. The following example demonstrates how to obtain specific bindings for multiple schemas. When an ANT script is used for generating classes, they are generated for all the schemas available in the directory from where the ANT script is invoked. In our example, the Java classes (POJOs) were generated for userProfilesDetailed schema and also the userApps schema. userApps schema stores the details for the different applications available in the user app store.

The schema definition is as follows:

```
{
"type" : "record",
"name" : "userApps",
"namespace" : "com.user.profiles",
"fields" : [ {"name" : "AppName",
"type" : "string"},
{"name" : "AppDesc",
"type" : "string"},
{"name" : "AppDetails",
"type" : {
"type" :"record",
"name" : "ApplicationInformation",
"fields" : [
{"name" : "Genre",
"type" : "string",
"default":"NONE"},
{"name" : "NumberOfUsers",
"type" : "int",
"default":0},
{"name" : "Publisher",
"type" : "string",
"default":"NONE"},
{"name" : "AvailableOn",
"type" : "string",
"default":"iphone,ipad,facebook.com,android"}
]
}
}
]
}
final AvroCatalog catalog = store.getAvroCatalog();
final SpecificAvroBinding<SpecificRecord> binding;
SpecificRecord specificRec;
binding = catalog.getSpecificMultiBinding();
```

The Avro catalog is obtained from the store and the specific multiple-schema bindings are obtained from the catalog. The keys are created and values inserted for the userProfilesDetailed and the userApps objects in much the same way as the previous example of single-schema specific binding.

```
Key myUserKey = Key.createKey("myUserProfile");
Key myAppKey = Key.createKey("myAppProfile");

store.put(myUserKey, binding.toValue(profileToInsert));
store.put(myAppKey, binding.toValue(appToInsert));
```

The real key difference, in handling the single-schema binding and multiple-schema binding, lies in reading the values from the key-value store. The different steps followed are

- Use the key to obtain a `ValueVersion`.

- Use the `toObject` method on the binding to assign it to an instance of a specific record.

- Compare the schema full name to the intended class name and typecast it accordingly.

```
vv = store.get(myUserKey);
if (vv != null) {
        specificRec = binding.toObject(vv.getValue());
if(specificRec.getSchema().getFullName()
   .equals("com.user.profiles.userProfilesDetailed"))
   {
            profileRead = (userProfilesDetailed)specificRec;
   }
System.out.println("The content read from the KVStore using specific
   bindings for the user profile details schema is the following:");
System.out.println("username:"+profileRead.getUserName());
System.out.println("user Full Name:"+profileRead.getFullName());
System.out.println("Profession:"+profileRead.getProfileDetails()
   .getProfession());
System.out.println("Number Of Likes:"+profileRead.getUsageDetails()
   .getAvgNumberOfLikes());
```

The piece of code that follows shows that the same binding can be used for the different schema, and after checking the type of the specific record and typecasting it, you can obtain its values and print it out.

```
vv = store.get(myAppKey);
if (vv != null) {

    specificRec = binding.toObject(vv.getValue());
    System.out.println("The class of the specific record is "+specificRec
       .getClass().toString());
    if(specificRec.getSchema().getFullName()
                 .equals("com.user.profiles.facebookApps"))
       {
            appReadFromStore = (facebookApps)specificRec;
       }
System.out.println("The content read from the KVStore using specific bindings for
  the user App Schema is the following:");
System.out.println("user App Name:"+appReadFromStore.getAppName());
System.out.println("user App Genre
  Name:"+appReadFromStore.getAppDetails().getGenre());
```

The output of the console is as follows:

```
The content read from the key-value store using specific bindings for
the user profile details schema is as follows:

username:wsmith
user Full Name:WillSmith
Profession:technical
Number Of Likes:14

The class of the specific record is class com.user.profiles.userApps.
The content read from the key-value store using specific bindings for
the user App Schema is as follows:

user App Name:Farmville
user App Genre Name:Games
```

This concludes the sample program, and you should now have a better understanding of specific bindings that are based on multiple schemas.

Generic Bindings

Generic bindings are a solution for multiple schemas and provide a wide range of support for Avro data types. Generic bindings treat the value in a key-value pair as a "generic record" and are useful when the schemas are not known ahead of time. Values are inserted into the fields by specifying them using the string name of the field and by using generic get and set methods. There are no specific methods, as there are with specific bindings, and type safety needs to be carefully handled for generic bindings. The object fields and methods are not known during the development of the Java client programs or during compile time.

To explain the concept of generic bindings better, let's consider the hypothetical use case of building a web application for exploring the different apps in the app store of the social networking website. Assume that the descriptions of every app are unique and are to be stored in the key-value store. The number of apps, the variation in the apps, and also the speed at which the apps get created are all high. The velocity, variety, and volume with which the new apps get added to the store are high and the schemas of the apps are constantly evolving with customer needs. So you cannot use specific bindings in this case because the classes have to be generated every time there is a change in the schema of the particular app. Also, many new apps may be created after the completion of the development of this application explorer. So the best possible solution for this situation is to use generic bindings.

Binding Type	Method on Avro Catalog
Single-schema bindings	`AvroCatalog.getGenericBinding()`
Multiple-schema binding	`AvroCatalog.getGenericMultiBinding()`

TABLE 7-4. *Methods for Obtaining the Generic Bindings*

As you look at the same example of the app explorer, assume that two new games, Autoville and Scrubsville, with different schemas, have been added to the user app store. We'll use these two games to explain the following aspects of generic bindings:

■ Single-schema generic bindings (using Autoville)

■ Multiple-schema generic bindings (using Autoville and Scrubsville)

Table 7-4 details the important methods that we will look into as part of the sample programs.

Single-Schema Binding Example

We explore single-schema bindings with the Autoville app schema. In the sample program, we insert a key-value pair into the key-value store based on the Autoville app schema using generic bindings and then read it back. The simple schema looks like this:

```
{
"type" : "record",
"name" : "autoville",
"namespace" : "com.user.appProfiles.games",
"fields" : [ {"name" : "ApplicationDescription","type" : "string"},
{"name" : "MaxNumberOfplayers","type" : "int","default":5},
{"name" : "NumberOfFreeLevels","type" : "int","default":0},
{"name" : "AgeRestriction","type" : "string","default":"NONE"}
]
}
```

Once we create the schema, we add the schema to our key-value store and verify that it is added by using the `show schemas` command:

```
kv-> ddl add-schema -file facebookApps-Autoville.avsc -force
Added schema: com.facebook.appProfiles.games.autoville.15
1 warning was ignored.
```

The schema parser reads the Avro schema file in the local machine:

```
final Schema.Parser parser = new Schema.Parser();

try{
    parser.parse(new File("C:/NOSQL/kv-2.0.26/bookExamples/avro/userApps-Autoville
       .avsc"));
    }catch(IOException e){e.printStackTrace();}

final Schema appSchema =
         parser.getTypes().get("com.user.appProfiles.games.autoville");
```

The Avro catalog is obtained from the key-value store, after which the generic bindings for the schema are obtained. We create a generic record based on the schema so that we can initialize it and then insert the generic record into the value portion of the key-value pair.

```
final AvroCatalog catalog = store.getAvroCatalog();
final GenericAvroBinding binding = catalog.getGenericBinding(appSchema);

final GenericRecord appInfo = new GenericData.Record(appSchema);

appInfo.put("ApplicationDescription", "This is a game with
activities surrounding an auto body shop");
appInfo.put("MaxNumberOfplayers",10);
appInfo.put("NumberOfFreeLevels",3);
appInfo.put("AgeRestriction","Yes");
```

Now to write this generic record into the key-value store as the value portion of a key-value pair, we need to serialize this information using the `toValue()` function of the generic binding handle we obtained. A simple key is created so that we can try to insert the key-value pair.

```
Key myKey = Key.createKey("autoville");
store.put(myKey, binding.toValue(appInfo));
```

We use the same key to obtain the value from the key-value store as a `valueversion` object. We deserialize the value into a generic record object. We typecast the values we obtain because we are using the generic bindings. The string input gets stored as UTF8 so we cast them back to a UTF8 object. We print the values that we obtained to the console to verify the contents. Finally, as a best practice, we close the key-value store.

```
final GenericRecord member;
Utf8 appDesc;
int numberOfPlayers;
ValueVersion vv=null;
```

```
vv = store.get(myKey);
if (vv != null) {

member = binding.toObject(vv.getValue());

// we are type casting the values we obtain since we are using the generic bindings
// which we do not know the type

appDesc = (Utf8) member.get("ApplicationDescription");
numberOfPlayers = (int) member.get("MaxNumberOfplayers");

System.out.println("Autoville Schema desc: "+appDesc);
System.out.println("Maximum number of players allowed: "+numberOfPlayers);

}

store.close();
```

The console output of the previous program is as follows:

```
Autoville Schema desc: This is a game with activities surrounding an auto body shop
Maximum number of players allowed: 10
```

This example has demonstrated how to use the single-schema generic binding method.

Multiple-Schema Binding Example

Now let's look at the use of multiple-schema binding by adding the Scrubsville app schema. We use a hash map to organize our schemas and we also create the bindings using the getGenericMultiBinding method. The new schema is as follows:

```
{
"type" : "record",
"name" : "scrubsville",
"namespace" : "com.user.appProfiles.games",
"fields" : [ {"name" : "Description","type" : "string"},
{"name" : "numberOfPlayers","type" : "int","default":10},
{"name" : "trialPeriodInMonths","type" : "int","default":0},
{"name" : "minAgeRequirement","type" : "string","default":"NONE"}
]
}
```

Now the schema is added to the key-value store:

```
kv-> ddl add-schema -file facebookApps-Scrubsville.avsc -force

  Added schema: com.facebook.appProfiles.games.scrubsville.14
  1 warning was ignored.
```

Now we are going to access information of two schemas: Autoville and Scrubsville. We present the key parts of our sample code to explain the concept of `genericMultiBindings`. A hash map is created to store all the schemas available in the store that need to be read from and written into.

```
HashMap<String, Schema> multiSchemas = new HashMap<String, Schema>();
final Schema.Parser parser = new Schema.Parser();

try {
parser.parse(new File("C:/NOSQL/kv-2.0.26/bookExamples/avro/
userApps-Autoville.avsc"));
} catch (IOException e) {
e.printStackTrace();
}

final Schema autovilleSchema = parser.getTypes()
.get("com.user.appProfiles.games.autoville");
multiSchemas.put(autovilleSchema.getFullName(), autovilleSchema);

try {
parser.parse(new File("C:/NOSQL/kv-2.0.26/bookExamples/avro/
userApps-Scrubsville.avsc"));
} catch (IOException e) {
e.printStackTrace();
}

final Schema scrubsvilleSchema = parser.getTypes()
.get("com.user.appProfiles.games.scrubsville");
multiSchemas.put(scrubsvilleSchema.getFullName(), scrubsvilleSchema);
```

The parser obtains the schemas and puts them in the hash map we created previously. The Avro catalog handle is obtained from the key-value store and the bindings are obtained by the `genericMultiBindings` method, which enables us to handle the multiple schemas using the same bindings:

```
final AvroCatalog catalog = store.getAvroCatalog();
final GenericAvroBinding binding = catalog.getGenericMultiBinding(multiSchemas);
```

We create a generic records for the Autoville app data and the Scrubsville app data and insert them into the key-value store. To verify, we obtain the value from the key-value store using the same key and print out the contents. We use the `toValue` and the `toObject` methods of the bindings to serialize and deserialize.

```
final GenericRecord avilleData = new GenericData.Record(autovilleSchema);

avilleData.put("ApplicationDescription", "This is a user game with activities
    surrounding an auto body shop");
avilleData.put("MaxNumberOfplayers",10);
avilleData.put("NumberOfFreeLevels",3);
avilleData.put("AgeRestriction","Yes");

Key myKey = Key.createKey("autovilleKey");

store.put(myKey, binding.toValue(avilleData));
```

Now that we have inserted the Autoville app data, let's insert the key-value pair for the second app:

```
final GenericRecord svilleData = new GenericData.Record(scrubsvilleSchema);

svilleData.put("Description", "This is a user game with activities surrounding an auto
    body shop");
svilleData.put("numberOfPlayers",10);
svilleData.put("trialPeriodInMonths",3);
svilleData.put("minAgeRequirement","Yes");

Key myKey1 = Key.createKey("scrubsvilleKey");

store.put(myKey1, binding.toValue(svilleData));
```

We have already inserted data using generic bindings, but the most important part of using the `genericMultiBindings` is reading the data from the key-value store. The data is read in the following way:

```
final GenericRecord avilleReadFromStore;
ValueVersion vv = store.get(myKey);
if (vv != null) {
    avilleReadFromStore = binding.toObject(vv.getValue());
    System.out.println("class:"+avilleReadFromStore.getClass().toString());
    System.out.println("schema:"+avilleReadFromStore.getSchema().getFullName());
```

The following is the console output for the two print statements:

```
class:class org.apache.avro.generic.GenericData$Record
schema:com.facebook.appProfiles.games.autoville
```

The only parameter that needs to be passed to the `get` method to read from the key-value store is the key. When you read from the key-value store based on `genericMultiBindings` you get a generic record back. The generic record can be of any specific type corresponding to the different schemas present in the schema map based on which we obtained the bindings from the catalog. The following are the different ways of identifying the type of the generic record:

- The key structure passed to read from the key-value store should be based on some application-specific knowledge so that we can identify the type from that.

- The schema name from the generic record object helps us identify the type of the generic record.

The class name is not helpful because it always gives the same result (as the preceding console output), and it does not help us identify what type the generic record holds from among the multiple schemas. Once we have identified the schema, then we can read and typecast based on the information from the schema.

Print code:

```
System.out.println("Autoville Description:
    +(Utf8)avilleReadFromStore.get("ApplicationDescription"));
System.out.println("Autoville Maximum Players Allowed:
    +avilleReadFromStore.get("MaxNumberOfplayers"));
System.out.println("Autoville Free Levels:
    +avilleReadFromStore.get("NumberOfFreeLevels"));
System.out.println("Autoville Is there Age Restriction:
    +(Utf8)avilleReadFromStore.get("AgeRestriction"));
}
```

Console output:

```
Autoville Description: This is a facebook game with activities
surrounding an auto body shop
Autoville Maximum Players Allowed: 10
Autoville Free Levels: 3
Autoville Is there Age Restriction: Yes
```

The second schema of Scrubsville can also be read in a similar way.
This concludes the example to explain the multiple-schema generic bindings.

How to Manage Multiple Schemas when You Do Not Know How Many

In the previous example, we were able to handle two different schemas because we knew that two different schemas existed. However, in the fast-paced business data environment of today, we may not know how many schemas exist ahead of time or when new schemas get added. The previous strategy of using a hash map to store all the schemas may require a lot of rework whenever a new schema is added. So as a remedy to the problem, we have the `getCurrentSchemas()` method available on the `AvroCatalog` object which will give us all the current schemas available.

```
final AvroCatalog catalog = store.getAvroCatalog();
final GenericAvroBinding binding = catalog.
getGenericMultiBinding(catalog.getCurrentSchemas());
```

The rest of the process does not change, so for the sake of brevity we move to the next topic.

JSON Bindings

JSON bindings is an effective Avro binding solution when JSON objects are involved. JSON (JavaScript Object Notation) is a collection of name/value pairs. In the web application world, JSON is popular. JSON objects might be directly provided to your NoSQL client application, and they need to be stored in the Oracle NoSQL key-value store.

To facilitate this, Oracle NoSQL has provided the JSON bindings so that you can serialize the JSON objects and store them directly into the key-value store. Using a JSON binding may be convenient for those applications that publish JSON objects to their clients and wish to streamline the return of objects directly from the key-value store. JSON bindings treat the value in a key-value pair as a JSON record. For example, applications that expose REST interface–based APIs tend to return data as JSON strings so they are a great use case for JSON bindings.

In a real-world scenario, the JSON objects may need to be written to your key-value store based on a call from another web service or web application, but in order to explain the concept in our sample program, we simply read the JSON object from the local file system. JSON bindings are very similar to the generic bindings, in the sense that they do not provide type safety. The schemas need not be known ahead of time at compile time. The JSON Avro binding has APIs to support single-schema binding and multi-schema binding. Table 7-5 lists the different methods of obtaining the JSON bindings.

Binding Type	Method on Avro Catalog
Single-schema bindings	`AvroCatalog.getJsonBinding()`
Multiple-schema binding	`AvroCatalog.getJsonMultiBinding()`

TABLE 7-5. *Methods for Obtaining the JSON Bindings*

The following sample program includes step-by-step information so you understand how JSON bindings are used to deal with values in the key-value pairs.

1. We use a parser to get the schema and this schema determines the JSON object:

```
final Schema.Parser parser = new Schema.Parser();
try {
parser.parse(new File(
"C:/NOSQL/kv-2.0.26/bookExamples/avro/gPersonSimple.avsc"));
} catch (IOException e) {
e.printStackTrace();
}
final Schema personNameSchema = parser.getTypes()
.get("avro.PersonName");
```

2. Obtain the Avro catalog and get the JSON bindings from the instance for the schema you obtained in Step 1:

```
final AvroCatalog catalog = store.getAvroCatalog();
final JsonAvroBinding binding = catalog
.getJsonBinding(personNameSchema);
```

3. Read the JSON object from filesystem and create a JSON record based on the object and the schema:

```
try {
final BufferedReader r = new BufferedReader(new FileReader("C:/
NOSQL/kv-2.0.26/bookExamples/avro/authors.json.txt"));
final StringBuilder buf = new StringBuilder(10000);
String line;
while ((line = r.readLine()) != null) {
buf.append(line);
buf.append("\n");
}

final ObjectMapper jsonMapper = new ObjectMapper();
final JsonNode jsonObject = jsonMapper.readTree(buf.toString());
final JsonRecord jsonRecord = new JsonRecord(jsonObject,
personNameSchema);
```

4. Serialize and create a value based on JSON bindings; create a key and store it in the key-value store:

```
final Value value = binding.toValue(jsonRecord);

Key myKey = Key.createKey("tennisStar");

store.put(myKey, value);

ValueVersion vv = null;
```

5. Obtain the value version based on the key, and by deserializing with the JSON bindings, create a `JsonRecord` and print out the value for verification:

```
vv = store.get(myKey);
if (vv != null) {

JsonRecord jr = binding.toObject(vv.getValue());

ObjectNode on = (ObjectNode) jr.getJsonNode();

System.out
.println("The toString() value obtained from the JSON record
read from the KVStore is "
+ on.toString());
```

The output from the console looks like this:

```
The toString() value obtained from the JSON record read from the
KVStore is {"FirstName":"Andy","LastName":"Murray"}
```

This section has provided a deeper understanding of JSON bindings using the sample code.

How to Manage Multiple Schemas when You Do Not Know How Many

In the above example, we have obtained JSON bindings for a single schema. We can also handle multiple schemas using the `getJsonMultiBinding` method. To address the situation of many schemas that are not known ahead of time, we have a method available called the `getCurrentSchemas()` on the `AvroCatalog` object which will give us the map of all the current schemas available in the catalog. This schema map can be passed to the getJsonMultiBinding method to get the JSON bindings.

```
final AvroCatalog catalog = store.getAvroCatalog();
final JSONAvroBinding binding = catalog.getJsonMultiBinding(catalog
  .getCurrentSchemas());
```

The rest of the process for reading the key-value pairs does not change, so for the sake of brevity we conclude this topic.

Summary

The value portion in a key-value pair may need to be based on a particular format and rules. The format and rules are described by the use of an Avro schema. An Avro schema is represented using a JSON object. You apply a schema to the value portion of the key-value pair using Avro bindings. The different kinds of bindings available are generic, specific, JSON, and raw. Different bindings have different characteristics which make them suitable to use in different real-world scenarios. Oracle NoSQL provides a rich set of APIs to enable the application programmer to effectively use Avro schemas and bindings.

CHAPTER
8

Capacity Planning
and Sizing

An essential step before installing Oracle NoSQL Database in a datacenter is to first understand the Oracle NoSQL Database application requirements and use this information to properly size and configure the underlying hardware. This ensures that the database can not only support the performance throughput required by the application, but also provide the right levels of availability and reliability, as these characteristics are heavily influenced by the choice and capacity of the hardware. This chapter discusses the best practices of capacity planning and sizing an enterprise-level Oracle NoSQL Database deployment.

Capacity planning is not an absolute science, and the process of estimating the sizing numbers is dependent on certain assumptions, such as the characteristics of the application workload, database disk space requirements, and high availability requirements. The assumptions help simplify the underlying estimation models (formulas and calculations) so they are generalized to work with a wide range of application requirements. Otherwise, you would be overwhelmed with complex formulas and theories, and might even consider dropping the capacity planning steps altogether.

Note that the sizing numbers obtained from this exercise are estimates at best, and are only as accurate as the inputs supplied and the estimation models used for the calculations. Therefore, these numbers should only be used as the basis for initial sizing, and should be validated by following proper performance and load testing methods, preferably under simulated or real-world workloads. The initial numbers may then be refined if necessary, which indicates that the capacity planning process is a bit iterative. The key here is to ensure that the findings are in line with the assumptions made earlier in the process, and, if not, you may need to adjust the assumptions accordingly.

NOTE
Microsoft Excel spreadsheets are provided by Oracle to assist you with sizing Oracle NoSQL Database. The spreadsheet takes input parameters such as the replication factor, disk capacity, key-value pair size, application performance requirements, and so on, and provides approximate sizing numbers. Refer to the Oracle NoSQL Database installation directory and the Oracle NoSQL Database manuals for further information.

Gather Sizing Requirements

One of the very first steps of capacity planning is the application discovery process, in which key metrics related to the characteristics of Oracle NoSQL Database application and the specifications of the available or reference hardware are captured. These metrics are later input into the sizing models and the topology of the Oracle NoSQL Database is architected.

Some of the metrics such as the Input/Output Operations per Second (IOPS) and the application *hot data* size (explained later) are difficult to estimate, as there are no standard, plug-and-play formulas available. However, there are industry standard best practices that can be followed to estimate such metrics, which are the focus of this section. Also keep in mind that the best practices are usually generic, and the initial estimates you may come up with by following them may be approximate and sometimes even a bit off, and not applicable to the specific type of workload you are dealing with. Therefore, testing and validating the sizing numbers and, if required, revising them iteratively to get the desired results, should be considered normal.

The following sections provide instructions on capturing application characteristics and the hardware specifications.

Application Characteristics

While it is relatively easy to capture the characteristics of existing NoSQL Database applications (both Oracle or non-Oracle), it is always tricky for brand-new applications because the application characteristics are not readily available and you have to work with estimates and heuristics at best.

For existing applications or systems undergoing a technology or a hardware refresh and moving to Oracle NoSQL Database, you can capture their characteristics using a variety of readily available tools and techniques. For example, transaction throughput, response times, and latency can be measured by using application workload metrics, and I/O performance, memory, and CPU utilization can be measured using OS utilities. You will also have a good idea of a reference hardware configuration utilized by the previous database, which can also serve as an initial baseline configuration for testing.

The intent of this section is to assist you with estimating the application characteristics of brand-new applications. Application characteristics of interest are mainly the key-value pair storage capacity requirements, the application performance metrics, and the replication factor to ensure high availability.

Key-Value Pair Size

The data stored within Oracle NoSQL Database is primarily a set of key-value pairs. In order to estimate the Oracle NoSQL Database storage requirements, determine the average size of a key-value pair (in UTF-8 bytes) and the total number of key-value pairs to be stored in the database. Multiply these two estimates to get the total size of the key-value store.

To accurately estimate the key-value size, it is important to understand the underlying design of its components. As you may recall, key-value pairs have a *key* component and a *value* component; keys in turn can consist of a *major* key and a *minor* key, and keys can be small or large. Basically, this means that the key storage requirements could be quite variable and depend mostly on the key design, the application access patterns, and the specific use case. Obviously, larger keys have bigger storage needs. Once you have determined a key design, estimate the average size in bytes of both the major and the minor keys, averaged over the total estimated number of key-value pairs in the store.

Similarly for the *value* component, estimate the average size of data in bytes, kilobytes, or megabytes for all the values to be stored in the database. Values are much larger than keys as they store the actual data, versus the path to get to the data, as keys do. Finally, estimate the total number of key-value pairs, as earlier indicated.

The database growth requirements over time would also need to be factored into these calculations. You would not want to be in a position where you have used up all the allocated hardware in only a few weeks or months after going live in production. Growth can be both planned and unplanned, and you can usually form a good estimate by speaking with the key stakeholders and data owners, and evaluating their past experiences and historical patterns.

For an example of estimating Oracle NoSQL Database key-value storage requirements, consider a scenario where the average key size is 32 bytes, the average value size is 1KB, and the total estimated number of records is 1 billion for the first year, with a 20 percent yearly growth projection. To estimate the Oracle NoSQL Database storage requirements for the next two years, use the following equation:

$$(\text{Avg. key size} + \text{avg. value size}) * (\text{Total records} + \text{Estimated growth})$$

$$= (32 + 1024) * (1{,}000{,}000{,}000 + (20\% \times 1{,}000{,}000{,}000))$$

$$= 1{,}267{,}200{,}000{,}000 \text{ bytes or } 1.15\text{TB}$$

NOTE
Keep in mind that the preceding number is the user data capacity and not the raw disk capacity. You will compute the raw disk capacity later in this chapter.

Performance Requirements

Typical workload characteristics of NoSQL Database applications follow patterns similar to that of OLTP systems. Therefore, the application performance metrics of interest are OLTP workload–specific, such as memory requirements and I/O throughput capacity requirements. More specifically, you can capture metrics such as *latency*, *block size*, *IOPS*, *read-to-write ratio*, and the *cache-hit ratio*, which are a common measure of OLTP application performance.

- *Latency* is the time for data travel from point A to point B, for example from hard disk platters to application memory buffers. Latencies from memory to memory are usually 100,000 times faster from disk to memory. This metric will help you decide if the latencies of hard disk are acceptable to the application, or if you need to consider flash disks or cache data in memory (DRAM). Just to give you an idea, hard disk latencies are on the order of 10–20 milliseconds, whereas latency of flash memory and DRAM are 2–4 milliseconds and 100 nanoseconds, respectively.

■ *Block size* is defined by the application and is a minimum unit of moving data between the storage and application buffers. The larger the block size, the longer it takes to move data. Typical block sizes used for measuring I/O performance by vendors vary between 4KB and 32KB. This should not be confused with the OS block size, which is defined at the OS level and is much smaller than the application block size (typically 512 bytes).

■ *IOPS (Input/Output Operations per Second)* is the rate of measure of small I/O reads/writes per second. The objective of measuring IOPS is to see how fast the storage is capable of writing (or reading) transactions that span a small number of disk blocks, usually of size 1 block size. IOPS numbers are primarily dependent on random seek time of storage devices, although rotational speed and latency also play an important role. IOPS can be measured for reads, writes, or a mix of read/write transactions, with a typical 4KB or 8KB block size.

Retrieval operations of key-value records are translated to short I/Os or random I/Os, a key characteristic of OLTP workloads. Short I/Os are quick reads (and generally writes as well) of small chunks of data, where the chunk is defined using the block size.

■ *Read-to-write ratio* is the ratio of the total read I/O requests issued by the application to the total I/O requests (reads + writes). For example, a read-to-write ratio of 60:40 indicates that three read I/Os are issued by the workload for every two write I/Os.

A typical OLTP workload contains a combination of reads and writes. It is important to estimate the read-to-write ratio of the application workload as they each have different performance characteristics. Reads can be cached in a faster memory such as DRAM, if the workload periodically issues repeated reads on the same data (*hot dataset*, discussed next), and cache access is much faster than the hard disk.

Oracle NoSQL Database write I/O requests, on the other hand, are usually much faster than the read I/O requests because the underlying engine of Oracle NoSQL Database can batch multiple writes in memory and issue one sequential write I/O per batch to the disk. This behavior occurs because of the log file–based write methodology used by the underlying Oracle Berkeley DB Java Edition, and will be discussed later in the chapter.

- When sizing memory requirements, it is important to know the size of the *hot dataset* and the *cache-hit ratio*. The data access pattern of typical OLTP applications is usually concentrated over a small subset that is frequently read or updated the most when compared to the rest. This active subset is commonly referred to as the *hot* dataset (also called the working set), whereas data that is infrequently or rarely accessed is referred to as the *warm* or the *cold* dataset. *Hot, warm,* and *cold* datasets are key aspects of all OLTP workloads.

  Estimating the size of the hot dataset of the application is an important factor for estimating its memory and I/O performance needs. Several studies suggest that hot datasets in OLTP systems as a rule of thumb are approximately 20 percent of the total database size. Just imagine if you were able to cache this 20 percent data in a faster memory such as the DRAM or flash; the I/O performance achieved could be multiple orders of magnitude greater than the performance of hard disks.

- *Cache-hit ratio* is the ratio of reads or writes from the cached dataset to reads or writes from the hard disk (physical I/O). The cached dataset could be the complete or a partial hot dataset. The cache-hit ratio plays a crucial part in sizing the application for performance, as you will see later in this chapter, so it is essential that you spend time to accurately estimate this metric to the best of your ability and knowledge.

NOTE
Sizing for CPU capacity is also critical for the capacity planning exercise. However, by following the best practices of balanced hardware configurations, CPU bottlenecks can be avoided especially when the application workload is I/O bound. The balanced configuration eliminates bottlenecks in the I/O path during the movement of data from the disk to memory, via the network, disk controllers, and CPU. If the workload is CPU-bound, then essential steps need to be followed to ensure that CPU capacity is also properly sized. CPU sizing is beyond the scope of this book.

Determine the Replication Factor

Oracle NoSQL Database contains one or more shards, and each shard contains one or more Replication Nodes. The shards can internally store multiple copies of the key-value pairs by specifying a storewide *replication factor* (RF). The RF specifies the total number of RNs contained in the shard. Also, one of the RNs within the shard is designated as the *master* node, and the remaining RNs are the *replica* nodes. For example, a replication factor of *three* indicates that each shard will have *three* RNs, out of which *one* RN is a master and *two* RNs are replicas.

A master node can handle read and write requests of key-value pairs, whereas a replica node can handle only read requests. The master node propagates the write requests to all replicas, so at any given point in time (or eventually at some point in time, based on the durability guarantees), all RNs within the shard will be synchronized to contain the same key-value pair data.

NOTE
If a master node is lost, a master election process is initiated using the industry standard set of Paxos protocols, and one of the existing replicas is elected as the new master.

There are several benefits to having a higher replication factor. First, the data availability is increased when you store multiple copies of the same data in different RNs. The key-value pairs are still available (albeit performance to retrieve them could be slow) to the application as long as there is one surviving Replication Node per shard, thereby providing a tolerance of (*RF*–1) failures within a shard.

Second, the higher the replication factor, the faster the read I/O performance as multiple RNs are available to serve application read requests. The Oracle NoSQL Database client driver directs the read request to the least busy Replication Node with the intent of getting the fastest response for the request.

Third, the total read I/O throughput capacity for the shard is also increased when the replication factor is increased. For example, if one RN has a capacity of 500 IOPS and the application requires a read throughput of 1500 IOPS, then a replication factor of 3 can satisfy the 1500 IOPS requirement. By having more RNs, you also get more disks that work in parallel to serve multiple I/O requests.

There are a few drawbacks to configuring a high replication factor as well. The write I/O performance does not scale by adding more Replication Nodes. In fact, it may degrade because the writes need to be synchronized across as many Replication Nodes as there are in the shard. You can configure durability guarantees in the application to propagate the changes asynchronously, but as far as the disks are concerned, all changes on the master will be pushed to all replicas, either sooner or later. Also, a higher replication factor results in a higher number of Storage Nodes needed for deploying Oracle NoSQL Database, thereby increasing the hardware cost.

As a best practice, you should configure a replication factor of 3 for Oracle NoSQL Database. You may consider a higher replication factor if the application read I/O performance dictates the need to go beyond 3. Keep in mind that the write performance may be affected with the increase as mentioned earlier.

A replication factor of 2 is generally discouraged for the following reasons. First, a single failure will result in too few Replication Nodes remaining to elect a new master, leaving the shard vulnerable to the possible loss of write availability. Second, the shard throughput capacity drops 50 percent when only one node fails, which is not ideal for any production-grade SLAs. Finally, as the shard node failure tolerance is limited to only one node, the risk of losing data runs high in your deployment.

A replication factor of 1 is definitely not recommended for any production-grade Oracle NoSQL Database deployment, as there is no inherent protection from data loss. A loss of a single disk or a node would warrant a recovery from a backup.

Hardware Specifications

Capturing the specifications of the available hardware is essential for calculating the shard I/O throughput capacity and the disk storage capacity, which are key elements in determining the total number of Storage Nodes required for Oracle NoSQL Database.

If the hardware has not yet been procured for the project, you may start with a baseline specification of a reference hardware normally used for projects of such types. It is important to start with a baseline; otherwise, it would be impossible to determine the Oracle NoSQL Database topology without knowing the individual configuration of the Storage Nodes.

Note that the hardware specifications may need to be revised once you undergo the capacity planning exercise and learn of the new sizing numbers. For example, you may start with a reference machine of 16GB of memory and three hard disks of 1TB capacity, and determine after the capacity planning exercise that to best satisfy the cost and performance requirements, it may be feasible to have a machine with 32GB of memory and six hard disks of 3TB capacity.

As mentioned previously, Oracle NoSQL Database application workloads follow typical OLTP access patterns. The IOPS is the most common metric for measuring OLTP performance; therefore, capturing the raw IOPS performance capacity of hard disks is important. The IOPS numbers will be used later for estimating the shard I/O throughput capacity. Other factors that may influence the choice of hardware are the availability and reliability requirements, and the total hardware cost.

NOTE
This section assumes that you have dedicated disks on the Storage Nodes for the key-value store. Although you may also use shared storage arrays such as SAN and NAS, dedicated disks are believed to provide better performance and are cost effective for deploying Oracle NoSQL Database.

Capture the following hardware specifications of the Storage Nodes:

■ The total number of disks per machine dedicated for the key-value store.

■ The total usable storage capacity of each disk. This specification along with the total number of disks is used to calculate the maximum number of key-value pairs that can be stored in the shard.

■ The disk IOPS capacity. This information is typically available in the disk specification sheet as the number of sustained random I/O operations-per-second capacity of the disk.

NOTE
If the disk IOPS capacity is not specified by the manufacturer, you can easily derive it from the other specifications such as the rotational speed, average latency, and average seek time, using the best practice formula 1/(Average latency in ms + Average seek time in ms). Alternatively, you may refer to external sources that publish averaged observed IOPS values for a variety of different types of disks.

Capacity Planning and Sizing

Now that you have the application requirements and the hardware specifications captured, the next step is to size Oracle NoSQL Database. Sizing is mainly a three-step process:

1. Determine the storage and I/O throughput capacity of a representative shard. The inputs to this step are the application characteristics and the hardware specifications. Memory considerations for caching frequently used objects are also included in this step.

2. Determine the total number of shards using the capacity number of a representative shard obtained from Step 1, and the storewide application requirements. Use the representative shard as a blueprint for this estimation.

3. Determine the Oracle NoSQL Database topology. This includes the total number of Storage Nodes and the number of partitions.

Once you have performed each of the preceding steps, you should test your installation under a simulated workload and refine the configuration as necessary. Testing is an essential step prior to placing Oracle NoSQL Database in a production environment.

Size a Representative Shard

The best practice of capacity planning and sizing the Oracle NoSQL database, or any database for that matter, is to first size for performance and I/O throughput capacity, and then for storage capacity. Most people leave out the "performance" part from sizing, as it tends to be complicated, especially for brand-new deployments, because you do not have a clear idea about the workload characteristics or the requirements. Omitting this important step will land you in trouble sooner or later, especially when the database chokes under production-level workloads and the application service level agreements (SLAs) get missed.

By now you should have a rough idea about the storage and performance requirements of your Oracle NoSQL Database. Application sizing metrics such as the read IOPS and write IOPS, read-to-write ratio, cache-hit ratio, replication factor, and the average key-value pair size should be readily available. Hardware specifications such as the total number of disks, disk storage capacity, and disk I/O throughput capacity must have been captured as well.

The process for sizing a representative shard includes the following:

- Estimating the maximum key-value pairs per shard

- Estimating the I/O throughput capacity per shard

- Memory considerations

- Network considerations

Estimate the Maximum Key-Value Pairs per Shard

It is important to remember that the storage capacity in the shard is the storage capacity of only one Replication Node (that is, the master node). The remaining Replication Nodes in the shard (the replicas) store the same data as the master. Thus, the maximum number of key-value pairs that can be stored in a shard is calculated by using the total disk capacity available per Replication Node, minus disk space overheads (described shortly), divided by the average size of a key-value pair, including a rough estimation of B-tree storage overhead per key-value pair. The following formula may be used for such calculations.

$$\frac{(\text{Total disk capacity per shard} - \text{Cleaner utilization} - \text{Safety margin})}{(\text{Key-value pair size} + \text{B-tree overheads})}$$

The variables used in the preceding calculation are described next.

Total Disk Capacity The total disk capacity is the total capacity of the disk storage available to the shard for storing the key-value pairs. For the purposes of this chapter, we will assume that the disk space required for the operating system and other software and utilities, including the Oracle NoSQL Database software, is separate—that is, residing on a separate disk or a partition.

The storage manufacturers specify disk storage capacity using the SI (International System of Units) interpretation of storage units such as gigabyte (GB) or terabyte (TB). The SI interpretation of 1GB is equivalent to 1 billion bytes, i.e. $1000 \times 1000 \times 1000$ bytes, and that 1TB is equivalent to 1 trillion bytes, i.e. $1000 \times 1000 \times 1000 \times 1000$ bytes. However, computer memory (RAM) is measured using the binary interpretation of these units in which 1GB is equal to 2^{30} bytes, i.e. $1024 \times 1024 \times 1024$ bytes, and 1TB is equal to 2^{40} bytes, i.e. $1024 \times 1024 \times 1024 \times 1024$ bytes.

As you are going to move data between storage and memory, it is essential to standardize your calculations using a common measure, and the preferred practice used by operating systems and the mathematics within computer software is to use the binary interpretation of GB or TB. This means you need to translate the SI interpretation of GB or TB to the binary interpretation. For example, if you have one disk of size 1TB (SI interpretation) the binary equivalent is equal to

$$\frac{1000 \times 1000 \times 1000 \times 1000}{1024 \times 1024 \times 1024 \times 1024} = 931GB \ (0.9095TB)$$

Cleaner Utilization   In order to better to understand cleaner utilization, it is essential to first understand the storage internals of Oracle NoSQL Database.

The underlying engine of Oracle NoSQL Database is the Oracle Berkeley DB Java Edition (JE). JE uses a series of log files to store the key-value pairs in an append-only mode. When new records are inserted or existing records updated or deleted, the log files are appended at the end of the log file with the new or latest data. This means that you may find stale as well as active records in the log files.

If the space used by stale records is not reclaimed from the JE log files, Oracle NoSQL Database will always be growing and never shrink, even if you have deleted all records. Therefore, to ensure a periodic cleanup of stale records, a process called the *cleaner thread* takes charge of cleaning and compacting the log files and reclaiming the disk space.

The cleaner thread is a background process that wakes up periodically and checks for the *cleaner utilization threshold*, a parameter that specifies the percentage of log file space to be utilized by active records. The cleaner thread picks a log file with the smallest number of active records, scans each record, and if the record is no longer active in the database B-tree structures, the record is skipped; if the record is still active, then the cleaner copies the record forward to a new log file. Once all the active records are copied to the new log file, the cleaner thread deletes the old log file, or, optionally, it can simply rename the old log file, in which case it will be manually cleaned up at a later time.

To illustrate the usable disk space you may have remaining after factoring the space for cleaner utilization, consider an example where you have one disk with

1TB capacity dedicated for key-value storage and have set a 60 percent cleaner utilization. This means that you may potentially waste a maximum of 40 percent of the total disk space due to stale records. Therefore, in this example, the total space available for storing active key-value pair records is 60 percent of 931GB (binary interpretation of 1TB), which is equal to 559GB. The default cleaner utilization threshold used by the Oracle NoSQL Database JE engine is 40 percent, and can be modified to suit your requirements.

Safety Margin A small percentage of disk space should be reserved for miscellaneous overhead such as temporary log storage when a replica node is down, and when the cleaner thread is running behind and needs to catch up. Typically, the best practice to follow is to reserve 10 percent of the total disk space to accommodate such scenarios. This overhead needs to be accounted for before the cleaner utilization overhead.

For example, consider applying a safety margin overhead of 10 percent to the 961GB disk from the previous example. The total disk capacity available before accounting for cleaner utilization would be:

$$(100 - \text{Safety margin percent}) \times \text{Total disk capacity}$$
$$= 90\% \times 931\text{GB} = 838\text{GB}$$

The total space available for storing key-value pairs after accounting for a 60 percent cleaner utilization overhead would be 60 percent of 838GB, which is equal to 503GB. Note that we started off with 1TB (SI interpretation) of raw disk capacity and ended up with 503GB (binary interpretation), which is roughly half of what we originally started with.

B-Tree Overheads Key-value pairs stored in Oracle NoSQL Database are internally organized as a B-tree structure. B-tree is a tree-like node structure comprising internal nodes (INs) and leaf nodes (LNs), with each node storing a portion of the key-value data. The internal nodes store the *key* portion of the pair, whereas the leaf nodes store the *value* portion. When database records are created, modified, or deleted, the modifications are represented in the B-tree's leaf nodes and sometimes also in the internal nodes. The B-tree data structure provides optimal data storage and retrieval mechanisms, and mainly because of this, it has been in use for many years as the storage structure of choice by many relational database management systems, including Oracle Database 12*c*.

Although minimal it may be, the internal nodes have an overhead for storing the metadata to speed up B-tree lookup operations, and this overhead should be reflected in your key-value pair sizing calculations. Discussing the internals of such metadata is beyond the scope of this book, so just keep in mind that you may want to add an additional 8 bytes to the average key size for storing a "prefix" to the key in the internal nodes. This prefix is used internally by the B-tree to speed up lookups.

Recall the example from the previous section. We started with a hard disk of 1TB raw capacity, and after factoring all overheads, we obtained a usable disk space of 503GB upon which the key-value pairs can be stored. Furthermore, consider that you have estimated the average key size as 32 bytes, and an average value size of 1KB. Using the formula provided earlier, and substituting the cleaner utilization, safety margin, and the B-tree overheads, the maximum number of key-value pairs that can be stored in this shard is approximately

$$(503 \times 1024 \times 1024 \times 1024)/(1024 + 32 + 8) = 507{,}605{,}392 \text{ pairs}$$

Estimate the I/O Throughput Capacity per Shard

The I/O throughput capacity of a shard is the sum of logical read I/Os and logical write I/Os supported by the shard. Logical I/Os are the total I/O requests originating from the application for which an actual physical I/O to the disk may or may not be required. For example, if a read I/O is issued by the application and the requested data was previously cached in memory, the data will be fetched from the memory instead of the disk, and a physical I/O can be avoided, thereby considerably increasing the throughput capacity of the read I/Os.

Similarly, for logical write I/Os occurring in Oracle NoSQL Database, the data is first written to memory buffers (depending on write durability guarantee settings), and the memory buffers are flushed to disk periodically in a batch and a single sequential I/O is issued for the whole batch. Sequential I/Os (Large I/Os) are much quicker than short I/Os (when transferring the same amount of data), which means that write I/Os are faster than read I/Os in most scenarios for Oracle NoSQL Database.

The logical read and write I/O capacity of the shard can be calculated using the Replication Node hardware specifications such as the total number of disks and the raw disk IOPS, and the application characteristics such as the replication factor, the read-to-write ratio, and the cache-hit ratio. Other factors such as latency and I/O batch size will also matter but they are beyond the scope of our discussion.

NOTE
To simplify the I/O throughput capacity estimations, the following assumptions have been made: I/O batch size is assumed to be for small I/O (4KB–32KB); random I/Os are measured using IOPS; IOPS are the main measure of short I/O performance, not latency; I/Os originating from background processes such as cleaner reads/writes and checkpointer writes are ignored; application read consistency is not ABSOLUTE; write durability guarantee setting is NO_SYNC and SIMPLE_MAJORITY.

The procedure outlined next for estimating the total logical I/O capacity of a shard takes a reverse approach in calculating the logical I/Os. In other words, given the application workload, it first calculates the percentage of total I/Os that translate to physical I/Os for the mix of read and write operations. It then extrapolates the total possible logical I/Os when the disk is pegged to its maximum, i.e. scaled up to 100 percent.

Use the formula that follows to calculate the percentage of total logical I/Os (reads + writes) that will require a physical I/O from the disk.

$$\text{Total logical I/Os} = \text{Physical read I/Os} + \text{Physical write I/Os}$$

$$= [\text{Read-to-write ratio} * (100 - \text{Cache-hit ratio})] + [\text{RF} * (100 - \text{Read-to-write ratio})/\text{Write batch size}]$$

Note that the ratios are expressed as a percentage to simplify the calculations. The formula uses the *read-to-write* ratio to estimate the percentage of read requests from the total requests. The first part of the formula calculates the total percentage of I/O requests that translate to physical I/Os because of read operations, whereas the second part calculates the total percentage of I/O requests that translate to physical I/Os due to write operations.

The physical read I/Os are calculated by eliminating any logical read I/Os that would be satisfied by the cache or memory using the *cache-hit* ratio. For example, consider each Replication Node in the shard containing one hard disk with a capacity of 300 IOPS, a replication factor of 3, a *read-to-write* ratio of 50 percent (i.e. one read I/O for every write I/O), and a *cache-hit* ratio of 10 percent. Using these assumptions, the total percentage of physical I/Os issued per Replication Node due to read requests is calculated using the previous formula as follows:

$$50\% * (100 - 90\%) = 45\%$$

As you can see from the preceding calculation, 45 percent of all I/Os originating from the application are translated into physical I/Os. Keep in mind that we have not yet accounted for any write I/Os.

When it comes to estimating the physical write I/Os for the workload, the calculation can be a bit complicated. However, considering that the write operations in Oracle NoSQL Database are performed in batches via sequential I/Os, very few physical I/Os are initiated when compared to the read operations.

A good estimate for the number of physical write I/Os is to divide the total logical write I/Os by the *write batch size*, which is the number of writes that are batched before being written to disk. Each batch is considered a single disk write operation for this estimation. The batching depends upon factors like write durability, FS cache dirty flush parameters, and JE buffer sizes (discussed later). A *write batch size* of 100 is a reasonable constant for a wide variety of conditions (refer to Oracle NoSQL Database documentation for details), which means that there would be 1 physical write I/O for every 100 logical write I/Os issued by the application workload.

The writes also need to be multiplied by the replication factor (*RF*) of the shard because the writes will eventually propagate to all the replicas. If an RF of 3 is used, each write operation will result in a total of three write operations in the shard. Using these assumptions, the total percentage of physical I/Os in the shard due to the write requests is calculated from the previous formula as follows:

$$(100–50)/100 * 3 = 1.5\%$$

The sum of the percentage of physical read I/Os and the percentage of physical write I/Os represents the percentage of logical operations that actually result in disk operations. From the preceding example, the total percentage of physical I/Os per Replication Node is calculated as

$$45\% + 1.5\% = 46.5\%.$$

The total logical I/O throughput per shard can now be extrapolated from the physical I/O throughput of each Replication Node using the following formula:

$$\frac{(\text{Disk 10PS capacity} \times \text{RF})}{(\text{Total percentage of physical 10s per RN})}$$

If you substitute into the preceding formula a replication factor of 3, disk IOPS capacity of 300, and the total percentage of physical I/Os per Replication Node computed earlier, you get the total logical I/O throughput per shard as

$$\frac{(300 \times 3)}{(46.5\%)} = 1935 \ \textit{10PS per shard}$$

NOTE
The preceding formula does not work well under pure insert or pure update workloads (when reads are zero). In such cases, a thorough analysis on the impact of batched writes (sequential I/O) under varying block sizes and write batch sizes, and the cleaner writes, will be required.

Memory Considerations

The amount of memory allocated to Replication Node (RN) processes will also affect the performance of Oracle NoSQL Database. The RN process, a Java-based engine behind Oracle NoSQL Database, resides on the Storage Nodes (SN) and is based on the Berkeley DB Java Edition (JE). The RN process runs within a JVM (Java Virtual Machine) and requires an optimal allocation of memory for JVM structures, mainly *Java heap* and *Java cache*. Java heap is the area of JVM memory dedicated to storing Java objects in order to enhance object sharing and reuse between multiple threads. Java cache holds a copy of frequently accessed data that is otherwise expensive to re-fetch or compute.

RNs internally use B-tree data structures to hold the key-value pairs. When the key-value pairs are fetched from disk, they are first stored in the Java cache and then transferred to the user process. Repeated reads on the cached key-value pairs can be fetched very quickly from memory, and costly disk I/Os can be avoided. The more fetches from memory, the better the performance of Oracle NoSQL Database.

It helps to understand the internal B-tree storage structures and their contents so that the memory can be optimally allocated to Java cache. The B-tree structures consist of internal nodes (INs) and leaf nodes (LNs). The INs contain the key portion of the key-value pair and the LNs contain the value portion. Caching the B-tree structures in the Java cache means caching the INs and the LNs. But as the LN size is very large compared to the IN size, you need a very generous allocation of memory to cache them both, which is impractical.

Therefore, the best practice for sizing the Java cache and also the default configuration used by the Oracle NoSQL Database RN is to size the Java cache at least as big to cache all INs in memory (not LNs). This would speed up *key* navigation and lookup operations, but the *value* portion may still need to be fetched from the disk (or the operating system disk cache as you will see later). The benefit of this setup is that you can size the Java cache much smaller and still benefit with fast key navigations.

Estimating the Java Cache Size   Improper sizing of the cache leads to performance issues; therefore, it is important to optimally size the Java cache and speed up access to key-value pairs, and hence improve performance. However, estimating the size of B-tree internal nodes and leaf nodes of a key-value store can be quite complicated. Thankfully, a utility called DbCacheSize is provided by the Oracle NoSQL Database installation to help you in estimating the size of INs and LNs, given the key-value pair sizing metrics.

The DbCacheSize utility requires the total number of records and the size of your keys as the input, and optionally you may also supply the projected data size (i.e., the value size). The utility then displays the minimum and the maximum cache size required for holding the INs and LNs in memory.

The main item of interest from the output of DbCacheSize is the information corresponding to the "internal nodes only" row from the "Database Cache Size" section. This row displays the minimum and maximum cache size required to hold the internal nodes in memory, along with a small overhead to account for B-tree optimizations; the estimates in the "Internal Node Usage by B-Tree Level" section do not include any overheads.

The information corresponding to the "internal nodes and leaf nodes" row includes the minimum and maximum cache size to hold both the internal nodes and the leaf nodes (i.e. the data of key-value pairs) in memory. As discussed earlier, this information is not used to size the Java cache for Replication Nodes.

To determine the JE cache size for an environment consisting of 100 million records, with an average key size of 12 bytes and an average value size of 1000 bytes, invoke DbCacheSize, as shown in the following example.

```
java -d64 -XX:+UseCompressedOops -jar je.jar DbCacheSize -key 12
-data 1000 -records 100000000
=== Environment Cache Overhead ===
3,156,253 minimum bytes
To account for JE daemon operation and record locks, a significantly
larger amount is needed in practice.
=== Database Cache Size ===
Minimum Bytes        Maximum Bytes         Description
---------------      ---------------       -----------
2,888,145,968        3,469,963,312         Internal nodes only
107,499,427,952      108,081,245,296       Internal nodes and leaf nodes
=== Internal Node Usage by Btree Level ===
Minimum Bytes        Maximum Bytes         Nodes        Level
---------------      ---------------       ----------   -----
2,849,439,456        3,424,720,608         1,123,596    1
38,275,968           44,739,456            12,624       2
427,512              499,704               141          3
3,032                3,544                 1            4
```

Default Memory Allocations of Replication Node JVM   It is important to know the default memory allocation of the Replication Node JVM. The default configuration of Oracle NoSQL Database allocates 85 percent of the total server memory to the Replication Node JVM. And within the JVM memory, 70 percent is allocated to the Java cache and 30 percent to the Java heap. The defaults can be very easily overwritten using various parameters. As a best practice, remember to use the DbCacheSize utility to estimate (at least) the size of the internal nodes, and configure the Java cache to hold the internal nodes in memory.

Role of Operating System Disk Cache   Operating system kernels store data on disk in multiple chunks called *pages*. The OS transparently caches frequently accessed pages in main memory in order to speed up reads and writes to disk, in an area reserved in RAM called the *disk cache* (a.k.a. *page cache* or *file system cache*). Applications benefit from the OS disk cache in a transparent fashion, when its data access patterns favor a subset of key-value pairs over others, i.e. the hot dataset of OLTP systems discussed earlier. The one characteristic that sets the OS disk cache apart from the Java cache is that the application cannot influence or control the pages that need to be cached. The frequently accessed pages as determined by the OS kernel are the primary beneficiaries of this cache and they will be paged out depending on the LRU (Least Recently Used) policies, without taking any application-specific patterns into consideration.

By now, you know that the OS disk cache speeds up reads and writes to disk when the application workloads are focused on the hot dataset, by caching frequently used data in a faster memory and benefiting from cache hits. The benefit of the OS disk cache over the Java cache is that the disk cache could contain both INs and LNs. Also, there are no Java object overheads in disk cache as there are in Java cache, which leads to better memory utilization. These features of a disk cache make it a popular caching mechanism and could help increase I/O throughput and reduce average read and write latencies.

NOTE
Disk controllers on most enterprise-grade servers also provide a caching mechanism commonly referred to as the disk buffer or the controller cache. The disk buffers are separate from the OS disk cache, and can further assist transparently in enhancing read and write I/O performance, using features such as read-ahead and write acceleration.

Network Considerations

A typical NoSQL Database deployment consists of multiple Storage Nodes with each node running a set of Replication Node (RN) processes. The RN processes need to communicate with the other RN processes in the cluster, and also the clients (applications) need to communicate with the Storage Nodes. To facilitate this communication, the NoSQL Database requires a reliable network that has a low and predictable latency, and is free of bottlenecks induced by other applications that do not access the key-value store.

Having a low latency network is more important than any other network performance metric. The goal of Oracle NoSQL Database inter-node communication is mostly to synchronize the replicated data between the Replication Nodes. The higher the latency, the longer the time it takes for the synchronization, assuming the bottleneck is on the network and not other components such as the disk. The client applications could end up waiting until the changes are synchronized across all replicas, in which case the application performance is impacted. However, the mode for synchronization can be configured by the client applications using durability guarantee settings, as you have seen in the earlier chapters.

The best practice for sizing the network for Oracle NoSQL Database is to ensure that the network capacity is at least 1 gigabit Ethernet and free of external bottlenecks. While a dedicated network is not a requirement from an installation standpoint, it would definitely help to eliminate "unknowns" due to third-party applications, which could induce unpredictable latencies to Oracle NoSQL Database applications. Also, as VLANs are becoming a popular choice for network administrators, it is okay to configure them as long as proper QoS (Quality of Service) settings are in place to ensure that Oracle NoSQL Database processes are allocated the required bandwidth.

Determine the Total Number of Shards and Partitions

So far in the earlier sections, we have estimated shard-level capacity metrics. Using these metrics, you can compute the total number of shards required to satisfy the application workload characteristics such as the I/O throughput capacity, and the storage requirements such as the total key-value pairs, using the estimation models provided in this section.

Total Number of Shards

The following are the inputs required to estimate the total number of shards:

- Application requirements captured using the best practices outlined in the "Application Characteristics" section earlier in this chapter:

  - The maximum number of the key-value pairs to be stored in the key-value store as determined by the application requirements (*Max key-value pairs per KVStore*)

  - The maximum transaction I/O throughput capacity (read IOPS + write IOPS) of the key-value store obtained by analyzing the application workload characteristics (*Max IOPS per KVStore*)

  - The shard-level capacity calculated using the best practices outlined in the section "Size a Representative Shard":

    - Shard-level I/O throughput capacity for the mix of read and write transactions, taking into account the read-to-write ratio and the cache-hit ratio (*Max IOPS per shard*)

    - Shard-level storage capacity (*Max key-value pairs per shard*)

The total number of shards is calculated using two different estimation models. The first model computes the number of shards required to satisfy the key-value store storage requirements (*Shards Required for Storage*), using the following formula:

Shards required for storage = (Max key-value pairs per KVStore)/(Max key-value pairs per shard)

The second model computes the required number of shards to satisfy the application I/O throughput requirements (*Shards required for throughput*), using the following formula:

Shards required for throughput = (Max IOPS per KVStore)/
(Max IOPS per shard)

The final number of shards will be the maximum of the two numbers obtained from the two models (*Total number of shards*). This number is sufficient to satisfy both the total storage and I/O throughput requirements of the application.

Total number of shards = Max (Shards for storage, Shards for throughput)

Total Number of Partitions

Oracle NoSQL Database employs a two-level partitioning approach with the first level being the shard and the second level, a *partition*. One-to-many key-value pairs are allocated to partitions, and each shard contains one-to-many partitions.

NOTE
The terms "shard" and "partition" are often used interchangeably when referring to database software, but in the context of Oracle NoSQL Database, they are associated with somewhat different (yet similar) concepts.

The key-value pairs are allotted to a partition based on a hash-based partitioning scheme. A hashing function is applied on the *key* portion of the key-value pair data to determine the partition to which the key-value pair would belong. All subsequent read and write operations on the key-value pair are directed to the appropriate shard/partition that holds the key-value pair. The hash function ensures that the keys are evenly distributed into the specified number of partitions and keeps the store well balanced during its lifetime when additions and deletions occur.

The total number of partitions in Oracle NoSQL Database is defined at the time of database creation, and cannot be changed and remains permanent for the life of the key-value store. The number of shards, on the other hand, can be increased or decreased. Changing the number of shards would initiate a process called *rebalancing the store*, which moves the partitions (and its associated data) to a different shard, followed by addition or deletion of shards. Although there is not a direct limitation on the maximum number of shards you can have in the key-value store, there is an indirect one, and this is equal to the number of partitions defined for the key-value store. Therefore, it is important to select the right number of partitions and accommodate any future growth requirements.

Technically speaking, it is possible to have a shard with one partition only, but it is best to configure the key-value store such that each shard always contains more than one partition. At a minimum, you need to configure the total number of partitions equal to the largest number of shards you ever expect Oracle NoSQL Database to grow. There is also an internal overhead (minimal) for having a very large number of partitions, but nevertheless it is quite a common practice to accommodate for future growth.

As a best practice recommendation, choose the number of partitions to about 100 times the maximum number that you would ever expect your shards to grow during the lifetime of the database.

Total number of partitions = (Total shards * 100)

Now that you have the estimated the total number of Storage Nodes, the key-value store partitions, and the replication factor, you may now proceed with deploying the key-value store. Refer to Chapter 4 for further instructions.

Summary

Capacity planning is an essential step to a successful deployment of Oracle NoSQL Database in an enterprise datacenter environment. Configuring the correct number of Replication Nodes, Storage Nodes, and the replication factor ensures that the key-value store can satisfy the right levels of application performance while guaranteeing the maximum store availability. The methods and guidelines provided in this chapter should give you a good place to start with initial sizing and then enable you to refine the estimates based on further tests.

CHAPTER
9

Advanced Topics

Enterprises have a mix of various technologies deployed in their environment, each serving a specific set of functional needs. Oracle NoSQL Database, when deployed in such a heterogeneous environment, has to work alongside these technologies to provide a complete and seamless integration. Customers deploy software and hardware solutions to solve their business needs. A technology that integrates with ease into existing data management infrastructures, and causes minimal disruptions to the business, leads to an improvement in return on investment (ROI) and lower total cost of ownership (TCO). In this final chapter, we cover multiple use cases that highlight how Oracle NoSQL Database can be integrated with Hadoop, Oracle Database, and Complex Event Processing engines. The chapter also provides details on the new functionality in Oracle NoSQL Database v2 for the support of RDF Graph, Avro format, and the new C-API support.

Hadoop Integration

Big Data deployments typically have two key requirements: The first is to be agile and responsive while receiving large volumes of data in real time; the second is to be able to analyze a large dataset in batch mode. The real-time capability allows the Big Data deployment to support a large number of users, sensors, or inputs, while the batch analysis capability brings the intelligence to make smart decisions for the Big Data problem at hand. These two requirements of a Big Data deployment are best explained through an example of an online retailer.

Let's look at the architecture of a sample online retailer, as shown in Figure 9-1. Customers access the website of the online retailer either through their mobile or desktop devices. These requests are routed to a bank of web servers that load balance these requests to multiple application servers. Fault tolerance and high availability are built into the application tier so that there is no single point of failure. As customers fill their shopping carts, the information needs to be quickly persisted so that it can be available at checkout or on the next visit if the customer does not finish the checkout process. Oracle NoSQL Database, with its high performance clustered architecture, is an ideal database to persist this information. Because of the seasonal nature of the retail business, the amount of customer traffic varies dramatically through the year. It is important to have a persistent store that can grow and shrink based on the load on the retailer's website. The elastic clustered architecture support in Oracle NoSQL Database means that new nodes can be very quickly provisioned, and once the peak load has passed, the number of nodes can be shrunk in an elastic fashion without any downtime. The elastic architecture is also relevant for cloud providers that need to quickly respond to the changing needs of their hosted customers.

Online retailers carry a large variety of products and customers are often lost in the myriads of choices and options available for each product category. It is therefore important to provide personalized recommendation of products to buy to the customers. To achieve this functionality, retailers will periodically send shopping cart information from their NoSQL database to a Hadoop cluster for further analysis.

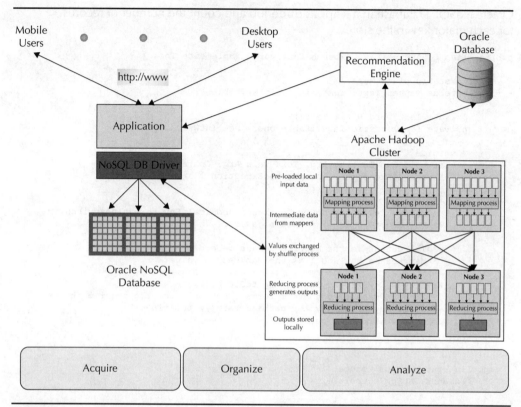

FIGURE 9-1. *Deployment architecture for an online retailer showing the integration between NoSQL and Hadoop*

The analysis provides insight into what products coexist on shopping carts across a large number of customers, and gives the retailer a good idea of what additional products to recommend.

In essence, the Hadoop cluster contributes to the building of a statistical model, which helps ascertain what recommendations to make to the customers; this in turn helps drive additional sales with each customer. A rules engine could help refine these recommendations further before sending them over to the application tier for display on the customer's browser or mobile application.

Oracle NoSQL Database provides an efficient mechanism to integrate with Apache Hadoop systems and has the capacity to move data in a bidirectional fashion. To read data from Oracle NoSQL Database, you use the `oracle.kv` `.hadoop.KVInputFormat` class and then prepare it for insertion into a Hadoop system. An example is included in the `<kvstore>/examples/hadoop` directory of the Oracle NoSQL Database installation, and it shows how one can read from

Oracle NoSQL Database in a Map/Reduce job and count the number of records for each major key in the store.

```java
public class CountMinorKeys extends Configured implements Tool {

    public static class Map
        extends Mapper<Text, Text, Text, IntWritable> {

        private Text word = new Text();
        private final static IntWritable one = new IntWritable(1);

        @Override
        public void map(Text keyArg, Text valueArg, Context context)
            throws IOException, InterruptedException {

            /*
             * keyArg is in the NoSQL Database canonical Key format described in
             * the Key.toString() method's javadoc.
             *
             * The Output is the NoSQL Database record's Major Key as the
             * Map/Reduce key and 1 as the Map/Reduce value.
             */
            Key key = Key.fromString(keyArg.toString());
            /* Convert back to canonical format, but only use the major path. */
            word.set(Key.createKey(key.getMajorPath()).toString());
            context.write(word, one);
        }
    }

    public static class Reduce
        extends IntSumReducer<Text> {
    }

    @Override
    public int run(String[] args)
        throws Exception {

        @SuppressWarnings("deprecation")
        Job job = new Job(getConf());
        job.setJarByClass(CountMinorKeys.class);
        job.setJobName("Count Minor Keys");

        job.setOutputKeyClass(Text.class);
        job.setOutputValueClass(IntWritable.class);

        job.setMapperClass(Map.class);
        job.setReducerClass(Reduce.class);

        job.setInputFormatClass(KVInputFormat.class);
        job.setOutputFormatClass(TextOutputFormat.class);

        KVInputFormat.setKVStoreName(args[0]);
        KVInputFormat.setKVHelperHosts(new String[] { args[1] });
        FileOutputFormat.setOutputPath(job, new Path(args[2]));

        boolean success = job.waitForCompletion(true);
        return success ? 0 : 1;
```

```
    }

public static void main(String[] args)
    throws Exception {

    int ret = ToolRunner.run(new CountMinorKeys(), args);
    System.exit(ret);
}
}
```

In this example, the `map()` function is passed the `key` and `value` for each record in the store, and it outputs the major path component as the output key and a value of 1. The `reduce()` step sums the value for each of the records with the same key. More complex map/reduce jobs can be written based on the needs of the application. To move data in the reverse, from Hadoop into Oracle NoSQL Database, you would read data from the Hadoop using the standard mechanisms. The data is then written to Oracle NoSQL Database using the APIs described in this book.

RDF Graph

With the advent of social networks, enterprises are looking at ways to benefit from the social and business relationships that customers are maintaining on social media sites like LinkedIn, Twitter, and Facebook. These relationship graphs and their corresponding arcs when traversed can unlock a treasure trove of information regarding the influence and clout of individual customers. Further, you can combine this information with enterprise content and domain vocabularies to provide a fuller context of your customer base and potential opportunities. This allows for a targeted outreach based on market segmentation and a high degree of propensity to buy. For example, if an enterprise were able to find the top 100 most connected and influential members of its customer base and through them reach out to prospects, it would have greater success with its sales campaign.

To store the information described in the preceding scenario, a database that uses graph structures to store objects as nodes and also captures the relationship between these nodes is required. The RDF (Resource Description Framework) Graph database provides a very flexible and efficient mechanism to store and retrieve associative datasets. RDF has its roots in the semantic web, and it has an abstract syntax that represents a graph-based data model. Oracle NoSQL Database Enterprise Edition supports this semantic technology, the SPARQL query language, and a subset of the Web Ontology Language (OWL), which collectively form the RDF Graph feature of Oracle NoSQL Database.

RDF represents data as triples, with a subject, predicate, and object, and RDF Graph supports named graphs by extending this triple. In the triple shown in Figure 9-2, the lender is the object and "loan products" is the subject. The relationship between the two is the predicate "is seller of." This basic paradigm of an RDF triple provides for a very flexible and intuitive way to store objects and the relationships between them.

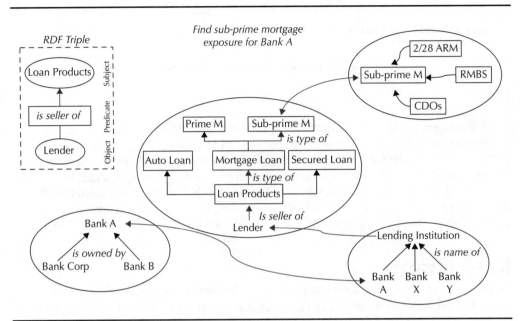

FIGURE 9-2. *RDF Graph concepts*

Further, as shown in the next paragraph, the capability to traverse RDF Graph can provide a very effective mechanism to analyze data.

Figure 9-2 also depicts a larger use case with multiple objects and relationships. This example showcases how RDF Graph can help detect risk liabilities for financial institutions. In this example scenario, a hypothetical Bank A has gone through mergers and, in the process, has acquired multiple other banks and lending businesses. Lenders in turn provide a variety of loans like Auto, Home Mortgage and Secured Loans. If you further look at the classification of the home mortgage loans, you see both Prime and Sub-prime loans. These final class of loans could have exposure to the sub-prime lending crisis that plagued the industry a few years ago. RDF has the capability to store relationships between entities, and it also provides the mechanism to traverse different relationships. This capability of RDF gives us a very elegant mechanism to find the exposure for Bank A to the sub-prime lending risk, something that otherwise could have been lost in the large amount of unstructured and disjointed data sets that exist in any large financial institution.

RDF Graph databases lack primary keys, making the relationship between tables completely arbitrary. The flexible schema evolves easily by adding new relationships and supports querying and discovery by graph patterns and traversal. Within Oracle NoSQL Database, to easily separate RDF-related data, the keys are prefixed

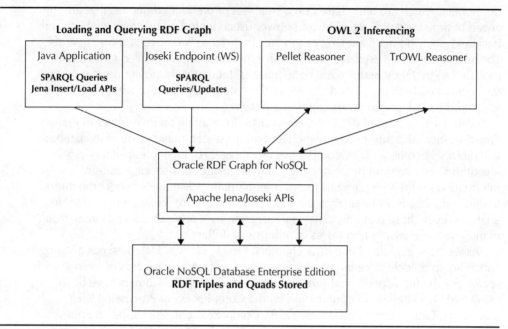

Loading and Querying RDF Graph

Java Application	Joseki Endpoint (WS)
SPARQL Queries Jena Insert/Load APIs	SPARQL Queries/Updates

OWL 2 Inferencing

Pellet Reasoner	TrOWL Reasoner

Oracle RDF Graph for NoSQL

Apache Jena/Joseki APIs

Oracle NoSQL Database Enterprise Edition
RDF Triples and Quads Stored

FIGURE 9-3. *The RDF Graph feature of Oracle NoSQL Database*

specifically for RDF Graph data. In addition to these basic features, the RDF Graph implementation in Oracle NoSQL Database features various enhancements to support incremental inserts and for loading large datasets through concurrent bulk loads. The massively parallel scalability of Oracle NoSQL Database makes it possible to process petabytes of triples, and run queries aggregating over the entirety of a large graph. For querying, the RDF Graph feature provides a Java-based interface to store and query semantic data. Also, web services endpoints such as Jena and Joseki SPARQL are supported. With the support of Apache Jena, it is possible to use tools for query, visualization, and ontology engineering. For a detailed diagram of the various RDF tools and technologies supported, refer to Figure 9-3.

Integration with Complex Event Processing

One way of viewing the evolution of business intelligence and analytics is by observing the kinds of BI users that exist today. There are two classes of users: the casual users who consume dashboards and reports generated by BI architects and developers, which are often based on a small set of predefined queries that are run ahead of time for rapid response; and power users, including business analysts and data analysts, who need analytic sandboxes in order to run novel, ad-hoc queries. The queries of power users are very iterative in nature and may need to be rapidly modified so that they perform the right analysis. Increasingly, power users work on data generated both inside and outside of the enterprise, much of which is a mix of structured metadata and unstructured main data.

With the evolution of Big Data, enterprises are making an investment in real-time analytics, and the speed at which an enterprise can make sense of its database will rapidly become a major competitive advantage. For example, risk analysis algorithms are often run by competing financial institutions seeking real-time information on their investments in order to maintain advantages over competitors. In this case, data must be analyzed rapidly as it streams in; inefficiencies in these analyses, even those that only delay a transaction by a few milliseconds, may result in massive price swings and losses of millions of dollars.

As we have explained in earlier chapters, Oracle NoSQL Database has a strong capability to quickly store large volumes of data and retrieve records of interest with speed. For the high-speed, real-time intelligence scenario, customers have been using NoSQL Database in conjunction with a Complex Event Processing (CEP) engine like Oracle Event Processing (OEP). Complex Event Processing engines provide the capability to analyze streams of data as they come in. They are the first line of defense when it comes to connecting the velocity of Big Data to value. CEPs can quickly detect patterns, and filter and correlate data. For example, in the case of detecting fraud in financial systems, the streaming transactions are passed through a Complex Event Processing engine, and to help detect fraud, the process requires a low latency lookup of recent transactions and user profiles and combining them with the output of CEP algorithms. In this scenario, Oracle NoSQL Database may be used to find recent transactions, authorization requests, account changes, and other indicators, which can then be analyzed in order to inform investigators and prosecutors as to whether the events merit further investigation.

Similar applications can be found in healthcare monitoring, where OEP captures incoming patient monitoring data and looks into Oracle NoSQL Database to find medical data, test results, monitoring trends, monitoring thresholds, or patient profile information—all of which contribute to determining whether an alert or notification should be sent, who should be alerted, and what the most likely treatment, if any, should be. Utilities sensor monitoring (telecommunications, water, power, and so on) is very similar. OEP captures incoming sensor data and looks into Oracle NoSQL Database to find recent sensor history, and alert thresholds, which helps engineers determine whether action should be taken and, if so, decide the course of this action.

Database External Tables

In Chapter 1, we discussed the use case for online advertisement and highlighted the stringent requirement of being able to decide which ad to display in less than 75 milliseconds. There are multiple parties involved in the successful rendering of an advertisement on a mobile device or desktop. To be effective, it is important for the publisher to track the behavior of its consumers, and with the help of the ad server make the right decision of which ad to display. A campaign management system is required to streamline the entire workflow, which includes launching an ad campaign, serving the advertisements, and reporting for billing purposes. This helps merchants, agencies, and marketers see the true value of their advertisement campaigns. The online advertisement scenario requires both Oracle NoSQL Database and Oracle Database because each fulfills critical functionality, and to be effective you also need to integrate the two databases.

In addition to the low latency requirements, online display advertising has to support extremely high data throughput of multimillion requests per second. The platform has to be highly available, and to maximize revenue it must deliver the most relevant ads. Oracle NoSQL Database is used in this scenario to store user cookies and associated behavioral patterns. The behavioral data includes timestamp and frequency. Also, to optimize ad delivery the recentness and frequency of ad display is stored.

A relational database such as Oracle Database 12c can be used to store campaign booking information and real-time business metrics for publishers and advertisers. Oracle Database also works well in order to store longer-term financials such as year-to-date revenues, quarter-over-quarter revenue changes, and the like.

Another use case where the two databases need to work together is a multiplayer online gaming application. Such games have very low latency requirements; player movements must happen in real time, while being tracked on the server. Popular games have tens of millions of active users, and have high availability requirements and heavy workloads. Many of these games also provide the capability for in-game micro-transactions, such as the purchase of power-ups or more advanced weapons with an in-game currency. With millions of players performing such transactions, they represent a major source of revenue for the customer.

Oracle NoSQL Database can be used to track the player movements with low latency, and can be used to store player usage statistics. For games that allow player communication via chat, Oracle NoSQL Database is used as a persistent message store for auditing and COPA compliance. There are various levels of consistency that the database needs to support in the online gaming scenario; for example, loose consistency is fine for some interactions such as player proximity sensing, while ACID transaction support is required for the in-game micro-transactions. Oracle NoSQL Database, with its flexible and configurable consistency model, is ideal for this purpose.

For business financials such as tracking credit card transactions, subscription billing, and payment in the gaming platform, relational databases are used. Oracle Database can be used as the master data store for all player information and payment processing. To better analyze usage trends, the combination of this master data with the micro-transactions stored in Oracle NoSQL Database is required. This could provide critical business information on which geographies and which in-game promotions are performing the best, and which product lines are bringing in the most revenues. The mechanics to do this elegantly is provided in version 2 of the product, through the use of NoSQL and Oracle Database external tables. This functionality provides an easy mechanism to access Oracle NoSQL Database as an external table to Oracle Database. No changes can be made to NoSQL Database content using this interface.

The next section will provide details on the architecture for NoSQL and Oracle external tables, as well as an example walk-through of this feature.

The Oracle Database external table feature allows a user to access data that resides outside of the database as if it were in a table in the database. This flexibility allows you to run SQL queries against the external dataset, and it provides you the mechanism to join data across internal and external tables for data analysis purposes. Oracle has developed functionality to work with Oracle NoSQL Database as an external source. The NoSQL database is read with the aid of a preprocessor utility.

Multiple steps need to be followed to configure the two databases to work together.

The first step is to build a PREPROCESSOR for the external table. You then define the external table with one or more Location Files and the name of the PREPROCESSOR. Let us assume you name the "publish utility" nosql_stream:

1. The next step is to invoke the PREPROCESSOR and have it save the configuration details in the Location Files specified. The PREPROCESSOR will need the connection information for Oracle Database and Oracle NoSQL Database instances, the name of the external table, details on which NoSQL Database records to process, and the name of any class that needs to be used to convert the key-value pairs from the NoSQL format to the external table format.

2. For the first time, you manually run the publish utility. After that, you only need to run the publish utility again if you want to change the way NoSQL Database is accessed (for example, using a different key prefix, or if you change the port or the rep nodes where you access the database).

3. After the publish utility has been run, you can query the external table in the same way as you would query any other Oracle database table.

Define an External Table

As a first step for the creation of an external table, you will need to specify where the Location Files reside and where the "publish utility" can be found.

```
sqlplus / as sysdba
SQL> CREATE DIRECTORY ext_tab AS '<exttab_pathname>';
SQL> CREATE DIRECTORY nosql_bin_dir AS '<bin_pathname>';
```

In the preceding SQL statements, exttab_pathname is the directory containing the Location File(s), and bin_pathname refers to the exttab/bin/ directory of the NoSQL Database installation where the nosql_stream utility is located.

You now need to grant permission to the Oracle user who needs access to the external table. Let's name this user nosqluser:

```
sqlplus / as sysdba
SQL> CREATE USER nosqluser IDENTIFIED BY password;
SQL> GRANT CREATE SESSION TO nosqluser;
SQL> GRANT EXECUTE ON SYS.UTL_FILE TO nosqluser;
SQL> GRANT READ, WRITE ON DIRECTORY ext_tab TO nosqluser;
SQL> GRANT READ, EXECUTE ON DIRECTORY nosql_bin_dir TO nosqluser;
SQL> GRANT CREATE TABLE TO nosqluser;
```

The next step is to define the external table:

```
SQL> CONNECT nosqluser/password
SQL> CREATE TABLE nosql_data (email VARCHAR2(30),
  2                            gender CHAR(1),
  3                            address VARCHAR2(40),
  4                            phone VARCHAR2(20))
  5      ORGANIZATION EXTERNAL
  6          (type oracle_loader
  7           default directory ext_tab
  8           access parameters (records delimited by newline
  9           preprocessor nosql_bin_dir:'nosql_stream'
 10           fields terminated by '|')
 11      LOCATION ('nosql.dat'))
 12      PARALLEL;

Table created.

SQL>
```

Let's assume that your NoSQL Database is loaded with the necessary data. For sample datasets, please refer to the Oracle NoSQL Database manual, or the LoadCookbookData program in the <KVHOME>/examples/externaltables directory.

Edit the Configuration File

Make a copy of the configuration file in `<KVHOME>/examples/externaltables/` `config.xml` and edit your site-specific values for the `oracle.kv.exttab` `.connection.url`, `oracle.kv.exttab.connection.user`, `oracle.kv` `.exttab.connection.wallet_location` (optional), `oracle.kv.kvstore`, and `oracle.kv.hosts` properties based on your Oracle Database and Oracle NoSQL Database installations.

Publish the Configuration

Run the `oracle.kv.exttab.Publish` utility to publish the configuration to the external table Location Files:

```
cd <KVHOME>
java -classpath lib/kvstore.jar:$ORACLE_HOME/jdbc/lib/ojdbc6.jar \
    oracle.kv.exttab.Publish \
    -config <pathname-to-edited-copy-of-config.xml> -publish
```

If you are using Oracle Wallet as an external password store, then you should also include `$ORACLE_HOME/jlib/oraclepki.jar` in your classpath. If the process executes successfully, there will be no output. If you have read access to the Location file(s), you can verify the Publish operation by looking inside one to see if the configuration XML is written there. You will see that two additional properties have been added to the XML: `oracle.kv.exttab.totalExternalTableFiles` and `oracle.kv.exttab.externalTableFileNumber`. Optionally, you can specify the `-verbose` argument to the Publish utility to see more verbose (i.e., debugging) output.

Test the nosql_stream Script

Edit the `<KVHOME>/exttab/bin/nosql_stream` script to have the correct values for `PATH`, `KVHOME`, and `CLASSPATH` when the script is run in the execution environment of the Oracle Database server. For this example, `CLASSPATH` should include the `KVHOME/examples` directory (in addition to the `kvstore.jar`).

Test the `nosql_stream` script by running it in a shell:

```
$ <KVHOME>/exttab/bin/nosql_stream <exttab_pathname>/nosql.dat
```

where `<exttab_pathname>` is the path of the Location Files specified earlier in the `CREATE DIRECTORY` command. You should see output similar to the following:

```
user6@example.com|F|#6 Example St, Example Town, AZ|666.666.6666
user1@example.com|M|#1 Example St, Example Town, AZ|111.111.1111
user9@example.com|M|#9 Example St, Example Town, AZ|999.999.9999
user0@example.com|F|#0 Example St, Example Town, AZ|000.000.0000
```

```
user7@example.com|M|#7 Example St, Example Town, AZ|777.777.7777
user8@example.com|F|#8 Example St, Example Town, AZ|888.888.8888
user5@example.com|M|#5 Example St, Example Town, AZ|555.555.5555
user2@example.com|F|#2 Example St, Example Town, AZ|222.222.2222
user4@example.com|F|#4 Example St, Example Town, AZ|444.444.4444
user3@example.com|M|#3 Example St, Example Town, AZ|333.333.3333
```

Use the External Table to Read Data from Oracle NoSQL Database

Using `sqlplus` (as `nosqluser` or whatever user you created the external table with), perform a `SELECT` on the `nosql_data` external table:

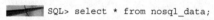

```
SQL> select * from nosql_data;

EMAIL                    G     ADDRESS                                  PHONE
------------------       -----  -------------------------------------   ----------------
user6@example.com        F     #6 Example St, Example Town, AZ          666.666.6666
user1@example.com        M     #1 Example St, Example Town, AZ          111.111.1111
user9@example.com        M     #9 Example St, Example Town, AZ          999.999.9999
...
SQL>
```

To improve the performance of your external table queries, consider using multiple Location Files, as this dictates the degree of parallelism possible when retrieving data.

Summary

Enterprises typically have a variety of technologies deployed in their data center. The success of their business is heavily reliant on the ease with which these heterogeneous technologies work together in a seamless fashion. With emerging technologies like Big Data, it is all the more important to fit into an existing IT environment. As we have seen in this chapter, Oracle NoSQL Database with its tight integration with Oracle Database and a variety of other complementary technologies is an enterprise-grade database offering for this space.

Index

J

K

L

M

S

Can I copy Java
code to an HTML
extension?

I want to improve
the performance of
my application...

Here's where you
can find the
latest release.

I coded it
this way...

Is the app
customizable?

How does
restricted task
reassignment
work?

Just watch the
live webcast on
virtualization.

The best way to migrate
Oracle E-Business
Application Suite Tier
servers to Linux is...

Where can I find
technical articles on
logging in Java ME?

Oracle Technology Network. It's code for sharing expertise.

Come to the best place to collaborate with other IT professionals.

Oracle Technology Network is the world's largest community of developers,
administrators, and architects using industry-standard technologies with
Oracle products.

Sign up for a free membership and you'll have access to:

- Discussion forums and hands-on labs
- Free downloadable software and sample code
- Product documentation
- Member-contributed content

Take advantage of our global network of knowledge.

JOIN TODAY ▷ Go to: oracle.com/technetwork